Cornish studies : 3

0859894762

**CORNWALL COUNTY COUNCIL
LIBRARIES AND ARTS DEPARTMENT**

INSTITUTE OF CORNISH STUDIES

Sardinia Pilchardus
(The Pilchard)

EDITOR'S NOTE

Cornish Studies (second series) exists to reflect current research conducted internationally in the inter-disciplinary field of Cornish Studies. It is edited by Dr Philip Payton, Reader in Cornish Studies and Director of the Institute of Cornish Studies at the University of Exeter, and is published by the University of Exeter Press. The opinions expressed in *Cornish Studies* are those of individual authors and are not necessarily those of the editor or publisher.

CORNISH STUDIES

Second Series

THREE

Edited by

Philip Payton

UNIVERSITY
of
EXETER
PRESS

First published in 1995 by
University of Exeter Press
Reed Hall, Streatham Drive
Exeter, Devon EX4 4QR
UK

British Library Cataloguing in Publication Data
A catalogue record of this book is
available from the British Library

ISBN 0 85989 476 2
ISSN 1352-271X

Typeset by Kestrel Data, Exeter, Devon

Printed and bound in Great Britain by
Short Run Press Ltd, Exeter, Devon

Contents

1 Introduction   1

2 Collective Action and the Cornish Miner in Australia:
An Early Repudiation of the 'Individualistic' Thesis
Mel Davies (University of Western Australia)   7

3 Not What They Seemed? Cornish Assisted Immigrants
in New South Wales 1837–77
Patricia Lay (Australian National University)   33

4 Cornish Emigration in Response to Changes in the
International Copper Market in the 1860s
Philip Payton (Institute of Cornish Studies)   60

5 The Great Western Railway and the Cornish-Celtic Revival
Philip Payton and Paul Thornton
(Institute of Cornish Studies)   83

6 Which Base for Revived Cornish?
Ken George (University of Plymouth)   104

7 Voice From a White Silence: The Manuscripts of Jack Clemo
John Hurst (University of Exeter)   125

8 The Significance of Cornish and Scillonian Natural History
Stella Turk (Institute of Cornish Studies)   144

9 The Importance of Metaliferous Mining Sites in Cornwall
for Wildlife (With Special Reference to Insects)
Adrian Spalding (Institute of Cornish Studies)   161

10 Movers and Stayers: A Comparison of Migratory and
    Non-Migratory Groups in Cornwall 1981-1991
    Malcolm Williams and Eric Harrison
    (*University of Plymouth*)   176

11 Housing in Cornwall: A Two-Tier System?
    Carol Williams (*University of Plymouth*)   194

12 Book Reviews   207

INTRODUCTION

The development of Cornish Studies as an area of academic inquiry has focussed, in the 1990s, on several key areas. Hand-in-hand with a vigorous historiographical debate concerning the nature of Cornish history and the perpetuation of 'difference' has been an emerging social science which has been concerned with a range of phenomena from ethnonationalism and language revival through tourism and economic policy to migration and housing. To these have been wedded literary and cultural studies of 'imaginings' and 'inventions' of Cornwall, together with an energetic environmental science which not only continues to emphasise the distinctiveness of Cornish flora and fauna but is increasingly willing to engage in inter-disciplinary debate on major issues such as landscape conservation.

Cornish Studies: Three continues the discussion in several of these areas, again emphasising an inter-disciplinary approach to Cornish Studies and reflecting that much recent academic work in the field has focussed on modern and contemporary Cornwall. It is worth noting here that elsewhere in the realms of 'Celtic Studies' there has been a similar shift in emphasis, with a desire to expand beyond traditional areas of study to embrace subjects with contemporary and applied relevance. In the Department of Welsh at the University of Wales in Cardiff, for example, issues of Welsh language policy and planning have emerged as part of a developing interest in territory and cultural diversity. At the Institute of Irish Studies in the University of Liverpool, recent research (especially in the Culture and Tourism Research Unit) has focussed on the regional dimension in Europe, with particular emphasis on regional culture, heritage and identity in the context of socio-economic development.

Against the background of the developing University of Exeter presence in Cornwall, it is crucial that the Institute of Cornish Studies should continue to play a leading role in this re-assessment of 'Celtic Studies'. Indeed, this comes at a time when the idea of 'the Celt' and the notion of 'Celticity' are themselves coming under close academic scrutiny. Malcolm Chapman has argued (*The Celts: The Construction of a Myth*, London, 1992) that such concepts are essentially English constructions, a romantic portrayal of 'Otherness'. Peter Berresford Ellis offers an opposing analysis (*The Celtic Dawn: A History of Pan Celticism*, London, 1993) but one which also intimates that 'Celticity' is a construction, albeit this time a politico-cultural device for emergent nationalist movements in the 'Celtic lands' in the nineteenth and twentieth centuries.

For linguistic purists, 'Celtic' remains an exclusively linguistic term but (as well as leading to unresolvable and ultimately meaningless debate about whether Galician claims to be 'Celtic' are to be considered 'authentic', or if Cornwall will cease to be 'Celtic' if it does not fully revive its language) such narrowness ignores the reality of both popular and academic usage. 'Celtic' is today a convenient short-hand for the territories and peoples of peripheral north-western Europe who exhibit elements of cultural affinity and whose historical experiences have been in several respects similar, leading in recent times to a limited but sometimes significant level of common consciousness. It is in this catholic, comparative European regional context that 'Celtic Studies' is likely to develop, and the emphasis is as likely (or rather, more than likely) to be on contemporary cultural or economic issues as, say, medieval Welsh and Irish literature.

Significantly, the whole notion of 'Celticity' and the current challenges that it faces were confronted energetically at the 10th International Congress of Celtic Studies, held at the University of Edinburgh in July 1995. In key-note addresses D. Ellis Evan (Jesus College, Oxford) stressed the need for a comprehensive historiography of 'the Celts' and their ethnogenesis, and Vincent and Ruth Megaw (Flinders University) drew a telling comparison between notions of 'the Celts' and 'the Aborigines' as externally-generated constructs which have none the less had a powerful impact on those two groups of people as they attempt to self-define their respective identities in the modern world. The same might be said, incidentally, for 'Red-Indians' (Native Americans) in North America, or perhaps even for 'Indians' in the Sub-Continent.

Cornish Studies: Three is evidence of this increasing willingness of 'Celtic Studies' to address modern and contemporary issues. Recognising that Cornwall's experience of industrialisation and rapid de-industrialisation has been perhaps *the* major factor in the creation of the condition of modern Cornwall (and its international identity), there are no fewer than three articles on aspects of the 'Great Emigration'. As 1995 is the 150th anniversary of the opening of the Burra Burra copper mine in South Australia (and—one might add—as the high standard of building and landscape conservation achieved at the Burra today is a model for those who are currently handling Cornish sites), it is appropriate that Mel Davies should concentrate in detail on the events of the 1848 Burra strike. In so doing he poses a number of significant questions, not only challenging the 'individualistic' thesis but also raising wider consideration of whether Cornish behaviour overseas was a reflection of the Cornish inheritance or an adaption to new conditions.

In an article which has wide comparative interest for the study of other emigrant ethnic groups, Patricia Lay examines the extent to which nineteenth-century Cornish emigrants to New South Wales lied to immigration officials (or misrepresented or exaggerated their credentials) to take advantage of government assisted passage schemes. Building upon work suggested by research at the Australian National University and facilitated at the Institute of Cornish Studies with the benefit of a grant from the Caroline L. Kemp Bequest Fund, this article shows how the techniques and micro-research of the family historian can be important in the elucidation of social history. Emigration is also the theme of a more wide-ranging discussion of Cornish behaviour during and after the 1860s, when massive changes in the international copper market precipitated an exodus of Cornish miners (often with their families) to America, Australia and elsewhere, a phenomenon both benefiting from and further enhancing the 'emigration culture' and 'emigration trade' that were already familiar aspects of Cornish life.

The 're-invention' of Celtic Cornwall takes centre-stage in a collaborative effort by Philip Payton and Paul Thornton, bringing together their hitherto separate interests in the history of cultural change and in tourism to argue that the touristic devices adopted by the Great Western Railway in Cornwall in the first half of this century represented a high degree of collusion with the image-makers of the Cornish-Celtic Revival. This focus on the ideology of the early Cornish Revivalists (not least their concern for the Cornish language as the central feature of the Cornish identity) anticipates the theme of Ken George who, in a robust response to international criticism of his 'Phonemic' revision of Cornish, argues that his recently introduced Kernewek Kemmyn ('Common' Cornish) is best placed to serve as the basis for the next stage of the Cornish language revival. As well as informing the continuing language debate, where the supporters of Unified, Kernuak (Modern) and Kemmyn (Common/Phonemic) advocate their particular forms of Revived Cornish, George's contribution is also of interest to those seeking an insight into the imperatives and motives of the contemporary Revivalist movement.

In marked contrast to the emphasis on Celtic Revivalism as the epitome of 'Cornishness', John Hurst's sensitive handling and appreciation of the late Jack Clemo's original manuscripts (deposited in the University of Exeter Library) reminds us of one of the many paradoxes in Clemo's life and work. Although growing-up in the midst of the china-clay country and representing it so faithfully in prose and poem, (a district still to this day overwhelmingly working-class indigenous Cornish in its make-up, where religious Nonconfomity is still a power and men still mine for clay, where brass bands, male voice choirs and even Cornish wrestling thrive) Clemo remained unmoved by the notion of 'Celtic Cornwall'. The clay-country might encapsulate all that is redolent of working-class popular Cornish culture, but for Clemo it was not 'Celtic'. He wrote, 'My Cornwall is different, at once more starkly modern and more radically mystical' (Michael Williams (ed.), *My Cornwall*, Tintagel, 1973). This modernity and mysticism was elaborated against the background of Clemo's twin disabilities of blindness and deafness, a process which—as Hurst explains—is laid bare in the manuscripts.

The theme of 'difference' in the context of Cornish natural history is emphasised by Stella Turk in an article developed from her Caroline L. Kemp Lecture, delivered in the Royal Cornwall Museum in 1994. She stresses the crucial, determining impact of Cornwall's geographic position and maritime context. Her perceptive comment that 'Within this paradox of land isolation and sea connections, there is a key to much that characterises Cornwall and the Isles of Scilly' is an explanation for the 'remarkable inventory' of Cornish flora and fauna but it has wider applicability to much else that makes Cornwall distinctive. Indeed, it is a phrase that all practitioners of Cornish Studies should have ready on their lips.

But, as Adrian Spalding makes clear in his article on the importance of metaliferous mining sites for wildlife, Cornwall's extensive experience of copper, tin and other metaliferous mining has left a distinctive landscape (so-called 'derelict land') which in itself forms a distinctive habitat for certain species. Thus, as Spalding argues, any environmental assessment with a view to 'reclamation' of derelict land sites in Cornwall should include careful consideration of the relationship between habitat and species. His article is, therefore, an important contribution to the growing debate on derelict land which, at its most stark, has seen a clash of opposing 'moral geographies'—on the one hand a desire to order, 'sanitise' ('anglicise'?) and make safe an unkempt, dangerous, abandoned wasteland; on the other, a determination to defend a unique and classic landscape which is not only a memorial to the past glories of Cornwall but a living and essential element of the Cornish cultural identity.

Contemporary controversies also inform the contribution of Malcolm Williams and Eric Harrison, and that of Carol Williams. Williams and Harrison investigate a paradox that has dominated much of post-war Cornwall, the continuing out-migration of indigenous Cornish against the background of massive in-migration which since the late 1960s has reversed the former century-long experience of declining population. They speculate that those Cornish who cross the Tamar are motivated, like their nineteenth-century forebears in the 'Great Emigration', by the prospect of material advance and conclude that there is indeed clear evidence that out-migrants 'do better' economically than their compatriots who remain in Cornwall. In-migrants, however, are less homogenous as a group. Williams and Harrison show that on the whole in-migrants are generally 'better-off' than the local population at the time of their move to Cornwall but that ten years later their economic fortunes have come to resemble those of the locals. However, Williams and Harrison caution against a conclusion that suggests in-migrants somehow become poorer than the Cornish but they do point to the contrasting experiences of different types of in-migrants—those deploying 'organisational' or 'cultural' assets (those relocated to Cornwall by their employers, or those with transferable professional skills) generally 'do well' while those with 'property' assets (those who accumulate capital from business and/or housing moves, and often move to Cornwall for 'life-style' reasons) are less successful in economic terms.

Carol Williams pursues the impact of in-migration in the area of housing in Cornwall, noting that increasing demand for accommodation has occurred at a time of a decreasing quantity of rented property, a fact that has prompted some to identify a 'housing crisis' in Cornwall. She concludes that in-migrants are generally 'better-off' than locals, and are thus better placed to compete in the Cornish housing market. However, she also notes that this advantage appears in general to be limited to those who sold properties outside of the region and have subsequently bought within Cornwall. And, in an intriguing echo of Williams' and Harrison's view that in socio-economic terms in-migrants come to resemble the Cornish with the passage of time, Carol Williams considers that the adult off-spring of in-migrants find themselves in precisely the same position as the indigenous Cornish when trying to penetrate the local housing market, and with the additional disadvantage of having few relatives locally to help smooth the way. This is clearly a proposition deserving of further research, and one might speculate that this socio-economic mechanism of 'assimilation' into the

Cornish community experienced by some in-migrant families could have wider cultural implications—from the propensity to self-define as 'Cornish' to perhaps voting behaviour.

Needless to say, the diversity of material in *Cornish Studies: Three* is reflected in the wider mass of publications, both popular and academic, on Cornish themes. An innovation in *Cornish Studies: Three*, therefore, is the introduction of a Book Reviews section. Although the flow of Cornish publications is so vast that to attempt a comprehensive reviewing policy would be doomed to failure (or at least warrant a separate review publication in its own right!), it is possible to identify those volumes that make contributions which either reflect the current development of Cornish Studies as a discipline or complement debate in the pages of *Cornish Studies*. With that in mind, a selective reviewing policy will be developed, and in this edition of *Cornish Studies* we discuss three quite different volumes which contribute to three areas of current concern—the historiography of early modern Cornwall, the language debate, and sources of data for research in the social sciences.

Philip Payton,
Reader in Cornish Studies and
Director,
Institute of Cornish Studies,
University of Exeter,
Redruth, Cornwall.

COLLECTIVE ACTION AND THE CORNISH MINER IN AUSTRALIA: AN EARLY REPUDIATION OF THE 'INDIVIDUALISTIC' THESIS

Mel Davies

INTRODUCTION

Only in recent years has the idea that 'Cornish individualism' presented an obstacle to collective action among Cornish miners in the nineteenth century, been questioned. Both Bernard Deacon and Gill Burke have shown that during the late 1860s and early 1870s concerted action was widespread, especially in the eastern reaches of the Duchy but that an embryonic union movement was stifled by adverse economic conditions which struck the copper and tin industries.[1] While 'individualistic' mentality has been questioned, it has also been claimed that tutwork and tribute systems which encouraged competition between workers compounded the individualistic trait[2] as did influential conservative Cornish Methodism which actively preached against any form of militancy.[3] By the 1870s (it can be claimed) traditional tribute and tutwork systems were breaking down[4] and Cornish Methodism was taking on a more liberal hue, with the added bonus that Cornish Methodism had brought to the fore lay preachers who through their discipline, powers of oratory and organisational abilities were able to lead union activity and labour movements throughout the Western world.[5]

This late dawning of collective action, is, however, difficult to reconcile with the strike at the South Australian Mining Association's (SAMA) Burra Burra mine, in the first half of the nineteenth century, an event that has hitherto been either ignored or downplayed.[6] In both its magnitude and organisation the strike that took place among a

predominantly Cornish workforce in 1848–49, must raise further questions as to the above reasons for lack of militancy and pushes back by
about twenty years the 'collectivist' thesis as pronounced by Burke and
Deacon. What the Burra Burra strike suggests is that while custom and
tradition associated with working practices might ordinarily have had
some restraining effect upon collective action, Cornishmen were just
as capable of joining ranks as workers in other occupations and
locations. This was as true in South Australia in 1848–49 as it was
during the Cornish events between 1871–74 upon which Deacon has
remarked that 'when the time was ripe, Cornish men and women, even
those involved in mining, were quite prepared to combine in defence
of their wages and conditions of work.'[7]

What is perhaps pertinent to the debate is that all methods of
mining, wage systems, rules and regulations, hours of work,[8] and even
the 'cost-book' form of ownership adopted by the South Australian
Mining Association at their Burra mine,[9] were based on Cornish
practice. It was virtually a transplant from Cornwall to the Antipodes.
This therefore begs the question, why should Cornish miners on this
occasion have behaved in concerted action against the mine owners in
a strike which involved a total of about 600 miners over a period of
three-and-a-half months?[10]

THE ASSAY DISPUTE

The strike was in fact based on two separate issues. The first was
associated with the assaying of ores, the second with a dispute over
wages.

Assaying procedures at the Burra were conducted according to
customary Cornish procedure. Parcels of roughly crushed ore were
made up into circular piles with a flat summit. One of the piles would
be cut across and samples taken from the 'rill' on both sides of the
cut.[11] Accompanied by the owner-tributer, the samples, under strict
observation by the 'grass' (surface) captain, would be taken to be dried
in a pan held over a fire so as to eliminate water weight. The ore was
then accurately weighed and samples placed in sealed bags.[12] One
sample was retained by the tributer for private analysis if he so wished,
another was taken to the mine-owners' assayer for immediate analysis,
while a third was retained by the captain for testing by an independent
assayer in the case of a dispute.[13] Such procedures and safeguards
appear to have kept generations of Cornish tributers quite content.
This was not to be the case at the Burra.

There is no doubt that the first problem brought to the attention
of the directors, in June 1848, involved skulduggery, for following

complaint by the pare of 'Penna & Co.' voicing dissatisfaction of the analysis of samples between their assayer, John Rowe, and the mine-owners assayer, a 'sealed' sample was sent to Adelaide for independent analysis. This revealed that when pieces of copper filings were removed, the assay value of the ore was brought down from fifty to twenty-three per cent! Not only did the pare fall under suspicion but so did Captain Samuel Penglaze and other persons involved in the sampling process.[14] Nothing was resolved but henceforth the mine's senior captain, Henry Roach, was ordered to personally take charge of sealing of samples.[15]

The problem did not go away, for a month after the Penna affair came to notice, George Crozer's ore recorded a difference of 14 per cent between the miners' assayer, John Rowe, and the mine superintendents' appointee James Hosken,[16] though this time there were no copper filings present. Captain Roach first put down the discrepancy to broken sieves and too much dirt in the ore which tended to produce bias between samples; then to the maldistribution of 'prills' of ore of extreme difference in quality which also caused bias; and also to the poor assaying procedure of Hosken the mine-owners' assayer.[17] Roach's suspicions regarding Hosken were probably warranted, as he had been allowed to take on the responsibility as assayer by the mine superintendent, despite having been rejected at an earlier date when he applied to the directors for the job.[18] Captain Roach's answer was to try to eliminate sample bias by finely crushing the sample ores and carefully mixing.[19] To keep the directors satisfied it was ordered that from July 1848, where there was a difference of under four per cent, settlement should take place at the mean difference between samples. All larger discrepancies were to be independently tested in Adelaide.[20] This meant that a large number of tributers were forced to have their ores independently assayed, causing them inconvenience and delay in eventual settlement.

Disturbed, however, by continuing large discrepancies, a deputation of directors hastened to the mine in early August.[21] They insisted on a thorough investigation which revealed, to their horror, that an estimated 6,500 tons of ore analysed by Hosken and paid for to the miners at an average thirty-seven per cent was actually only twenty-eight per cent.[22] Fraud on a large scale by the miners was now suspected but the focus of the directors' attention fell upon Thomas Burr who was held ultimately responsible for the problem, being accused of gross neglect in his supervisory position in the assaying division and other areas of responsibility.[23] Burr, the former Surveyor General of South Australia had been recruited to the position of superintendent in August 1847, on attractive salary terms and a three year contract.[24] On

8 September 1848, the directors wrote to inform him of his immediate dismissal.[25]

In the meanwhile there was discontent in the ranks of the tributers who rankled at the inconvenience and delays in having their ores assayed and settled, and also at the greater time, effort and expense involved in having to dress their ores to a higher standard than hitherto.[26] They also grumbled that Elphick, the directors' Adelaide-based 'independent' assayer, was recording biased and unfavourably low assays. The directors further aggravated the miners when they ordered that all of Hosken's previous assay certificates were to be ignored and all unpaid-for-ores re-tested.[28] This was because of the suspicion that the miners had taken advantage of Hosken's (described by the directors as only a young lad whom Burr had allowed to assay without supervision)[29] inexperience by carefully and fraudulently selecting the samples which were passed over for sealing.

The scene was set for a show-down, and this occurred when following Burr's refusal to resign,[30] a deputation consisting of Mine Secretary Henry Ayers, and directors Charles Beck, Captain John Ellis and George Kingston arrived at the mine township of Kooringa on 13 September 1848, to personally dismiss him. According to Ayers, the tributers,

> fearing they would lose a good *friend* . . . partly to intimidate the Directors from dismissing Burr and partly on their own account *Struck* and would not go to their pitches, they then forced all the others to leave off work and in fact, took possession of the Mine, and carried on such games, that I was obliged to despatch 'an express' to the Governor.[31]

The 'express' was despatched on Friday 15 September and took eleven hours to reach Adelaide. It contained news of alarming proportions:

> of acts of the most violent character and actual force having taken men up from the shafts tied together and carried them off the mine . . . (warrants had been obtained) against two of the ringleaders but the police prevented from making the capture by a mob of about one hundred and sixty men. The total number of men now in revolt is about three hundred. The men have virtual possession of the Mine and have prevented the ore from being carted away. The only work permitted to go on is the Whim at the Water Shaft which they threaten to stop . . . unless means are taken to stop this . . .

the Mine will be ruined . . . This being the first time that anything like this has occurred in the Province the Deputation feel that it is necessary to act with energy and decision or otherwise we should be entirely in the hands of the people.[32]

As news also reached Adelaide that Ayers had been assaulted and that the miners boasted of 'having as much powder as the Association, and . . . (were) determined to have their rights',[33] it is little wonder that Adelaide readers were faced with the startling news headline 'Revolution at the Burra Burra Mines'.[34]

As a result, a party of twenty-six armed mounted police, headed by G. S. Dashwood, Commissioner of Police, arrived at the Kooringa township on the afternoon of 17 September.[35] Dashwood soon discovered that Ayers' alarm was unwarranted, and reported that there was no intent by the miners to resort to violent measures, having 'evinced that disposition, by (the miners) consenting that the two men referred to (i.e. in Ayers' letter) . . . should appear before the Resident Magistrate tomorrow'.[36]

The events, as subsequently revealed, showed that, anticipating the arrival of the directors, the miners had called a mass meeting. A committee was elected and the Chairman of this committee had, after leading those gathered in prayer, carefully detailed grievances to the crowd. He emphasised to them:

> the purpose of the frequent quotation that 'labour is capital', and the oft proved fact that aggression on the part of the *monied* capitalists on their subservients must sooner or later find their level in the reciprocal return of the latter (tread on a worm and he will [be] sure to recoil), and finished by inviting his fellow-sufferers to give language to their own opinions in this, to them, all-important subject.[37]

This appears to have been rather radical language for a Methodist lay-preacher, for it was from such ranks that the leaders of the miners were drawn. These leaders were later applauded by the editor of the *South Australian Register*, John Stephens, himself an ardent Methodist and of Cornish descent, when he welcomed the 'pastoral efforts of the various Reverend Gentlemen for having drained the flocks in so admirable a manner'. The 'draining' was in reference to the prohibition placed on drinking during the strike and the discipline that was instilled among the ranks by their efforts.[38]

At conclusion of the meeting it was agreed that the directors be approached by a delegation to seek redress of grievances, and if unsuccessful a 'general strike' was to take place.[39] The directors, however, ungraciously refused to even meet the delegation, stating that as tributers were individual contractors then they would only be received as individuals.[40] Failing this, the directors threatened to close the mine for four months.[41] Being frustrated by the directors' response, a further mass meeting was called which determined to strike immediately and to 'prevent any straggling delinquent from proving a stumbling block in the way', they forthwith headed for the mine to dissuade would-be recalcitrants. Eight were caught in the act, and two who proved unresponsive to persuasion 'were *hauled up to grass*', tied back-to-back in a wheelbarrow carried on the shoulders of four able men, and preceded by the other six recalcitrants, were paraded with vociferous 'Hurras' and exposed 'to the gaze and ridicule of about 1800 laughing souls'. The whole was carried out in perfect good humour.[42]

The incidence of 'violence' referred to by Ayers was later tried by the Court. James Henswood and William Stevens were accused of using threatening language to William Cock Snr. and John Reed, preventing them from entering the mine, and for threatening to destroy their property. Corporal Brooks of the Mounted Police arrested one but deemed it wiser to let the other go when faced by a large crowd of miners.[43] When the case was presented, both men were reproved for 'being ignorant in not being able to write' and were each released on a recognisance of £30 each with thirty-four shillings costs.[44] Another, William Sprague (an Irishman), was accused of assaulting the directors but at that time he was so 'stupidly drunk' he had been under the impression that he was attacking Captain Roach who had sacked him some months previously. He too was given the same penalty as Henswood and Stevens. All were quickly released following payment of costs and recognisances by the Burra miners.[45] By their apparent ignorance, it is obvious that none of these men were from among the miners' leaders.

With Police Commissioner Dashwood acting as arbitrator, the directors eventually agreed to meet the miners' delegation, on condition that there was no coercion and that they were approached in a respectful manner.[46] The 'Committee Men' as they were called, subsequently brought their grievances to the fore. These not only embraced the assay question but also the matter of compulsory deductions for the 'Club & Doctor Fund', and exorbitant charges for tools, fuses, powder, and candles.[47] The latter was probably a perpetual grumble among all Cornish miners and the directors argued that their charges were no higher than those made in other copper mines in the Province.[48] In respect to the Club and Doctor fund, it was the contribution of six pence per week for the mine doctor that especially rankled, for the cover did not extend to families, and the combined contribution of the miners meant a very handsome salary of £17 to £20 per week for the doctor, in whose appointment the miners had no say.[49] On a previous occasion the miners had argued that they had their own benefit societies. These could provide cheaper and more adequate medical care, and also cover for sickness benefits at a lower charge than paid to the mine club (the latter cost the miner one shilling per week).[50] This argument was rejected by the directors who insisted that retention of Cornish practice would ensure that all workers were compulsorily insured and that skilled medical attention would always be at hand on the mine site. They did suggest, however, that the miners might discuss details such as family charges with the doctor concerned.

On the assay question it was agreed that arrangements as outlined in a previous miners' memorial would be accepted. It was determined that in future any samples tested by the mine assayer should be sealed and returned to the miner for testing by a 'practical assayer', and that numbers should be substituted for names on samples. The directors, however, insisted that all samples differing by more than one per cent, rather than the old agreement for a four per cent differential, should be re-analysed.[51] The miners, it is reported, were at first delighted, especially as the directors benevolently allowed a return to work without fining the miners for breach of contract which was within their power.[52] However, this news was spiced with the less palatable information that a drop in the price of ores on the Swansea market would lead to a reduction in wages.[53]

The emergency over, the directors' party headed post-haste back to Adelaide. When making a dramatic exit from Kooringa their coach overturned with Beck, Ellis and Kingston suffering minor injuries. Ayers, falling on top of the others, only dented his dignity! So ended the first incident in what was to become a long, drawn-out industrial dispute.

WAGE CUTS

On Wednesday 20 September, just six days following the beginning of the first strike, Ayers wrote to William Challoner, accountant and temporary superintendent at the mine, instructing him to pin up a notice to announce a reduction in wages from thirty-five to thirty shillings per week for miners, and from twenty-five to twenty-one shillings for labourers, carters and other grass workers. Carpenters, blacksmiths, sawyers and mechanics also saw substantial wage reductions.[55] On 2 October, 'rumour' reached Ayers in Adelaide that the surface men had again struck and that the tributers had refused to bid for pitches at the

October letting. The directors were unperturbed for there were about 15,000 tons of ore on the surface.[56] Their only concern was that the drays carrying ores to Port Adelaide should not be detained.[57] They also believed that with miners from Cornwall arriving at Port Adelaide every day, the strike would be short lived.

The reductions in wages were not without precedent[58] and in Cornwall, as in South Australia, wage levels tended to relate to shifts in supply and demand for labour and with the 'Standard' determined by the price of copper. While tributers had a chance to ride such fluctuations by greater work effort and possible extension of the working day (though it generally resulted in a lower average wage), this was not possible for the surface worker unless he happened to work on a contract basis as an ore dresser, though few did. There are two interpretations of this new strike, the first, that tributers and tutworkers came out in support of their lower paid brethren and the second, that coming on top of the aggravations of the earlier strike, and in light of the *peculiar* situation of the mine in terms of its earning capacity, that all miners, imbued with a feeling of gross injustice, struck to challenge the owners.

The 'peculiar' circumstance was highlighted by the editor of the *South Australian Register* when he attacked the directors for their extreme avarice. This attitude was in contrast to the *South Australian*, an establishment newspaper, which believed the directors had acted rationally 'according to the law of supply and demand'.[60] The point being made by the *Register* was that the Burra Burra was proving the richest copper mine in the world. Between September 1847 and 1 September 1848, dividends amounting to 800 per cent had been paid to shareholders. The last payment of 200 per cent had been paid just two weeks before the first strike. The directors had also announced on that occasion that another 200 per cent would be paid in December, a forecast based on expected receipts and on fabulous new finds. In August, for example, there had been discovered a lode of red oxide measuring '8 fathoms by 48 feet which had gone down and true as if it had been driven in. There were men blasting away as if it was a Stone quarry and raising blocks of this ore at 12/- per ton. It requires no cleaning or dressing . . . I could scarcely believe what I saw.'[61] Another discovery in Kingston's shaft 'of compact green carbonate yielding 50% . . . ten feet wide (had an estimated value of) . . . one hundred thousand pounds!!!'[62] Despite this good fortune, the directors made their decision to cut wages, only a few days after their September dividend payment, in response to the news that thirty-five per cent ores had dropped between £4 and £5 per ton on the Swansea market.[63]

During the ensuing struggle, it was John Stephens, editor of the

South Australian Register and the *Adelaide Observer*, who rose to champion the mine workers. Stephens was well qualified to do so. His father, who in 1827 had gained the presidency of the Methodist Conference, was Cornish, which probably gave Stephens an empathy with the miners. The editor's brother, Joseph Raynor Stephens, a Wesleyan Minister forced to resign from the connexion, has been described as the first Chartist martyr.[64] His often violent tirades in the 1830s helped split the Chartist movement into 'moral force' and 'physical force' factions. While later he dropped his support for the political charter itself, he continued to champion the cause of the oppressed against tyranny and exploitation.[65] In Joseph Raynor Stephens' most turbulent years, his younger brother John (supporter of the cause of the Burra miners) had given him active support as editor of the Wesleyans' most influential journal the *Christian Advocate*, until removed from that position by the reactionary forces within the connexion led by their secretary, Jabez Bunting.[66]

John Stephens' advocacy of the Burra miners' campaign cost him the advertising revenue of the South Australian Mining Association[67] and was the cause of writs for libel served upon him by the mine's nine directors.[68] It also gained him the gratitude of the Burra miners who contributed £50 towards the cost of fighting the libel cases,[69] and public acclaim as the champion of independent journalism at a 'Monster Meeting' called in Adelaide.[70] From 29 September, when surface workers gave notice that they would refuse to work at the reduced rates and when tributers and tutworkers refused to accept pitches at the captain's price, Stephens constantly urged them on and solidly supported their cause. The refusal to bid for pitches was, of course, one of the rare cases when Cornish copper miners failed to compete against each other for mining pitches.[71]

On 4 October Stephens printed the miners' grievances,[72] pointing out that deductions of at least seven shillings per week for Club and Doctor, candles, gunpowder and rent, when added to the heavy cost of living 100 miles inland from the port,[73] made the new rate of wages unacceptable. 'In solidarity', all workers, even 'whim boys and ore-pickey boys' determined to dress their ores, settle accounts and leave the mine, unless the directors reconsidered their wage decision. The public declaration was signed by the 'Committee members' (although only twelve of the names were printed in the *Register*), headed by John Davy Hailes and Malachie Deeble.[74] On 8 October it had been reported that some miners had already left for New Zealand but that most were prepared to stay and fight. A fighting fund with more than 400 workers contributing one shilling per week was set up to support the families of poorer workers.[75]

At this juncture, some two to three weeks after the beginning of this second strike, another development occurred to strengthen the resolve of the strikers. Indeed, previously their position had been one of weakness for the directors were quite content to note the huge stockpile of ore at grass ready for conveyance to the port and shipment to the Swansea market.[76] Thus when the teamsters who drove the bullock drays struck in support of the miners and to protest their own case, the chance of victory rose appreciably.

The teamsters were led by a remarkable character, an Irishman, Captain William Chace.[77] Chace, some months prior to the strike, had been blacklisted by the directors from their carrying trade because he refused to convey back-loading from the port to the mine at sub-market price. Ores to the Port were paid for at forty shillings per ton but the return goods at only twenty-five shillings. 'We must be determined with these gentry' stated Ayers, but Chace was made of stern resolve and when the opportunity arose he answered the miners appeal to join the strike.[79] Claiming to represent 500 drovers, Chace, under his pseudonym of 'Teamster' called for action: 'On Tuesday morning, the 17th October, I hoist my flag with "Free Trade and Bullock Drivers' Rights" and "Keep drays at Home" upon it . . . now my lads, stick to it and come under your Captain's flag and never let us furl it until we get our price . . .'.[80]

Under the standard of the Red Flag, Chace set up his blockade at Sod Hut some thirteen kilometres from the Burra, and with strong support from fellow bullockies, plus the occasional threat (for bullockies were not renowned for their finesse),[81] traffic to and from the mine was reduced and came to a complete stop by 31 October.[82] Over the next three weeks not one ounce of ore was removed from the mine.[83]

While the directors mulled over possible demurrage charges on sixteen ships engaged and waiting for ore cargoes at Port Adelaide,[84] a situation of which the workers were well aware,[85] a war of words continued in the local press. The rhetoric also suggested widespread support for the striking workers.

Noting the 'Warfare of Right against Might', one commentator was pleased to note that:

> Out of the quagmire of oppression . . . our brethren (from Kapunda, another copper mine, largely manned by Cornishmen) . . . are prepared to forward £100, or more, if required, in proof of their unity in the common cause with the club fund in Kooringa, Burra Burra. We cite this one instance only that the public may see, at a *coup d'oeil*, the 'Union, Strength,

and Communion' which now so happily reign throughout the mining districts of this colony.[86]

Another correspondent reminded readers that: 'The "rights of labour" are even more to be respected than the "rights of capital", for as labour is the foundation of all wealth, it follows . . . that no wealth can be created without labour.'[87] From a less radical source, the correspondent from the General Agency Office, Adelaide, warned the directors: 'they had better beware attempting to over-reach the miners. I shall not be surprised hearing before long of one universal strike all over the colony—one thing is certain, that to a great extent, a species of "Trade Union" has been established amongst the miners of several mines'.[88]

The situation was almost too much for another commentator who saw in the strike the dreaded seeds sown by the revolutions taking place in Europe. Stephens, who it was claimed goaded on and encouraged the miners and teamsters,[89] was virulent in his attack on the directors, accusing them of abusing 'their unlimited power . . . by which the honest labourer of South Australia will be brought down to the level of home drudgery and starvation from which he hoped he had escaped when he touched our free shores . . . There is here a disposition to grind the faces of the poor'.[90]

A letter from 'Teamster' placed the situation in radical terms and appealed not only to bullock drivers and miners but all workers to fight for their rights: 'Workmen what did you come here for? You came here, I presume to escape the bondage and the serfdom that labour is under to capital in Europe . . . the exaggeration of capital in a few hands is an embodiment of tyranny as sordid as it is powerful. "Awake, arise, or be for ever fallen." '[91]

Despite this rhetoric the directors remained unabashed. To illustrate the point, on 4 November it was moved at the board meeting that a dividend of 100 per cent should be paid on 1 December. The motion was narrowly defeated, for conditions were considered 'not expedient'.[92] This reluctance had nothing to do with the feelings and sensitivities of the strikers but with the fact that the directors had just discovered their financial position resulting from overdrawn accounts on their foreign consignments due to the incorrect assays.[93] It was this fact which had strengthened their resolve to force down wages.[94]

The miners, meanwhile, continued their resistance. On 11 November, observed by Ayers and three directors, Captain Roach offered twenty-one pitches on the basis of a thirty shilling wage.[95] This offer rubbed salt into the wounds of the tributers, for the limited number of pitches would have seen at least fifty pares face the indignity of having to work at owners-account. The 400 assembled miners refused all offerings 'by Rebel advice'.[96] The resistance was soon to be weakened though not among the miners' ranks. On 22 November, the first crack appeared in the edifice of solidarity when the teamsters, driven by divisions between large carrying contractors and the independent drovers (mainly Irish), went back to work at the old rates.[97]

Now in a stronger position, the directors began to react. Lists of what the mine accountant, Challoner, called 'obnoxious persons', were drawn up, and it appears that even the public mail was tampered with to obtain information on individuals.[98] Agents at the port also attempted to recruit penniless immigrant miners as blacklegs even before their feet touched shore.[99] There were few prepared to act as scabs but in December Challoner noted dwindling resolve among the miners and announced that he had been approached by one large family of miners who, desperate for accommodation, had agreed to work at the advertised rates, 'if protected from the "Old Hands".'[100] Hamstrung by the fact that many of the 'old hands' were still awaiting settlement of their ores, Ayers ordered that the processing of these ores be expedited[101] and notices to quit given to those who lived in Company cottages, 'for it is plain that until the Committee men and Ring Leaders are off the property no work will go on'.[102] Protection was also to be offered by the magistrate to any strike-breakers, for, as Ayers remarked, 'some one must be the first to begin, as with the Draymen'.[103] Two days before Christmas, Ayers wrote to instruct Challoner that Joe Trevean, A. Penna, Thos. Cocking, M. Rogers and F. Polkinghorne were to be offered the chance of starting immediately, either on tutwork or tribute. His Christmas message for Messrs. Bosance, Robins, Hoskins and Stephens was immediate notice to quit their premises.[104] Challoner was also instructed to vet all applicants carefully to ensure that no undesirables were re-employed.

The first week of January 1849 heralded the end of the strike, despite a last minute attempt by twenty-eight miners to continue with the action. As the *South Australian* gleefully announced:

> the refractory were those who had made a few hundreds in the golden age of the mine, while those who had arrived more recently are now penniless, and, as the rich would not be *social* and divide their funds, it was according to the old adage, 'ill talking between full men and fasting'.[105]

Stephen's sympathetic interpretation, under the title 'The Burra Burra Martyrs', however, told a different tale. He appealed for a subscription: 'in aid of the rightly-intentioned but unfortunate men who, with their families, (had) been thrown out of bread by the issue of the last strike . . . We learn their situation is already trying, and likely to become pitiable unless prompt relief be arranged.'[106]

As another commentator pointed out, the miners had been forced after sixteen weeks to return 'under the influence of fair promises and need'.[107] Not only were the ringleaders and Committee men forced from their premises and refused re-employment at the Burra but they were also blacklisted from other mines[108] and related industries in the Colony.[109] A list of 'Obnoxious men' was, for example, given to the Superintendent of the Patent Copper Company[110] which had begun constructing a copper smelting establishment at Kooringa.[111] Those now employed went back to work at the reduced wage rate announced before the strike.

TAKING STOCK

In tackling the Board of Directors, the Burra miners had taken on a formidable foe. Their approach to the workers was not in terms of perceived exploitation but rather in terms of 'natural rights' to be exercised by those prepared to take risks with capital. Faithful proponents of the 'iron-law of wages' and the guiding-hand of 'demand and supply', they were captive to the 'scientific' political-economic thought of the day. Such beliefs and the promise of the unfettering of the forces of *laissez-faire* had attracted these 'Radical' members of the middle class to the nascent Colony of South Australia.[112] As Secretary to the Board, Henry Ayers, a self-made man, and future Premier of South Australia, guarded the interests of shareholders with great tenacity of purpose. In facing such opponents the miners had for over three months faced immovable objects.

Ayers' response at the end of the strike was predictable in that he saw the battle in terms of the triumph of capital over labour:

> altho' we had vessels in the Port on which we were almost daily expecting to pay demurrage—no quarter shewn—rather pay demurrage for a month than acknowledge the power of men to raise their wages when they like . . . We have gained such a triumph to ourselves and the employers of men here that scarcely any sum would equal. We have shewn men that they cannot do as they like.[113]

Facing the directors was a core of men equally determined. Stephens described them as men who were chosen to lead by their fellow workers 'in consequence of their moral and general standing . . .

(and) their mental superiority', men who had stood up for 'the preservation of the just rights of labour employed in a dangerous calling'.[114] Their rationale for the strike was their ardent belief in fair play and the dignity of labour which also explained their determination to carry it through. While in Cornwall they had seen wages rise and fall according to the Copper Standard, never had they, in all probability, experienced wage cuts made with such apparent callousness. In Cornwall it was understood that the tributer was a partner in speculation, but when the owners of capital were jubilantly flaunting dividends of almost unbelievable magnitude,[115] and promising shareholders even greater rewards, then this, along with the nagging complaint of compulsory deductions and the upset of the assaying disagreements, was enough to turn the supposed 'individualistic stoicism' into active combination and resistance. Adding fuel to grievances was, no doubt, that the miners had been attracted to South Australia by publicity which promised them fair play and a high standard of living.[116] The timing was also significant, for most of the miners had fled Cornwall during and after the appalling destitution and food riots of 1846–47.[117] Such ingredients provided an adequate recipe for revolt.

The success in keeping the strike going for so long (fourteen weeks, excluding the break for work between the two strikes) must lie with the leaders who, as the documentation shows, time and again exhorted their weaker brethren to continue the fight. Part of their effort also went into keeping the peace, for there is little doubt that rioting or damage to property would have called down the full and bloody wrath of the authorities. As contemporaries noted, what was remarkable was the orderly way in which the strike had been conducted. There was an absence of any 'unruly or vindictive outrage',[118] for a principal part of the Committee's duty had been 'to see that good and peaceable order was maintained among the constituents'.[119] Emphasised by onlookers was the role of Methodist leaders in keeping their flocks sober and calm.[120]

The seeds of indiscipline and riotous behaviour were certainly present in the community. One commentator reported that three of his acquaintances had left the mine in disgust in an earlier year because 'there was such a drunken black guard lot there'.[121] Another described Kooringa in 1846 as having been a 'hell on earth'. Frederick Hayward described activities at a local hostelry in 1847: the publican tired of handing out one pint pots of malt, liquor or spirits, began to serve his mining customers in buckets:

A roaring trade was driven where the roughest characters congregated, breaking windows, singing and fighting, and where the landlord used a cricket bat to clear his house at night. On pay nights, Saturdays, fights would be coming off all the afternoon and evening, the Ring formed and kept by two Policemen, who were powerless to do anything but see fair play.[123]

By 1848, according to some authorities, 'backsliders' among the Cornish miners had been tempted back to join the various Methodist denominations as the raw 'frontier' community began to settle down. Chapels and Teetotal Societies were being established and laymen preachers from among the miners were being appointed to look after the spiritual welfare of the community and to bring a less roisterous complexion to the mining town.[124] It was in this calmer, perhaps more typical Cornish environment, that the strike took place.

While the strikers were eventually defeated in their objectives, the spark of defiance casts new light upon 'non-militant' Cornish miners and their lack of will or ability to act collectively. At the Burra, facing destitution, twenty-eight of them stood out in defiance even when others, including new arrivals, were forced to work due to need. While the strike had no apparent long-term effect upon union activity (it was not until 1864 that the next strike of copper miners took place at the Moonta Mines), the organisation at the mine and the strong support from other copper miners in the colony indicates that the radical spirit was early experienced in South Australia, a fact which is difficult to reconcile with the picture usually presented of Cornish workers.

In explaining the militancy of the miners, the influential role of John Stephens must also be recognised. Accused by the directors of encouraging defiance among both miners and teamsters, he bolstered the miners' morale. His powerful voice through the medium of the *South Australian Register* which railed against the mine's employers was born out of a radical past and belief in the dignity of man. Whilst it has been claimed that Stephens was no Chartist[125] his language and advice was certainly in accord with Chartist sentiments of the time, and he was Cornish by descent.

CONCLUSION

The outcome of the strike was not a clear cut victory to the owners, for, on balance, they had surprisingly few cards in their favour. Because the miners were recent migrants and therefore relatively unsettled, this tended to dilute the mine directors' power over the mining population. As already noted, the relative mobility of the miners was witnessed in the early days of the strike when a number took the line of least resistance and left for New Zealand. Although there was a large in-flow of overseas labour during the strike period, the directors were initially unable to manipulate the situation. While Cornish miners were renowned for their strike breaking activities, the recently arrived Cornish miners refused to scab on fellow countrymen, most of whom would have known the strikers as workmates, friends, or even relations, among the close-knit communities in Cornwall. This was a source of frustration to the directors who underestimated the solidarity among the Cornish immigrants.

The management also had little power in terms of its threats over accommodation and welfare. The latter, as noted, was the source of much discontent by the miners. The former was provided for only a few miners, for most men and their families at this time (the census of 1851 recorded 1,800 creek dwellers out of a total of 4,300 people in the township) lived outside the confines of the company property in rent-free dug-outs excavated into the banks of the Burra Creek.[126] While the directors had an advantage in holding a large stockpile of ores which reduced urgency to negotiate or repudiate their wage decision, the miners recognised that distance from the mine to the port was a weakness which could be exploited to advantage. With co-operation and apparent collusion of the teamsters who also had grievances, the miners knew they could gain the upper hand.

The apparent strength of the directors in terms of their ability to hold out against the strikers was in fact illusory, for their propensity to pay out profits in dividends and the methods adopted to market their produce had placed them in a position where they faced em-barrassing financial problems. Unfortunately the strikers were not to know this. The winning stroke by the directors was to force divisions within the ranks of the teamsters. It was basically this that attained them victory over the striking miners. In the light of this interpretation, the strategy of the miners can be read as a well-organised attempt to attack the power of capital.

While Ayers interpreted the result as a triumph over the workers, and while demand and supply as well as copper prices continued to determine wages, it is notable that a more conciliatory approach to employees was adopted by the directors of the mine thereafter, especially in terms of communication and consultation. There is little doubt that the event had shaken the employing class out of their belief that in South Australia there was a new harmony between the classes. This is witnessed, for example, by the fact that the strike impressed upon the employing class the need to close ranks and, while the blacklist appears to have been successfully applied during the strike, it is claimed that the experience persuaded them to form the Adelaide Chamber of

Industry to amplify and coordinate the voice and strength of employers in the colony.

In respect to some of the characters involved in the strike, Stephens died in November 1850, aged 44 years, a sad loss for radical causes in early South Australia. Of the 'Committee men' little is known and most of them probably left the colony.[127] In 1851, one of their number, Andrew Robins, attempted to seek re-employment at the Burra Mine but the directors, vindictive to the end, refused his application.[128] Three years earlier, at the close of the strike, Challoner, the acting super-intendent, had requested the directors to reconsider Robins' case along with Messrs Bosnance and Hoskens, because they were 'quiete and industrious men', but from the 1851 response it appears doubtful that any of them would have been reinstated.[129] In 1863 Malachie Deeble was appointed underground captain at the Moonta Mine which replaced Burra Burra as South Australia's major copper ore producer. He retired in 1887 having gained a reputation for being the arch-enemy of local trade unionism.[130] Another of the Committee men, William Moyle, shifted to Victoria during the 1850s Goldrush but proved more successful in saving souls at Bendigo and Ballarat than in winning gold.[131] Hosken, the mine assayer, and Captain Penglaze who had been in charge of ore-dressing were both sacked. Elphick, the assayer who was appointed to replace Hosken, enjoyed long and trouble-free employment at the mine and 'gave general satisfaction both to men and employers'.[132] Chace, the teamster, was blacklisted by the directors and became a stockman of some repute. Burr, the deposed super-intendent, gained a victory over the directors when he obtained £1,763 in compensation and costs, after he took them to court for breach of contract.[133] In 1854, Burr took part in Australia's most celebrated uprising when gold miners took up arms at the Eureka Stockade. Perhaps, ironically, the man described in 1848 as the 'miners' friend' was highly commended for his efforts in support of the establishment in putting down the rebellion![134]

All these characters contributed to an industrial conflict in South Australia that denies the stereotype picture that has previously been drawn regarding the inability of Cornish miners to act collectively before the late 1860s.

NOTES AND REFERENCES

1. Bernard Deacon, 'Attempts at Unionism by Cornish Metal Miners in 1866', *Cornish Studies*, 10, 1983, pp. 27–36; Bernard Deacon, 'Heroic Individualists? The Cornish Miners and the Five Week Month 1872–74', *Cornish Studies*, 14, 1986, pp. 39–52, who also quotes Gill Burke, 'The

Cornish Miner and the Mining Industry, 1870–1921', Unpublished PhD.,
University of London, 1982; see also Philip Payton, 'Labour Failure
and Liberal Tenacity: Radical Politics and Cornish Political Culture,
1880–1939', *Cornish Studies* Two, 1994, pp. 83–95; Philip Payton, *The
Making of Modern Cornwall*, Redruth, 1992, esp. Introduction and Ch.
7; for the 'individualistic' thesis, see, A. K. Hamilton Jenkin, *The Cornish
Miner: An Account of His Life Above and Underground from Early
Times*, 1927, reprinted David & Charles, 1972, p. 199.

2. G. D. H. Cole, *The Payment of Wages*, London, 1928, p. 77, saw such
piece work methods as 'a crude appeal to individualism . . . it is generally
agreed among Trade Unionists that where they are adopted the morale
and sense of solidarity among workers are often lowered. They tend to
set one man's hand against the other's and inaugurate a system of
cut-throat competition between worker and worker.'

3. For the schism that rent Methodist ranks in 1849 and for Cornish
'conservatism', see: David Hempton, *Methodism and Politics in British
Society 1750–1850*, London, 1984, p. 211; John Rule, 'Methodism and
Politics 1791–1851', in Robert D. Storch (ed.), *Popular Culture in
Cornwall in Nineteenth Century England*, London 1982; Thomas Shaw,
The Bible Christians 1815–1907, London, 1965; Thomas Shaw, *A History
of Cornish Methodism*, Truro, 1967, p. 100; E. R. Taylor, *Methodism
and Politics 1791–1851*, Cambridge, 1935, pp. 12–13; J. T. Ward,
Chartism, London, 1973, p. 246; Robert F. Wearmouth, *Methodism and
the Working-Class Movements of England 1800–1850*, London, 1937,
pp. 176–7. For a brief overview of the issue see, Mel Davies, 'Australia's
First Mining Strike: The Burra Burra Mines, South Australia, 1848–49',
in Klaus Tenfelde (ed.), *Towards a Social History of Mining in the 19th
and 20th Centuries, Papers presented to the International Mining History
Congress Bochum, Federal Republic of Germany, September 3rd–7th,
1989*, Munich, 1992, pp. 694–95.

4. For Comment and reasons for the lack of militancy see, J. R. Leifchild,
Cornwall and Its Mines and Miners, 1857, reprinted Newcastle-upon-
Tyne, 1968, p. 146; John Taylor, 'On the Economy of Mining' (1837),
reprinted in Roger Burt (ed.), *Essays on the Organisation of Cornish
Mines and the Cornish Mining Economy*, Newton Abbott, 1969, p. 39;
L. L. Price, 'West Barbary or Notes on the System of Work and Wages
in the Cornish Mines' (1891) reprinted in Burt, 1969, pp. 154–5; D. B.
Barton, *Essays in Cornish Mining History*, Truro, 1968, (2 vols), vol. 1,
p. 46. For breaking down of the tribute and tutwork systems see, D. B.
Barton, *A History of Tin Mining and Smelting in Cornwall*, Truro, 1967,
p. 199; Deacon, 1986; Payton, 1994; Payton, 1992; p. 142.

5. R. E. Lingenfelter, *The Hardrock Miners*, Univ. of California, 1974, p. 6;
Payton, 1992, pp. 148–49 who lists such leaders in South Africa, the
United States and Australia.

6. A notable exception to this comment is the account in Ian Auhl, *The Story
of the 'Monster Mine'. The Burra Burra Mine and Its Townshops*

1845–1877, Burra Burra, 1986, ch. 10, and a brief account in Jim Moss, *Sound of Trumpets. History of the Labour Movement in South Australia*, Adelaide, 1985, pp. 22–28; In the most recent comment, Payton, 1992, p. 147, talks of the strike as being an 'incoherent protest' and contrasts this with the 'more telling stoppage at South Australia's Moonta and Wallaroo copper mines' in 1864. This author would suggest that the Burra strike was the more coherent in that it pitted capital against labour on industrial matters, whereas the 1864 strike which was of much smaller duration, involved a personality clash, involving miners who objected to the activities of two captains of the mine.

7. Deacon, 1986.

8. In respect to the limited militancy of Cornish miners nothing has previously been said about hours of work. In the nineteenth century some of the bitterest industrial conflict was associated not with working conditions or wages but with the fight to reduce hours. In Cornwall the eight hour 'core' appears to have been the established norm in the mining sphere which might explain some of the lack of industrial unrest, see Barton, 1967, p. 29. At the Burra, miners enjoyed the eight hour day, and a 44 hour week from its inception in 1845, see, South Australian Archives, BRG 22, 960, Directors' Out-letter books (hereafter SAA BRG 22, 960) No. 40, 5/11/1845. Note, Deacon, 1986, p. 41, refers to the fight for the nine hour day in Cornwall in 1872, but his examples do not include mining activities.

9. See, Mel Davies, 'The Cost-Book System in Australia with Particular Reference to the South Australian Mining Association', *Discussion Paper*, No. 85:15, November 1985, Department of Economics, University of Western Australia.

10. The vast majority of the 250 to 300 underground workers were Cornish. At the surface about half the 300 workers were of German origin but it was the Cornish underground workers, the 'elite' in the mine who dictated events over the period. The duration of this strike may be compared with the longest single strike during the 1866 events in Cornwall, which involved a period of three-and-a-half weeks at the South Caradon and Glasgow Caradon; see, Deacon, 1983, p. 32.

11. Jenkin, 1927, p. 230.

12. Auhl, 1986, quoting reminiscences of Solomon William, Miner, *Burra Burra Record*, 26 April 1934.

13. *South Australian*, 19 September 1848, *South Australian Register*, 20 September 1848; Burt, 1969, pp. 25, 189–90.

14. SAA BRG 22, 96, *Letters to Mine Officials* (hereafter SAA BRG 22, 961) No. 75, 21/6/1848, to Thomas Burr; SAA BRG 22, 961, no. 78, 1/7/1848.

15. SAA BRG 22, 961. No. 84, 22/7/1848, to Thomas Burr.

16. SAA BRG 22, 961, No. 84, 22/7/1848, to Thomas Burr.

17. SAA BRG 22, 961, No. 84, 22/7/1848; SAA BRG 22, 961, No. 87, 2/8/1848; BRG 22, 961, No. 94, 26/8/2848, all to Thomas Burr; BRG 22, 957, *Letters to Mine Officials*, (hereafter SAA BRG 22, 957) 8/8/1848, pp. 214–15.

18. SAA BRG 22, 961, No. 67, 31/5/1848, to Thomas Burr.
19. SAA BRG 22, 961, No. 85, 26/7/1848, to Thomas Burr.
20. SAA BRG 22, 961, No. 85, 26/7/1848, to Thomas Burr.
21. SAA BRG 22, 961, No. 88, 5/8/1848, to Thomas Burr.
22. *South Australian Register*, 4 November 1848, 'Burr v Beck & Others';
    SAA BRG 22, 961, No. 94, 26/8/1848, to Thomas Burr.
23. SAA BRG 22, 961, No. 94, 26/8/1848, to Thomas Burr; SAA BRG 22,
    961, No. 4, 5/10/1848, to Wm. Challoner, Accountant; Burr was accused
    of allowing the private use of company property, of failing to supervise
    the construction of cottages which were found to be substandard, of
    raising ores of too low quality, and of general neglect of duties. His
    morality was also questioned: 'his wife and himself both get drunk and
    not satisfied with his own wife but must have the mens wives—as well
    as the young girls in the open days'. Not all the directors saw this as a
    flaw, for Captain Allen's opinion was that 'a man has a right to get his
    greens when he can'. See, South Australian Archives, papers of John
    Benjamin Graham, Microfilm, PRG 100 (hereafter SAA PRG 100),
    16/9/1848, Diary Mr. Adams.
24. SAA BRG 22, 957, 18/8/1847, p. 167.
25. SAA BRG 22, 960, No. 618, 8/9/1848, to Thomas Burr.
26. SAA BRG 22, 961, No. 84, 22/7/1848, and No. 97, 7/9/1848, both to
    Thomas. Burr.
27. SAA BRG 22, 961, No. 94, 26/8/1848, to Thomas Burr.
28. SAA BRG 22, 961, No. 97, 7/9/1848, to Thomas Burr.
29. SAA BRG 100, No. 7, 14/2/1849, H. Ayers to J. B. Graham.
30. *South Australian*, 19 September 1848.
31. SAA PRG 100, No. 7, 14/2/1849, H. Ayers to J. B. Graham.
32. SAA GRG, 24, series 6, Colonial Office Correspondence, A (1848) 1432,
    15/9/1848, Ayers' letter was supported by a deposition from W. Lang,
    the Resident Magistrate, based on information furnished by the directors.
    Lang was incapacitated at the time.
33. *South Australian*, 19 September 1848.
34. *South Australian*, 19 September 1848.
35. The directors remaining in Adelaide suggested that a detachment of
    troops should also be despatched, see SAA BRG 22, 960, No. 621,
    16/8/1848, to G. F. Dashwood, Commissioner of Police.
36. SAA GRG 24, series 6, C/O Correspondence, A (1948) 1477.
37. *South Australian Register*, 20 September 1848.
38. *South Australian Register*, 23 September 1848; *South Australian*,
    22 September 1848, reported religious services being conducted at the
    mine and cynically suggested that this was a ploy to keep the miners
    sober.
39. *South Australian Register*, 20 September 1848.
40. *South Australian*, 19 September 1848; *South Australian Register*, 20
    September 1848.

41. See SAA BRG 22, 960, No. 622, 16/9/1848, Adelaide directors to H. Ayers at Kooringa.
42. *South Australian Register*, 20 September 1848.
43. SAA GRG 24, series 6, C/O Correspondence, A. (1848) 1432, 15/9/1848, from Resident Magistrate, Kooringa; *South Australian*, 19 September 1848.
44. H. Ayers had noted earlier in the year that 'in nine cases out of ten, the men cannot write', see SAA BRG 22, 961, No. 37, 9/2/1848, to Thomas Burr; Note that the sentence in the above case appears extremely lenient when contrasted with the two months hard labour meted out to eight miners at the Callington Petty Sessions in 1866, for seizing blacklegs who were paraded through the village of Gunnislake in Cornwall. See, Deacon, 1983.
45. *South Australian*, 19 September 1848.
46. SAA GRG 24, series 6, C/O Correspondence, A (1848) 1477, G. Dashwood to Governor, Henry Young.
47. SAA BRG 22, 960, No. 652, 9/10/1848, to Mr Charles Reed, Miner, Burra Burra Mines.
48. That the Company made a handsome profit on such items is borne out by figures which show that the candles purchased at 2 pence per dozen were sold to the miners for 12 pence. Fuses purchased at 2/6d to 3 shillings per coil were sold at 4/6d. See SAA BRG 22, 961, No. 36, 21/9/1846 and SAA BRG 22, 961., No. 37, 26/9/1846, to Samuel Stocks; South Australian Archives, *Superintendent's Letter Books*, BRG 22, 966, (hereafter BRG 22, 966) No. 1060, 14/3/1863, from W. H. Challoner.
49. However, at an earlier date, in 1847, following complaints from the miners, one doctor, A. McThompson, was replaced by the directors. See SAA BRG 22, 960, No. 343, 22/7/1847; Jenkin, 1927. p. 268, states that in some Cornish mines the 'doctors club' was so lucrative that many medical men took shares in the mines merely to render themselves more eligible for appointments.
50. SAA BRG 22, 80/65, 11/7/1847, To H. Ayers from Allen H. Thomas, M.D., Burra Burra Mines; Note, in 1851 the German operatives requested special dispensation so as to appoint their own doctor, but this too was refused. See BRG 22, 960, No. 1366, 8/8/1851, to Mr A. F. Friedlander.
51. *South Australian Register*, 20 September 1848.
52. *South Australian Register*, 23 September 1848. For Cornish practice see John Rowe, *Cornwall in the Age of the Industrial Revolution*, Liverpool, 1953, p. 27; Barton, 1960, p. 17 notes that up to the mid 19th century, contract breakers in Cornwall and Devon were liable for up to three months hard labour. Leifchild, 1857, pp. 143–48, provides a less harsh picture, stating that should a pitch turn out badly, the tributer had a right to abandon his place of work upon payment of a 20 shilling fine.
53. *South Australian Register*, 23 September 1848; The decision to reduce wages and the Standard had actually been made on 8 September. SAA BRG 22, 957, 8/9/1848.

54. SAA PRG 100, 25/9/1848, Diary of Mr Adams; *South Australian*, 26 September 1848.
55. SAA BRG 22, 961, No. 2, 28/9/1848, to Wm. Challoner, Accountant.
56. *Mining Journal*, 27 January 1849, p. 45. This figure is consistent with that provided in July 1848, when reported that 12,000 to 14,000 tons lay at grass. See, SAA BRG 22, 960, No. 614, 7/7/1848, to Marshaall MacDermott, Manager, Bank of Australasia.
57. SAA BRG 22, 961, No. 2 [sic] 2/10/1848, to Wm Challoner, Accountant; SAA PRG 100, No. 7, 14/2/1849, H. Ayers to J. B. Graham.
58. See for example, SAA BRG 22, 957, 6/1/1847, and 13/7/1847, p. 161, where recorded that miners' wages were reduced from 35 to 30 shillings, and labourers' from 25 to 23 shillings per week.
59. This attitude was also adopted by the editor of the *Sydney Morning Herald*, 28 October 1848.
60. *South Australian*, 17 October 1848.
61. SAA PRG 100, No. 15, 23/8/1848, H. Ayers to J. B. Graham, reporting comments of Captain Henry Roach.
62. SAA PRG 100, No. 6, 21/8/1848, H. Ayers to J. B. Graham.
63. SAA BRG 22, 961, No. 97, 7/9/1848, to Thomas Burr.
64. Ward, 1973, p. 110.
65. For bibliographical details and accounts of his vociferous outpourings, see Ward, 1973, Robert F. Wearmouth, *Methodism and the Working-Class Movements of England 1800–1850*, London, 1937, p. 129; Leslie Stephen, Sidney Lee (eds), *The Dictionary of National Biography*, 1917; George Jacob Holyoake, *Life of Joseph Rayner Stephens Preacher and Political Orator*, 1881, reprinted London, 1986; T. M. Kemnitz and F. Jacques, 'J. R. Stephens and the Chartist Movement', *International Review of Social History*, 19, 1974.
66. Holyoake, 1881, p. 47; p. 155; For further details on his life and also on his brothers Samuel Stephens, first Colonial Manager of the South Australian Company, and Edward Stephens, Manager of the South Australian Banking Company, see *Australian Dictionary of Biography, vol 2, 1788–1850*, Melbourne, 1967; Douglas Pike, *Paradise of Dissesnt. South Australia 1829–1857*, Melbourne, 2nd edn 1967, pp. 134–35; Rev. James Haslam, *The History of Wesleyan Methodism in South Australia from its Commencement to its Jubilee*, Adelaide, 1958, p. 10.
67. SAA BRG 22, 957, 7 October 1848, p. 219. Advertising was denied for both the *Register* and the *Observer*.
68. Pike, 1967, p. 336 states that the libel cases were not pressed in the Supreme Court.
69. SAA PRG 100, 7/11/1848, Diary of Mr Adams.
70. Pike, 1967, p. 395.
71. SAA BRG 22, 967, 29/9/1848, W. H. Challoner to H. Ayers.
72. *South Australian Register*, 4 October 1848.
73. Correspondence in the Adelaide Press varied as to the estimates of the cost of living at the Burra compared with Adelaide. Estimates varied

from twenty-five per cent to fifty per cent above Adelaide prices.
However, Henry Ayers believed this to be untrue, pointing out that while
some items such as tea and sugar were higher at Kooringa, dairy and
meat products and rents were cheaper, thus evening-out the discrepancies. For newspaper comments see, *South Australian Register*, 18
October 1848, letter from 'Teamster'; *South Australian Register*, 28
October 1848, letter from 'G. P.'; *South Australian Register*, 1 November
1848, letter from 'Teamster'; *Adelaide Observer* 7 October 1848; the *South
Australian*, 21 October 1848, letter from 'A Foreman'; For Ayers'
remarks, see, SAA BRG 22, 960, No. 700, 29/11/1848, to Peter Cumming
Esq., St Andrew's Society.

74. *South Australian Register*, 4 October 1848.
75. *South Australian Register*, 18 October 1848.
76. SAA PRG 100, No. 7, 13/2/1849, H. Ayers to J. B. Graham.
77. Unfortunately little is known of his background nor as to the origin of
    the appellation 'Captain'. His activities following the strike are better
    known than his antecedents, and he is remembered by his pioneering
    activities in the Flinders Ranges which resulted in a number of prominent
    landmarks bearing his name, see Hans Mincham, *The Story of the Flinders
    Ranges*, Adelaide, 1964, pp. 261–62, 267.
78. SAA BRG 22, 961, No. 79, 5/7/1848, to Thomas Burr.
79. This was according to Ayers, see SAA PRG 100, No. 7, 14/2/1849,
    H. Ayers to J. B. Graham.
80. Auhl, 1986, p. 161, quoting *South Australian Register*, 13 October 1848.
81. Auhl, 1986, p. 162 noted one teamster who having broken the blockade
    by taking a detour found his eighteen bullocks missing. Some hides were
    later discovered 'with nothing in them'. One of the largest cartage
    contractors, Bell Freeman, later apologised for withdrawing his services,
    stating that it was fear of what the miners and drovers would do to his
    bullocks that had caused him so to act. SAA BRG, 22, 967, No. 20,
    15/11/1848, Wm. Challoner to H. Ayers.
82. SAA BRG 22, 967, No. 17, 4/11/1848, from S. W. Humble (for Super-
    intendent).
83. SAA PRG 100, No. 7, 14/2/1849, H. Ayers to J. B. Graham.
84. See, *Mining Journal*, 27 January, 1849, p. 45.
85. *South Australian Register*, 1 November 1848, letter from 'Teamster'.
86. *South Australian Register*, 8 November 1848, letter from 'Observer'.
87. *South Australian Registre* 28 October 1848, letter from 'G.P.'
88. *South Australian Register*, 4 October 1848, from 'General Agency Office,
    Adelaide (Share Market)'.
89. See SAA PRG 100, 14/11/1848, Diary of Mr Adams.
90. *South Australian Registr*, 15 November 1848, editorial, 'The Rights of
    Labour'.
91. *South Australian Register*, 25 November 1848, letter from 'Teamster'.
92. SAA BRG 22, 957, 4/11/1848, p. 225.
93. If there was any consolation for the miners it was that they had been

well overpaid for their ores due to the inaccurate assays. As a result the directors had drawn on their overseas agents on the basis of high percentages, a situation which found them in a most embarrassing position. See, SAA BRG 22, 960, No. 755, 6/2/1849, to Messrs Duncan Dunbar & Sons, London. For account of the drawing procedures and relationships with overseas agents, see, Mel Davies, 'Copper and Credit: Commission Agents and the South Australian Mining Association 1845–77', *Australian Economic History Review*, XXIII, 1, 1983.

94. SAA PRG 100, No. 7, 14/2/1849, H. Ayers to J. B. Graham.
95. *South Australian Register*, 15 November 1848.
96. SAA PRG 100, 14/11/1848, Diary of Mr Adams.
97. *South Australian Register*, 22 November 1848, For details of the structure of the carrying trade and breaking of the strike, see, Mel Davies, 'Bullocks and Rail – The South Australian Mining Association 1845–70', *Australian Economic History Review*, XVII: 2, 1977.
98. SAA, GRG 24.4.21, No. 1572, 24/10/1848, Colonial Secretary to Postmaster General, Adelaide, re. Mr Brody, Postmaster at Kooringa who had opened mail addressed to John Stephens of the *Register*.
99. SAA RG 22, 960, No. 688, 15/11/1848, to Captn Beal, Ship *Poitiers*.
100. SAA BRG 22, 967, No. 23, 29/11/1848, from Hy Challoner.
101. SAA BRG 22, 961, No. 22, 11/12/1848, to Wm Challoner.
102. SAA BRG 22, 961, No. 20, 4/12/1848, and No. 22, 11/12/1848 to Wm Challoner.
103. SAA BRG 22, 961, No. 18, 27/11/1848; No. 19, 30/11/1848, and No. 26, 28/11/1848, all to Wm. Challoner.
104. SAA BRG 22, 961, No. 26, 23/12/1848, to Wm Challoner.
105. *South Australian*, 9 January 1849.
106. *South Australian Register*, 24 January 1849.
107. *South Australian Register*, letter from 'Spectator.'
108. *South Australian Register*, 'The Burra Burra Martyrs'.
109. There is a great deal of evidence of collusion among mine proprietors. In 1846 it was stated 'There is a sort of understanding among the proprietors of the mines that wages should be reduced . . . and I think if we all understand each other then there will be no difficulty with it.' See SAA BRG 22, 961, No. 43, 23/11/1846, H. Ayers to Samuel Stocks. In 1854, despite shortages of labour associated with the goldrush, the Burra directors refused to employ miners who wished to leave the Kapunda Mines. See, SAA BRG 22, 961, No. 545, 20/3/1854, to Captn Hy. Roach.
110. SAA BRG 22, 967, No. 27, 13/13/1848, from Wm. Challoner; In SAA BRG 22, 961, No. 18, 27/11/1848, to Wm. Challoner, Ayers mentioned a reciprocal agreement with the Patent Copper Company to blacklist dismissed men.
111. The parent of the Patent Copper Company was the Spitty Works, Loughor, South Wales, owned by the Schneider Bros. The smelter opened in April, 1849, just four months after the Burra strike ended.

112. See, Pike, 1967, Grenfell Price, *The Foundation and Settlement of South Australia 1829–1845. A Study of the Colonisation Movement, Based on the Records of the south Australian Government and other Authoritative Documents*, Adelaide, 1924.

113. SAA PRG 100, No. 7, 14/2/1849, H. Ayers to J. B. Graham.

114. *South Australian Register*, 24 January 1849.

115. For example, at this time a great deal of publicity was given to John Benjamin Graham, the largest shareholder of the Association, who in the twelve months to September 1848 had netted over £16,000 in dividends. See *The Times* (London), 7 September 1848; This sum can be compared to the mine labourers' net wage of about £55 to £65 per year.

116. See, Philip J. Payton, 'The Cornish in South Australia: Their Influence and Experience from Immigration to Assimilation, 1836–1936', Unpub. Ph.D., University of Adelaide, 1978, (2 vols), vol. I, esp. pp. 54–89; John Cashen, 'Social Foundations of South Australia Owners of Labour', in Eric Richards (ed.), *The Flinders History of South Australia* Adelaide, 1986, (3 vols), vol. 1, pp. 109–10; Pike, 1967, pp. 135, 314, 317. Pike notes the propaganda published for emigrants in the *South Australian Colonist*, a journal edited by John Stephens. Stephens also published a book which was also used for publicity purposes, *The Land of Promise*.

117. Rowe, 1953, pp. 152–64, but especially pp. 157–8.

118. *South Australian Register*, 24 January 1849, 'Burra Burra Martyrs'.

119. *South Australian Register*, letter from 'Spectator'.

120. See for example, *The South Australian*, 22 September 1848; *South Australian Register*, 23 September 1848. During the 1846–47 Cornish corn riots, Rowe 1853, p. 231 noted a similar role for Methodist laymen preachers when they organised 'orderly protests'.

121. SAA BRG, D4057/1(L), 20/6/1847, John Dickens to relatives.

122. *South Australian Register*, 3 January 1849.

123. SAA 842, Diary of Johnson Frederick Hayward, 1846–56, p. 8.

124. For the rising fortunes of Methodism in the vicinity of the Burra Burra Mines, and for the alleged improvement in manners by the end of 1848, see: Arnold D. Hunt, 'The Bible Christians in South Australia', *Journal of the Historical Society of South Australia*, No. 10, 1982, p. 18; Rev. James Haslam, *The History of Wesleyan Methodism in South Australia from Its Commencement to Its Jubilee*, 1886, reprinted Adelaide, 1958, pp. 10, 101–2, 115, 121–2; Rev. Harry Alvey, *Burra: Its Mines and Methodism: A Lecture Given to the South Australian Methodist Historical Society*, Adelaide, 1960, pp. 7, 10–12; *South Australian Register*, 14 June 1848, 9 August 1848, 19 August 1848, 8 January 1849, 14 March 1849.

125. Pike, 1967, p. 394.

126. See Auhl, 1986, ch. 12.

127. No complete list appears to exist of Committee men and others placed on the directors' blacklist. The only ones identified are: John Hailes, William Mitchell, William Moyle, John Mill, Andrew Robins, S. Penglaze, Messrs Bosance, Robins and Hoskens, Malachie Deeble, Charles Reed,

Richard Tresize, Richard James, James Wallace, Hugh Bowden, Richard Cocking and Charles Burn.

128. SAA, BRG 22, 961, No. 275, 2/6/1851, to Captn Hy Roach.

129. SAA, BRG 22, 967, No. 29, 20/12/1848, Hy Challoner to H. Ayers.

130. Payton, 1978, pp. 187, 202.

131. Payton, 1978, p. 273.

132. SAA, PRG 100, No. 8, 12/3/1849, H. Ayers to J. B. Graham.

133. See report of trial in *South Australian Register*, 4 November 1848, 'Burr v Beck & Others', the *South Australian*; 3 November 1848, and 7 November 1848. In SAA PRG 100, 4/11/1848, Diary of Mr Adams, it was claimed that the Judge was Burr's friend 'and shewed all along decidedly in his favor'.

134. L. J. Blake, *Gold Escort*, Melbourne, 1971, p. 9. f.24, quoting *Victorian Parliamentary Papers, 1855–56*, 'Report of Goldfield's Commission on Inquiry, 1855'.

NOT WHAT THEY SEEMED? CORNISH ASSISTED IMMIGRANTS IN NEW SOUTH WALES 1837–77

Patricia Lay

INTRODUCTION

Emigration was a major Cornish experience during the nineteenth century, not least for miners and those in associated trades who settled together in Cornish communities across the world. Cornish immigrants to New South Wales settled in 'Cornish clusters' across the colony but it was predominantly a pastoral and agricultural economy, unlike the mining destinations usually chosen by the Cornish. Colonists were anxious to sponsor further immigrants who could come out to work for them, particularly as farm labourers. But emigrants wishing to qualify for free or assisted passages to New South Wales had to be skilled in the occupations needed in the colony, or at least able to claim to be in these categories even if in reality they were not. Contemporary opinion in nineteenth-century New South Wales held that, despite the apparent stringency of assisted immigration regulations, many of the immigrants were in fact unsuitable for the employment opportunities that awaited them. One explanation for this state of affairs was that many immigrants did indeed lie about or misrepresent and exaggerate their occupational skills (and other attributes, such as age) to secure assisted passages.

The purpose of the research that underpins this article was to test the reliability of occupational and other claims by Cornish assisted immigrants, through investigation of the origins and backgrounds of a sample group of the 4,000 Cornish assisted immigrants who arrived in New South Wales between 1837 and 1877.[1] If such claims were found to be unreliable, then (in addition to confirming the suspicions of nineteenth-century colonists in New South Wales) some doubt could well be cast on the the reliability (or at least uncritical use) of the shipping lists as a source for historians.

Where possible, the research sought to make comparison between the actual backgrounds of Cornish assisted immigrants and the backgrounds they claimed on arrival.[2] The sample consisted of 390 persons who arrived in Sydney between 1838 and 1857. They represented 10 per cent of the total Cornish assisted emigration to New South Wales between 1837 and 1877, and 21 per cent of all assisted emigrants aboard the seven selected ships. Since the New South Wales colonists' main complaint was the unsuitability of assisted immigrants because of their occupations, this was the focus of research, but the reliability of answers to other questions was tested where possible. Cornish emigrants aboard the following ships formed the sample.

	Year of arrival	Total Assisted immigrants	Cornish Immigrants
Florentia	1838	15	9
William Metcalfe	1844	241	43
Harbinger	1849	287	77
Lord Stanley	1850	308	23
Lady Ann	1854	288	128
Lord Hungerford	1855	321	25
Fitzjames	1857	429	85
TOTAL		1899	390

These ships were selected because the years of arrival cover the period before, during and after the discovery of copper and gold in New South Wales, and because the majority of Cornish assisted immigrants arrived during this period. Moreover, during these years the places of birth of assisted immigrants were recorded precisely in official documents. Also, varying additional information exists for these particular voyages in government, parliamentary and private papers.

EMIGRATION TO NEW SOUTH WALES
The Australian colonies were just some of the many worldwide destinations chosen by Cornish emigrants, so to place Cornish emigration to New South Wales in context, a summary of conditions affecting nineteenth-century emigration to the colony is necessary.

Australia was a group of discrete British colonies until Federation in 1901. Each colony developed separately, with its own immigration system and regulations which evolved according to its own changing needs. New South Wales began as a penal colony in 1788 and developed as a pastoral and agricultural economy throughout the nineteenth century, although gold, copper and tin mining did become important in the second half of the century. Cornish people were amongst the earliest settlers in the colony, but those choosing to emigrate to New South Wales before the 1830s needed sufficient capital to establish themselves in the colony. They were from the Cornish landowning classes, and it was not until the later part of the 1830s that assisted passages became widely available to the labouring classes.[3] At that time, the system had expanded to include families, as well as single men and women, from all over Britain, who would be useful employees in the rapidly expanding colony. Free and assisted passages were financed by the sale of Crown land in New South Wales. Understandably, colonists were interested in contributing to the costs of the voyages of potential servants and labourers only.

As the colony and its requirements changed, so the immigration regulations altered. At all times, however, the main criteria for assistance focused on the type of labour needed in the colony, and on healthy and respectable individuals who offered value for the money spent on their voyages. Changing immigration schemes and administrative regulations operated within these unchanging expectations.

During the period from 1837 to 1877, 4,000 assisted immigrants arriving in New South Wales stated that their birthplace was Cornwall but many others came unassisted. Theoretically, assisted emigrants met strict criteria relating to their health, strength and usefulness to the colony. In theory these emigrants were the cream of their generation but in practice assisted emigrants could only be selected from those who wished to go, and generally both assisted and unassisted emigrants only left their homeland if the prospects in New South Wales were better than in Cornwall. Such prospects were publicised by family and friends already in the colony, and decisions to emigrate were influenced by a variety of other push-pull factors. They included economic conditions in Cornwall and in New South Wales, the availability of employment and land, and the regulations governing free and assisted passages.[4]

Several events in New South Wales strongly influenced the course of assisted immigration to the colony. When the transportation of convicts finally ceased in 1842, a supply of free labour that had always been available to colonists also ended. Employers were forced to look elsewhere for labour and this encouraged an influx of free (as distinct from convict) labour. In 1851, the discovery of payable gold (near Bathurst in western New South Wales) began the Australian Goldrush. This brought a flood of willing immigrants, but they preferred the goldfields to the wheatfields, and many workers previously employed in farm labouring work also rushed off to the goldfields. In 1856 the introduction of responsible government in the colony affected its immigration policy. The new government favoured assisted immigration, but tried to decrease government involvement. During the 1850s, the railway network began to spread out from Sydney, opening up more farming land and bringing markets closer.

So, Cornish individuals and families requesting financial assistance for their journey to New South Wales were emigrating to a distant land which offered opportunities not available in Cornwall. If they were to have help with their travelling expenses, they had to be accepted as assisted emigrants, which meant meeting the criteria laid down by the government. The government would only give financial help to those whose occupation, health and respectability would ensure that they would become useful servants or labourers on arrival. Those who did meet these criteria travelled under the regulations of the current assisted passage scheme.

ASSISTED PASSAGE SCHEMES

In testing the claims made by assisted immigrants, it is necessary to understand the regulations in force at the time of arrival of each of the seven sample immigrant ships, and to discuss briefly the assisted passage schemes. It is estimated that fewer than half the nineteenth-century immigrants to the Australian colonies travelled as assisted passengers[5] but detailed records were kept on all assisted immigrants because government money was being invested in them.

A restricted form of assisted immigration to New South Wales operated from 1832, following the New South Wales Legislative Council vote of £10,000 from the sale of land.[6] Later two separate assisted systems, the Government and the Bounty schemes, operated concurrently.[7] Assisted immigrants were questioned on arrival by an Examination Board in an attempt to verify their claims for eligibility. Eligible adult males were respectable agricultural labourers or mechanics. Married couples aged under 30, unmarried females between fifteen and thirty years, and unmarried males between eighteen and twenty-five years (no more in number than the unmarried females) were acceptable. The most preferred immigrants were young married couples under thirty years of age, with no children, because it was thought that these people would immediately increase the labour force in New South Wales. Young children were a poor risk because they were most likely to become ill or die on the voyage.[8] Single women were eligible if they were travelling under the protection of immediate family, or married relatives or friends, and advertisements appeared in Cornish newspapers publicising the opportunities in New South Wales for respectable, unmarried female domestic and farm servants.[9]

Under the Government scheme (1837 to 1840) surgeons from New South Wales went to Britain to select suitable emigrants; mechanics, craftsmen and agricultural labourers. The Bounty system (1835 to 1841) allowed the colonists to choose suitable emigrants themselves or through an agent, and then to receive a bounty usually equal to the cost of the passage if the immigrants were passed as satisfactory at the examination on arrival. Colonists criticised the Government system because of its costs and selection procedures and the amount of illness occurring on the voyages, and it ceased in 1840. The Bounty scheme regulations remained basically the same throughout its operation, but it was suspended in mid-1842 because of deteriorating economic conditions in New South Wales, to resume in a modified form from the end of 1843 until 1845. In 1837 the age limits were relaxed for married men and half bounties were allowed to men and women above the age limit who travelled with their younger families. Immigrants aboard the sample ships *Florentia* in 1838 and *William Metcalfe* in 1844 were travelling under Bounty regulations.

The colonists preferred the Bounty system to alternative schemes of assisted immigration, but it became almost a commercial scheme operated by shipowners who were accused of accepting ineligible occupants, and sometimes providing them with forged documents to satisfy the Examination Board. In 1841 new regulations from the Land Board in London ensured tighter control of selection procedures in Britain and over the comfort and safety of emigrants. Immigration was suspended again in 1845 because of serious economic depression in the colony. When it resumed in 1847 under the control of the newly-formed Colonial Land and Emigration Commission, the regulations remained basically the same. Assistance was offered to agricultural labourers, female domestic and farm servants and a few mechanics. The most acceptable people were still young married couples without children. Families with more than three children under seven were not eligible.

Optimistic reports of the investment and other opportunities available to Cornish emigrants appeared in local newspapers,[10] and the need for labourers was emphasised:

> Every ship from Australia brings papers containing (news of) the depressed state of the colonies from the want of an adequate supply of labourers, with earnest appeals to the Home Government for thousands of the starving people here to be sent to where they can find immediate employment.[11]

Immigrants aboard *Harbinger* in 1849 and *Lord Stanley* in 1850 travelled under the new regulations. Emigrants made a deposit payment towards their passage, and a larger payment was required from those who were less acceptable because of age or occupation. The rules regarding the protection of single women emigrants were altered and large numbers travelled in groups under the supervision of a matron. She was responsible to the Surgeon-Superintendent, the officer in overall charge of all matters relating to the emigrants. Selected emigrants were paid a gratuity to assist officials on the voyage, and included constables, cook's assistants, schoolteachers, and hospital attendants. The new regulations did not include proper facilities for verifying credentials, and criticism of the new regulations still concentrated on the numbers being sent who were unsuited to agricultural work, and on the quality of single women who were likewise unsuitable for domestic service.

After 1851, the Goldrush encouraged many Cornish individuals to travel privately to New South Wales, as well as those recruited by private companies. Items in the Cornish press regularly reported the discovery of new goldfields, or of Cornish emigrants who had prospered in the colonies, and advertised prospectuses for mining companies and employment for miners.[12] Australian gold nuggets were exhibited in Cornwall, and 'an extensive moving panorama of the goldfields'[13] was displayed.

Cornish immigrants aboard the *Lady Ann* were affected by new immigration regulations which had come into force during 1854,[14] differing from those in force in other Australian colonies. Emigrants paid a deposit before embarkation, with the choice on arrival of paying the balance of their passage money or of hiring themselves for two years to an employer approved by the Immigration Department. No deposits were required for wives or for children under fourteen as it was considered that this would reduce payments when the emigrant was least able to afford them. It was thought that high wages and high demand for labour in the colony would enable such immigrants to find satisfactory work easily. Single males (ineligible in other colonies) were accepted as immigrants, even when not part of a family on board.

With the introduction of responsible government in 1856, regulations were relaxed to include as eligible anyone who worked for wages, and allowing employers to use a British agent to select and nominate employees for an assisted passage. But the immigration vote was drastically reduced between 1857 and 1860, and even before the arrival of *Fitzjames* in 1857 concern was being expressed in the colonial Parliament on the continuing unsuitability of assisted immigrants, it being said that colonists should be selected according to the needs of New South Wales rather than those of Great Britain.

To summarise, although regulations controlling the selection, transport and disposal of assisted immigrants altered between 1838 and 1857, the complaints in New South Wales remained constant in relation to the unsuitability of many immigrants, particularly in regard to their occupational skills and their respectability. Many immigrants claiming to be farm labourers were said to be incapable of agricultural work, while often single women accepting assisted passages as domestic and farm servants were either not from the respectable backgrounds they claimed or were unused to domestic service.

RELIABILITY OF CLAIMS

Like other assisted immigrants, the Cornish on arrival in Sydney were examined by government officials at an Immigration Board. The officials recorded each person's name, age and place of birth, occupation, religion, literacy, parents' names and abode, state of health, names and whereabouts of relatives already in the colony, and whether immigrants had any complaints about the voyage. It was impossible for all these answers to be verified by colonial officials 12,000 miles from Britain, although some who lied were caught, or at least the suspicions of the officials were noted.

At the Immigration Board's examinations, Cornish immigrants gave a variety of occupations but these fell into three main categories. A minority (413) of the 4000 assisted Cornish arriving between 1837 and 1877 said they were miners, copper miners, tin miners or (even) coal miners, while 755 said they were agricultural labourers, labourers, or farm labourers, and 436 said they were tradesmen or in other trained occupations. The variety of women's occupations showed that many of the 630 women who stated their occupations had skilled work such as milliner, nurse, needlewoman, tailoress, teacher, safety-fuse maker. The miners came in several waves, particularly in 1849, 1853 and 1877. In 1849, they arrived in response to changes in the immigration regulations and after the discovery of copper in New South Wales. The 1853 influx was as a result of the Australian Goldrush, and in 1877 many Cornish-American miners were aboard four immigrant ships which came from New York.[15]

The age of assisted immigrants was obviously an important factor, since colonists preferred young, healthy workers. Almost 80 per cent of immigrants were under thirty years of age. The remainder were between thirty and seventy years old. As in Cornwall, the majority were Methodists but the answers given by immigrants regarding their religion did not support this. The Methodist sects combined to give a surprisingly low 1103 members, of a total of 3898, the majority stating they were Church of England. Thus only 30 per cent admitted to being Methodist, while the expected percentage would have been closer to 70 per cent. This discrepancy could be the result of the way in which officials phrased their questions (for example, merely asking if an immigrant was Protestant or Catholic), or it might be an instance of immigrants supplying the answers most likely to benefit them in the colony. Two hundred and fifty three said they were Protestant, and there were sixty-one Catholics (mostly of obvious Irish descent). Only forty-three had no religion recorded, and these were generally children with their families.

Few of the 4,000 Cornish made official complaints in their Immigration Board examinations about their voyages, and when they did it related to the quality or quantity of rations issued, or the surgeon's neglect of a family member. Thomas Toms per *Victoria* in 1849 complained that the surgeon had called his wife Eliza 'a damned humbug and a beggar', and Eliza supported him in his complaint. Other Cornish complaints were more substantial, for example those of immigrants aboard *Lord Hungerford* in 1855.

Occasionally, ineligible Cornish individuals who had slipped through the selection process were discovered during the Immigration Board's examination at Sydney. Ann Gilbert, aged twenty-one, who came with her parents aboard *Ascendant* in 1858, was said to be 'idiotic and unfit for serving'. Officials were suspicious of Richard Hooper aboard *Plantaganet* in 1857, a Wesleyan aged forty-three, who said he was a labourer. It was noted that he was obviously above the class of farm labourer and that he had admitted to previous employment as a storekeeper and a farmer—occupations which may not have qualified him for assistance. The five children of stonemason William Knight aboard *Plantaganet* in 1857 were undersized and it was said by officials that the family would find difficulty living on its earnings in the colony.

Some immigrants who had relatives already in New South Wales stated that they did not. Perhaps this was because they did not plan to be dependant on these relatives, or it could be an example of Cornish suspicion of bureaucracy in that they had no intention of disclosing information if they were unsure why it was being requested. In some cases, such as Mary Blight aboard *Fitzjames*, there was an obvious ulterior motive for reticence. Her attempt at deception failed (as we shall see below), but others were successful.

In general, in comparing their claimed backgrounds with their actual backgrounds, discrepancies have been found in answers from a wide range of Cornish immigrants but they were particularly obvious on certain, specific ships. Although conditions in New South Wales changed in the period between 1838 and 1857, and the selection procedures and regulations affecting assisted immigrants altered to accommodate these changes, the physical conditions on the emigrants' journey remained much the same. The length of the voyage was about 100 days under sail and the route was basically the same. Food and accommodation conditions on the vessels were similar throughout the period. It is interesting, then, to compare the differing experiences of each sample voyage, and to note and compare the discrepencies in answers given by Cornish immigrants from the various ships on their arrival in Sydney. Although a small number of discrepencies came to light at the time, most remained undiscovered and have been identified by the present author as a result of recent research.

THE *FLORENTIA* 1838

The *Florentia*, of 453 tons, which left Plymouth on 4 April 1838 and arrived in Sydney on 3 August 1838, carried twenty-six crew and eight-five passengers. They were a mixture of bounty emigrants and paying steerage and cabin passengers. At least twelve of them were Cornish.[16] There were no deaths or serious illnesses on the voyage, and only one convalescent passenger on arrival. The cabin passengers had more luxury in their accommodation and diet than the steerage passengers, but otherwise the experiences of the Cornish steerage passengers were similar to those of the cabin passengers.

Storms at sea were to be expected on the long, cramped and often monotonous voyage. Off the Cape of Good Hope a gale blew up, involving the crew in hours of frantic preparation as it approached. Hatches were battened down, the carpenter built protective covering over every possible place where the wild seas might enter, and extra crew were ordered to the wheel. In spite of the careful precautions:

> as quick as thought there was a general cry to 'hold on' when she gave a terrific lurch to larboard and fairly buried herself in the waves, the water rushing in at the ports—over the bulwarks & in every direction—the cuddy door was forced open & in an instant was knee deep in water the chairs actually floating about & everything in the greatest possible confusion —the scene at this time beggars description, what with the cries & fainting of the women, the scurry of the men, jumping on the table, anywhere to get out of the way, the laughter of the sailors, the rushing backwards & forwards of the immense

body of water in the cabin—the howling of the wind & sea,
altogether formed such a scene as cannot easily be imagined
. . . an immense quantity of the water found its way down . . .
going down like a cataract & deluging all the births (sic)
below.[17]

The master, William Deloitte, had captained six earlier emigrant
voyages before settling in Sydney as a merchant and shipping agent.[18]
Amongst the *Florentia*'s steerage passengers were George Hawke of
St Eval (one of the pioneer farmers of Cornish Settlement near Bathurst
in New South Wales), his wife Jane and his fifteen-year-old nephew
Frederick. Nine of the fifteen bounty emigrants on board were Cornish.
William Rowe of Bodmin, aged thirty-four, a house carpenter and
joiner, was accompanied by his wife Eleanor aged thirty-four and their
children Mary and Rebecca. The family was Wesleyan. The single male
bounty immigrants were Edward Nicholls aged twenty-six, a farm
overseer of Treglossack, St Keverne, John Rogers aged twenty-two of
Manaccan and Robert Smith aged twenty-five, a farm overseer of St
Keverne. Nicholls and Smith were Church of England and Rogers a
Methodist. The two single women were Ann Wills Tristrain, a dress-
maker aged twenty-five of Truro, and Mary Grace Vercoe aged fifteen,
a nursemaid of St Columb. One said she was was Wesleyan, the other
Methodist. Both were under the protection of George Hawke. All these
emigrants were literate. Ann Tristrain accompanied the Hawkes to
Bathurst, and married Samuel Bray, a Cornish tailor and draper in
Bathurst, in May the following year.[19] It is likely that George and Jane
Hawke already knew the Cornish bounty passengers, and that George
had organised a group to travel together as he had done on his first
voyage to the colony in 1828.[20]

Reliability of answers
Evidence showed that all the Cornish assisted emigrants aboard
Florentia were who and what they claimed to be. They probably had
no need to lie because they did meet the criteria in force for assisted
emigrants at that time, and all seemed the type of immigrant the
colonists preferred. Also, it was highly unlikely that George Hawke,
as organiser of the group, would have condoned any dishonesty because
he was known as a man of the greatest integrity. For example, he took
his nephew with him as a paying steerage passenger and made no
attempt to pass him off as an assisted emigrant.[21]
Captain Deloitte, master of the *Florentia*, gave evidence relating
to emigration soon after his arrival in the colony. He stated that it was
'rather difficult to induce such persons to Emigrate as would come

within the terms of the Government Regulations'. He had found that most emigrants were:

> persons who had a little money, but not enough to pay their own expenses, and have had some assistance to enable them to join their friends here. Those friends have often sent home for such parties; giving the owner of the vessel a guarantee to pay on arrival here the difference between the bounty allowed and the actual expense.[22]

The assisted Cornish aboard the 1838 voyage fitted this description. The Hawkes were travelling steerage with the assisted passengers and it seems that these were all known either to the Hawkes or to friends of the Hawkes in the colony, and most of them settled in the Bathurst district. The Rowes from Bodmin were close friends of the Hawkes in Cornish Settlement, where William Rowe was the school-teacher and—like George Hawke—an active member of the Wesleyan community. The Hawkes took his daughter Rebecca in as a daughter following her mother's death in 1851.[23] Robert Smith was a brother of John Smith of 'Gamboola' near Bathurst, who had been friendly with the families at Cornish Settlement since his arrival in New South Wales in 1832.[24] Smith, Nicholls and Rogers came from the Lizard Peninsula and doubtless knew each other before embarkation; they made no attempt to conceal the fact that they all came from relatively prosperous farming families,[25] and two gave their occupations as 'farm overseer'.

The assisted Cornish aboard *Florentia*, then, seem to have been a well-organised group, with a definite destination (Bathurst and Cornish Settlement) in mind. They were known to each other, or at least had friends in common. There were no obvious discrepancies in their answers to immigration officials, probably because they were who and what they claimed to be and so did not need to lie.

THE *WILLIAM METCALFE* 1844

The *William Metcalfe*, of 447 tons, arrived in Sydney on 13 March 1844, after a voyage of 110 days. Aboard were two cabin and six intermediate passengers, twenty-eight crew and 241 bounty immigrants, of whom forty-three were Cornish. The Cornish contingent consisted of eight separate families (sixteen adults and twenty-three children) plus two single females and two single males (who were in fact older children from these family groups). There was no evidence to suggest that they were a group organised by one person, in contrast to the group aboard *Florentia*. However, there were common areas of origin. The Evans,

Nance, Phillips, Rowe and Warren families all had Penzance connections, the Warren and George families had Redruth connections. Only
the Julians, from Truro, seemed unconnected to other immigrants.

The *West Briton* of 19 July gave friends and relatives in Cornwall
news of the ship's safe arrival and noted that all were well.[26] Although
there had been no contagious illness during the voyage, one adult and
two children had died. Three children had been born during the voyage.
The Immigration Board report stated that the vessel was well-suited to
her purpose, and that the accommodation and fittings were acceptable.
Immigrants had made no complaints about the voyage, the officers were
complimented for their efficiency, and the quality and health of the
immigrants was good. 'We have rarely inspected a body of Immigrants
with whose appearance & demeanour we were so well pleased'.[27] The
local New South Wales press was not quite so enthusiastic, commenting
'there are but few agricultural labourers, being mostly mechanics'.[28] It
is interesting to compare the employment accepted by *William Metcalfe*
immigrants on arrival compared with their occupations stated at the
Board's examination (given here in brackets): agricultural labourers 48
(53), shepherds 7 (3), male domestic servants 6 (0), female domestic
servants 24 (24), mechanics engaged in building or building materials
13 (18), tradesmen making or selling articles for consumption 1 (0),
and other mechanics 6 (7).

Reliability of answers

Evidence that all eight Cornish families were who they claimed to be
was was found by the author in the British census records, the Mormon
International Genealogical Index (IGI), and various sources in New
South Wales. However, the families were not all what they claimed to
be in regard to their occupations and ages. In this period, regulations
required that they provide evidence of their baptism as well as
references from respected people in Cornwall. It is likely, therefore,
that the misrepresentations evident here were condoned by Cornish
worthies who generally regarded emigration very favourably.

Several men gave incorrect information about their occupations.
Joseph Evans stated he was an agricultural labourer but appeared
in the 1841 census as a carrier in Penzance. He told immigration
officials in Sydney that his family was going directly to Hobart Town
(Tasmania) but in fact they went straight to Tumbarumba in southern
New South Wales to join his brother who already had a large pastoral
holding there.[29] He also told officials that he had no relatives in the
colony.

John Phillips stated he was a farm labourer, but in 1841 he was a
gardener of Penzance prosperous enough to employ a servant. Samuel

Warren also claimed to be a farm labourer, but in 1841 he was a tin miner in Ludgvan, Penzance. John Julian claimed to be a farm labourer, husbandman and shepherd, but was employed from the ship as a miller and farm servant, which suggested that milling was probably his main but undeclared skill. The Nance and Phillips families were not able to find employment on arrival. They were maintained on board ship for eleven days and then taken into temporary employment by the government, while other Cornish families had been kept on board for some days before eventually finding private employment. This suggests that they may not have had those eagerly sought-after skills that they had claimed.

There were also several discrepancies between the claimed and actual ages of immigrants. Samuel Warren was thirty in the 1841 census but thirty-one in 1844. There were discrepancies in the ages of Alice and Joseph Evans, and of one of the children of William and Mary George. Some understandable discrepancies in place of birth occurred, for example Madron as opposed to Pendeen, or Ladock instead of St Austell, and this could simply signify that there had been a family move between birth and baptism.

All individuals found in the census by the author matched correctly with the parents they had claimed. But an unusual discrepancy occurred in the Rowe family. When questioned, James and Mary Rowe of Madron (Penzance), admitted they had left two children in Cornwall in the care of their grandfather, who would send them on. This practice was strictly forbidden under immigration regulations. In fact James and Mary Rowe had married the previous year[30] and James appeared in the 1841 census in Madron with his first wife Margaret and two daughters aged five and one. There was also an unusual discrepancy in the Warren family. One of Samuel Warren's stepsons, John Bray (said to be aged twelve) did not appear with the family in 1841. It is possible that nine-year-old John Bray was away from home on census night, but also possible that he was actually the child of another family, thus travelling illegally with the Warrens.

To summarise, many of these discrepancies relating to age and occupation amongst immigrants arriving on the *William Metcalfe* occurred when individuals did not in fact meet the immigration criteria for assistance. As noted above, that immigrants were required to produce testimonials from reliable referees and yet resorted to deception suggests a high degree of collusion in Cornwall, where emigration was seen as a means of both avoiding distress at home and 'getting on' abroad.

THE *HARBINGER* 1849

The *Harbinger*, of 751 tons, arrived in Sydney on 12 February 1849 after a voyage of 118 days from Plymouth. It carried merchandise, thirty-eight crew and 288 government immigrants, of whom seventy-seven were Cornish. There were thirteen Cornish families consisting of twenty-six adults and forty-two children, plus three single females and six single males.[31] The majority of Cornish on board had some connection with the Gwennap district, with the remainder from Truro and Redruth, Helston and St Keverne, and St Erth.

Officials in Sydney recorded that two of the Cornish single women were of questionable character. One was reported to be of very bad character, and known to have been a prostitute in Falmouth, and the surgeon suspected that the second girl had also been a prostitute in Cornwall. Several other immigrants were considered ineligible for free passages,[32] and probably included the seven Cornish miners on board. From the reintroduction of emigration in 1847 until the end of 1848, fifty-two persons had been objected to, on arrival, because of their occupations. They were miners, blacksmiths, bricklayers, carpenters, wheelwrights and gardeners and females other than domestic servants:

> Of the 33 miners we find that some were passed by us as 'Agricultural Labourers', or as 'agricultural labourers and miners', it being a common practice in Cornwall to engage in farming as well as mining pursuits; nor do we find any reason to doubt that this representation of their calling is correct. Some however, were passed simply as miners. A few of these seem to have been accepted through our officer at Plymouth, to fill up those occasional vacancies which will continually occur in our ships at the last moment, but we had also good reasons for supposing, that a small number of this class of persons might not be unacceptable in the colony.[33]

The reason for this supposition was the possibility that additional copper mines could be opened if more miners came to the colony, following the discovery of copper in several places in the Bathurst district. Since seven Cornishmen aboard *Harbinger* made no attempt to falsify their mining occupation, it is likely that they came into this category and so had no need to lie.

Reliability of answers

Research has uncovered evidence that all but one family, and all but one of the six single men, were who they said they were. However, none of the three single women could be traced. One of these was a widow travelling with her married daughters and their families and although she was not found in census returns, it is reasonable to assume she was the person she claimed to be. The other two single women were said to be of questionable character, and may have given false information intentionally about their ages, their parents and their places of birth. In fact, one of them did not give a parish of birth at all, just 'Cornwall', and with the undistinctive name of Elizabeth Brown there was no way she could be traced—either then or today. It is interesting that both these women, who were known prostitutes (and had probably been informed on by someone on board who knew their reputations), claimed to be Wesleyans—perhaps in the hope of adding a touch of respectability.

Although there seemed little need for miners to claim to be of some other occupation on this voyage, James Collins of Gwennap apparently did so. He said he was a farm labourer, but in the 1841 census both he and his father were copper miners. A single man, Thomas Roscrow, also of Gwennap, claimed to be a farm labourer, and although he came from a mining family he was an apprentice grocer in 1841. There were five instances of age discrepancy. James Collins was twenty-six, not twenty-three as he claimed. Others were in the Bosanko and Mortimore families, and two single men who claimed to be several years younger than they actually were. It is difficult to identify false claims about religious denominations, but the Nettle family who said they were Church of England were associated with the Wesleyan Church after they had settled in Bathurst.

Apart from the fact that many on board *Harbinger* came from the Gwennap area, there was definite evidence that some people were closely related, or were part of a chain of migration to New South Wales which had begun years before. The Northey, Blamey and Trenemon families were clearly related, as were the Roscrow and Phillips families. The Thomas brothers were nephews of Robert Smith who had arrived aboard *Florentia*, and they went to the Bathurst district where he was living. Joseph and Susannah Wearne and their eleven children were part of a more subtle chain migration which had begun with the first Cornish Wesleyan missionaries to the colony, Benjamin Carvosso and Walter Lawry, early in the century. This chain had continued through contacts with the Wesleyan Tom, Lane and Hawke families at Cornish Settlement, and others. The Wearnes were staunch Wesleyans, and also friends of Benjamin Carvosso and his family in Ponsanooth, and their employment with a Wesleyan miller in Sydney had been arranged prior to their emigration.[34]

Occupational, age and 'respectability' discrepancies occurred amongst Cornish immigrants aboard *Lord Hungerford* when individuals did not meet the immigration regulations, and were presumably deliberate ploys to take advantage of or 'beat' the system. An unusually liberal interpretation of the regulations by officials allowed assistance to a sprinkling of miners and enabled all but one of the miners to admit this occupation.

THE *LORD STANLEY* 1850

The barque *Lord Stanley*, of 769 tons, arrived in Sydney on 26 August 1850 after an uneventful voyage of 114 days,[35] carrying a majority of farm labourers amongst the 307 immigrants of whom twenty-three were Cornish. There were four families (eight adults and five children) plus one single woman and nine single men. There was no evidence of a particular place of birth or residence shared by a majority of them, or of any organised group emigration. The parishes of origin were Landrake and Saltash, Lewannick, St Wenn and St Columb, Helston, Ladock and Truro.

The *Lord Stanley* had been visited in Plymouth Sound by members of the Plymouth Emigrant Employment Society, who reported that the ship was a beautiful and well-ordered vessel, and that their gifts of books and work to occupy the emigrants on the voyage, together with the prayers and advice they had offered, had all been gratefully received.[36]

On arrival in Sydney, as required, the *Lord Stanley's* surgeon presented a health report. He stated that no epidemics had occurred on the voyage, that illnesses suffered had been diarrhoea, dysentery, catarrh and rheumatism, and that on arrival two were suffering from scurvy and three from rheumatism. One adult and three children died on the passage. No immigrants made complaints about the voyage. After immigration formalities were completed, the *Lord Stanley* anchored at the entrance to Sydney Cove and, as was customary, the public was notified of the categories and numbers of immigrants for hire. The single women were taken to Hyde Park Barracks for interview by prospective employers, and the married people and single men remained on board to be interviewed.

Information on the occupations of immigrants aboard *Lord Stanley* was advertised in the *New South Wales Government Gazette* for the benefit of potential employers.[37] Overwhelmingly, the male immigrants available for hire were said to be agricultural labourers (thirty-eight of the fifty married individuals, and seventy-six of the eighty-seven unmarried), although there was a smattering of other occupations such as shepherd, miner, groom and weaver.

Reliability of answers

Research has shown that three of the four family groups, the single woman and seven of the nine single men were who (but not necessarily what) they claimed to be. However, the one family group which was not found by the author was not necessarily making false claims. They were John and Maria Hawke, and their two small children who had been born at Landrake. John's place of birth was North Hill and his parents were both living there. Maria had been born in Landrake and her parents (surname not given) were living at Callington. They were Wesleyan so the children's baptisms are not on the IGI. They had not been married in 1841 and by 1851 they were in New South Wales. So, although they cannot be found, there is no evidence to suggest they were not what they claimed.

As in the earlier voyages, there were some interesting discrepancies, mostly in occupation and age. James Jolly claimed to be a farm labourer, but was a blacksmith and came from a family of blacksmiths. Edward Mount also claimed to be a farm labourer but he appeared in a Sydney directory in 1851, the year after his arrival, as a dyer, living in an inner city area.[38] George Striberley was at least two years older than the thirty years he claimed. William Chapman claimed to be Church of England but had been baptised in the Bible Christian denomination.[39]

Most of the Cornish immigrants aboard *Lord Stanley* were what they claimed to be, and so had no need to misrepresent themselves to fit the criteria, except for a few who did not fit exactly and thus falsified some of their answers. There is no evidence to suggest that any of these immigrants had adopted false identities, or had told blatant or deliberate lies in the way that had happened on some earlier voyages.

THE *LADY ANN* 1854

In the year following the *Lord Stanley*'s arrival, the Australian Goldrush began, bringing a flood of people to New South Wales. In 1851 the *West Briton* reported that emigrants were leaving Britain at the rate of 930 per day, and that in a recent three-month period, 2,779 had left from Plymouth alone.[40] Those aboard the *Lady Ann* in 1854 were travelling to a colony which had been changed by the Goldrush and which was quite different from the agricultural and pastoral destination it had been when the *Lord Stanley* had arrived. New South Wales had become a highly attractive destination for miners and others hoping to 'strike it rich'.

The *Lady Ann* itself, of 745 tons, arrived in Sydney on 29 September 1854 having left Plymouth on 26 June and passed Land's

End four days later. It carried three cabin passengers and 290 government immigrants of whom 128 were Cornish.[41] The Cornish were twelve family groups (twenty-four adults and nineteen children) plus eighty-five single men and two single women. They came from all over Cornwall; from Redruth, Illogan, St Agnes, Camborne, Crowan, Gwennap, Truro, Merther, Ruan, and Stithians, from Mevagissey and Charlestown, from St Keverne, Helston, Falmouth and Penryn, from St Buryan, Sancreed, Penzance, St Ives and St Erth, and from Mawgan, Wadebridge, Padstow and Davidstow.

The number of 148 single men (of whom eighty-five were Cornish) on this voyage was unusually high for a ship carrying assisted immigrants. As well as being a response to take advantage of the new regulations, this high number was doubtless due to the enthusiasm of many single men to join the Goldrush.

Reliability of answers

Evidence indicates that all twelve Cornish families, and seventy-five of the eight-five single men and one of the two single women were who they claimed to be. However, there were many discrepancies in occupation and age. Two of the married men, thirty-seven (almost half) of the single men and one single woman were not in the occupation they claimed. The married men, Anthony Hammill and John Jackson, both claimed to be farm labourers. In the 1851 census, one was a copper miner and the other was a miner. The single woman, Jane Martin, who claimed she was a housemaid aged twenty-five, was a straw bonnet maker aged thirty-two.

Occupational discrepancies amongst the single men varied from those like Job Curnow of Ludgvan who claimed to be a farm labourer, but whose father was a farmer prosperous enough to employ a servant, to discrepancies which were obviously deliberately false, like James Pool who claimed to be a farm labourer from Phillack aged nineteen, but was actually a mason (from a family of masons) aged seventeen.

There were four age discrepancies amongst the families, one amongst the single women, and twenty-four amongst the single men. For example, William Carah of Crowan, claiming to be a farm labourer aged twenty-one was in fact fifteen and the son of a copper miner.

There was some evidence that groups of people aboard *Lady Ann* were either travelling together from the same part of Cornwall, or were related to one another. The two single women, Jane Martin and Maria Simcocks, were both from Penzance, and both said they had an aunt, Mrs Kerno, living in Sydney. They were probably cousins, travelling with yet another cousin, Job Curnow, also from Penzance.

John Hicks had been born in St Eval and had known George

Hawke there. On arrival, his family went directly to the Hawkes at Cornish Settlement and settled in the neighbourhood. Travelling with them were John Watts and his family.[42] The Hicks and Watts families had both been living in Camborne for some years prior to their emigration (the Hicks and Watts children were born in Camborne) although John Watts had been born in Merther. Also travelling on *Lady Ann* with his family was John Varcoe of Merther, whose parents were neighbours of Joseph Watts' parents in Merther in 1851.

Simon Richards (aged twenty-two) said he was a Methodist and a miner from Perranzabuloe. He was not challenged about his answers on arrival but his later life in New South Wales indicated that some of his claims had been false. He was employed from the ship by a farmer, but as soon as he could he became a shoemaker in a nearby town. Some years later, after land became available to small selectors in the area in 1861, he selected 320 acres and eventually expanded his property to 7,000 acres.[43] He was also three years older than he claimed on arrival.

At least two other Cornishmen aboard *Lady Ann* attempted to 'beat' the emigration system to their own advantage. In August 1855 an anonymous informant from Sofala, near Bathurst, notified the Immigration Department that John James and Francis Painter (who had absconded from the Maitland emigrant depot without paying their passage money or hiring with a suitable employer for two years), 'were making their best of turning the double on the government agents' as goldminers at Sofala, earning from £8 to £10 per week. The informant suggested that the authorities should find them and force them to pay their passage money.[44] The emigrant depot in Maitland was one of several in rural areas such as Parramatta and Bathurst to which immigrants were despatched directly from ships.

The Cornish people travelling on board *Lady Ann* had given a high number of unreliable answers. Like those on earlier ships, some were what the regulations stipulated and thus had no need to lie. However, many others told outright lies, or deliberately exaggerated the truth. Some instances were borderline discrepancies, as in the case of Job Curnow. James' and Painter's escapades after arrival indicated that although they fitted the immigration criteria, and gave truthful answers to Immigration officials on arrival, they had no hesitation in misusing the system to their advantage when it suited them.

THE *LORD HUNGERFORD* 1855

The *Lord Hungerford*, of 936 tons, arrived in Sydney on 20 March 1855, carrying 321 government immigrants of whom twenty-five were

Cornish. These comprised four families (eight adults and seven children) plus two single women and eight single men. There is no evidence that members of the group had arranged to emigrate together. They were from Truro, West Penwith, Saltash, Mevagissey, Perranzabuloe, and from Wadebridge, Withiel, St Enoder and St Columb.

On this occasion many of the Cornish, as well as other immigrants, complained about the supply and quality of rations, and about the rolling of the ship throughout the voyage. An investigation conducted by immigration officials reported that although the ship was well built and ventilated, a large quantity of railway iron being carried as cargo had been loaded improperly. This had caused rolling of the ship, sending rushes of water down the hatchway into the immigrants' quarters, and causing dampness in the between decks accommodation throughout the voyage. The wet conditions were blamed for many of the passengers suffering from scurvy on arrival. The immigrants in general had an unhealthy appearance and the ship's standard of cleanliness was unsatisfactory. The cookhouse had been placed on the quarter deck, covering with soot the space which should have been available to the immigrants for exercise. Immigrants frequently had difficulty actually having their food cooked, and because of the negligence of the officer responsible, were not properly issued with their rations. Towards the end of the voyage the butter, raisins and suet ran out completely. Although the health of the immigrants on arrival caused official concern,[45] they were said to be of 'a useful class'.[46]

Reliability of answers

There is evidence that three of the four family groups, six of the eight single men and one of the two single women were who they claimed to be. However, there were some discrepancies in the claims of what they were. For example, two of the married men's occupations were not what they claimed. Joseph Bennett said he was a farm labourer, but in 1841 he was a grocer in Chacewater. Christopher Bottrell said he was a farm labourer but in 1841 he was an engine man in St Just and in 1851 he was a farmer of fifteen acres in Madron. It is possible that he was a borderline case, an example of the mining-farming dual occupation which occurred in Cornwall. However, he gave false information to other questions (about the ages of himself, his wife and two of their children), and Immigration officials in Sydney considered that he was 'sickly looking'. He was hardly the type of immigrant intended by colonists to qualify for assistance.

Two single men were not strictly in the occupations they claimed. William Bullock of St Enoder and William Trebilcock of St Columb said they were farm labourers. Bullock came from a farming family sufficiently prosperous for all the children to be living at home and so probably should not have qualified for assistance. Trebilcock falsified his occupation completely. He was a tailor, living at home with his father who was a woolcomber. Both single women's occupational claims were suspect. Mary Juleff of St Columb said she was a housemaid, but in 1851 she was living with her family, with no occupation given. Matilda Benney, said to be a housemaid aged eighteen of Chacewater, could not be found. There was no entry for her or her alleged parents in Chacewater in 1851. There was no Matilda Benney baptised in Chacewater between 1835 and 1840. In fact, there was no child named Matilda baptised there during this period.

There were discrepancies in answers given by family groups regarding their ages, four in the Bottrell family and two in the Bennett family. One single man, Thomas Over, claimed to be twenty-one, but was actually only seventeen.[47] The Bennett family claimed to be Church of England, but there is no record that any of their children, said to have been born in Kenwyn, were baptised in that parish between January 1835 and May 1846. They have been baptised elsewhere, but it is also possible that they were Nonconformists.

Those immigrants aboard *Lord Hungerford* who fitted the regulations had no need to lie. Those who did not fit the regulations had little hesitation in doing so. As on earlier voyages, some individuals produced several discrepancies.

THE *FITZJAMES* 1857

The *Fitzjames* of 1307 tons, which arrived in Sydney on 1 April 1857 after a voyage of ninety-nine days from Liverpool and Plymouth, brought a majority of immigrants who stated they were (the preferred) farm labourers or domestic servants. The ship carried one passenger and 429 immigrants of whom eighty-five were Cornish, comprising seventeen families (thirty-three adults and twenty-eight children, plus seven single females and seventeen single males).[48] They came from all over Cornwall, from Truro, St Agnes, Redruth, Illogan and Camborne, from St Neot, Cardinham, Duloe, Lanreath, St Veep and Calstock, and from St Austell and Mevagissey. They were also from Breage, Mabe, Mawnan and Penryn, from St Just in Penwith and Penzance, and from St Enoder, St Columb and Newlyn East.

Susanna Austen from Devonshire (the forty-four year old matron in charge of the single women's compartment) was responsible for six women over fifty, two little boys under the care of their mother, two other married women and ninety-six single women.[49] From the very beginning she had difficulty in exercising any effective control over her charges. She had used the influence of friends in Britian to obtain the situation in the hope of securing extra privileges on the voyage, but found the opposite to be the case. On the second night at sea she had to contend with three separate dramas: 'the young women imagined the ship was on fire', then 'a choping (sic) is heard and fancy has made it the cutting down of the masts and rigging'. Finally:

> The lights went out at 4 o'clock and now I never can describe
> the confusion that took place, hearing the noise of the sea
> they took it in the dark for the rushing in of the water at the
> portholes. Here every man and woman I believe were calling
> on their God and declaring that if spared they would never
> do as they had done before.[50]

Early in the voyage the weather temporarily ensured 'the tempers of all are hushed by the storm', but soon she was in the midst of a riot amongst the young women who demanded extra water above their daily allowance. An emigrant constable called to assist quickly summoned an officer who threatened to remove the lamps unless the women behaved.

> But no they determined to brave all and compel us to bring
> the water. The lights were at last taken away, the Surgeon and
> Captain were sent for and I was really alarmed . . . most
> of those who were engaged in prayer one little hour before
> or appeared so humble were now in their fury like Tiger
> and Hyenas, tearing down the woodwork . . . and yelling
> horribly.[51]

The matron blamed the girls' behaviour on the unaccustomed spare time available to them, on the novelty of shipboard life and on the evil influence of a few 'thoroughly depraved'. She was relieved to be able to distribute the knitting and needlework provided to keep the single women occupied, and each girl made herself a bonnet as protection against the heat of the sun. Such occupation did not prevent quarrelling and malicious gossiping, and she was constantly concerned at the immodest behaviour of some. A Cornish girl, Grace Hocking, was reported to the surgeon for her laziness in remaining in bed after breakfast.

> I told her she must get up before 7 o'clock or I should get the
> bed taken from her, or get some water used for her for a

shower bath. She replied this way—if you were to do so you should never breathe again. Can she really mean this? Her general conduct answers yes I fear so.[52]

No other Cornish girls were singled out for adverse comment, and two were said to have been amongst the best behaved, having 'resisted every inducement to do what is wrong'. They were Mary Blight of St Austell and Elizabeth Sawle of Ladock (whom Miss Austen considered 'a most clever young woman'). She made no comment about Mary Jenkin of Camborne, but letters written by Mary from the Emigrant Depot in Sydney to a crew member of the *Fitzjames* left little doubt that she and her friends had associated with crew members during the voyage. This was completely forbidden under the regulations and, if discovered, resulted in loss of the crew member's gratuity.[53]

Reliability of answers

Evidence suggests that eleven of the seventeen family groups, six of the seven single women and fifteen of the seventeen single men were who they said they were. Two of the family groups not located consisted of Irish Catholic parents and their small children, some of whom had been born in Cornwall. However, there were many discrepancies in answers about occupation and age.

Four of the family groups, three single women and five of the single men had occupational discrepancies, while five of the families, three of the single women and five of the single men had age discrepancies. Several, but not all, had discrepencies in the answers about occupation and age. This again suggests that discrepancies only occurred when they were necessary for individuals to appear to fit the requirements.

One single man, Samuel Bennett aged twenty, said he was a farm labourer who had been born in Calstock, and that his parents Samuel and Mary were living in Calstock. None of them appear in the census in Calstock in 1851, and there is no record of his baptism in Calstock Parish between 1834 and 1840. It is difficult to assess just how much this man had falsified. He made have constructed an entirely false identity for himself. Alternatively, he might have been who he claimed but perhaps much older or younger. He may have been a Nonconformist, and it may be that he and his parents had visited another parish on census night.

Joseph Salmon of St Columb was three years older than the twenty-six he claimed. John Davey of St Neot was a tin and copper miner claiming to be a sawyer, but although he was forty-two and his wife forty, they did not attempt to falsify their ages, only his occupation.

Brothers James and William May of St Erme also exaggeraged their occupations. Both were living with their father, a farmer of sixty acres, in 1851, and so were probably from a relatively prosperous family and should not have qualified for assistance. William was the nineteen years he claimed but James was twenty-four, not twenty-two. Grace Hocking was twenty-two as she claimed, but it is very unlikely she was a cook. In 1851 she lived with her parents in Pool, Illogan, where her father was an assayer of copper ore. With this background, she should not have been eligible for assistance. If she was not from a working class background, and was unused to waiting on others, it is not surprising that she did not take kindly to Matron Austen's commands to rise early!

Although Mary Blight of St Austell had impressed Matron Austen as a 'respectable' immigrant, Mary had in fact misrepresented her age—she was thirty, not twenty-seven. More significantly, while strictly correct in advising that she had no relatives in New South Wales, she did not mention that she had a sister in neighbouring Victoria whom she intended to join. In other words, she was taking advantage of the New South Wales assisted immigration scheme to travel to an adjoining colony. This came to light when her sister's enquiry to the immigration authorities concerning Mary's whereabouts prompted a terse memo:

> She . . . took service in Sydney and stated she had no relatives in the colony. I see no object in appending this information as it is evidently required with the intention of sending the girl to the Colony of Victoria.[54]

CONCLUSION

Each voyage and each group of immigrants in the sample was composed of individuals who needed to fulfil certain criteria to qualify for financial assistance for the voyage. Those who did match these criteria generally did not lie, because they had no need to do so, while those who almost fitted the criteria exaggerated their credentials in the areas where they were lacking. Some individuals and families needed to bend the answers to more than one question to qualify, and these cases indicated premeditated and deliberate attempts to misuse the immigration regulations for their own purposes. Here the collusion of officials and referees in Cornwall was significant, the assisted passage schemes being seen as devices that could be taken advantage of to promote the 'improving' cause of emigration. The group experience of emigration, of events and circumstances on board ship, may have coloured the answers that were given in Sydney and occasionally 'exposed' the deceit (or lack of 'respectability') of some assisted immigrants.

Deficiencies in the occupational skills and respectability of assisted immigrants were the most common complaints from colonists in New South Wales. It is evident that many Cornish immigrants did falsify or exaggerate their occupations during examination by immigration officials on arrival, while 'unrespectable' immigrants tried sometimes to affect a veneer of respectability (for example, by stressing religious affiliations). In extreme cases, there seem to have been attempts to misrepresent individual identities.[55] To this was added common mis-representations of age, an apparently common misrepresentation of religion (for whatever reasons), and the occasional non-disclosure of other relatives in the colony.

For emigration historians none of these discrepencies should come as a surprise, for in areas such as Cornwall where emigration had become a major way of life by the mid-nineteenth century, it was inevitable that individuals and communities should wish to bend the rules to their own advantages. However, the extent to which this happened in the sample discussed above is an important demonstration and reminder that shipping lists and other emigration documentation should not always be taken at face value. A more critical examination of such documents will not only yield a more accurate picture of what actually happened but will also afford new insights into the charac-teristics and culture of the emigration process itself.

NOTES AND REFERENCES

1. See Patricia Lay, 'One and All: The Cornish in Nineteenth-Century New South Wales', unpub. MA thesis, Australian National University, Canberra, 1992.
2. The principal sources used in this study are those in the Archives Offices of New South Wales (*Shipping Lists* and *Ships' Papers*), *Parliamentary Papers* and the *New South Wales Government Gazette*, UK Census 1841 and 1851, newspapers (especially the *Sydney Morning Herald* and the *West Briton*), the *Mormon International Genealogical Index* (IGI), and selected baptism and marriage records.
3. See R. B. Madgwick, *Immigration into Eastern Australia, 1788–1851*, 1937, repub. Sydney University Press, 1969.
4. There was also the competition of other Australian colonies,particularly South Australia whose mining industry andNonconformist background drew the majority of Cornish in Australia, where at least 13,000 Cornish immigrants between1836 and 1886 formed some 8 per cent of all emigrants to that colony(see Philip Payton, *The Cornish Miner in Australia: Cousin Jack Down Under*, Redruth, 1984, p. 12).
5. Eric Richards, 'Poverty and Immigration', in Eric Richards (ed.), *Poor*

Australian Immigrants in the Nineteenth Century: Visible Immigrants: Two, Canberra, 1991, p. 3.

6. Madgwick, 1937 and 1969, pp. 94–95. Emigration was organised through the London Emigration Committee whose chief agent was Mr John Marshall. There was criticism of his selection methods and dissatisfaction in the colony with the general quality of these emigrants.
7. Madgwick, 1937 and 1969, p. 112, pp. 126–129.
8. Madgwick, 1937 and 1969, pp. 150–168.
9. *West Briton*, 12 January 1840.
10. *Plymouth, Devonport and Stonehouse Herald*, 7 July 1849.
11. *West Briton*, 12 May 1848.
12. *West Briton*, 16 April 1852, 21 May 1852, 1 October 1852, 3 December 1852, 11 February 1853, 14 October 1853.
13. *West Briton*, 4 March 1853, 27 May 1853.
14. *New South Wales Government Gazette*, 11 July 1854.
15. For a detailed discussion of Cornish immigration into New South Wales, see Lay, 1992.
16. Archives Offices of New South Wales (AONSW) Shipping Lists, *Florentia* 1838, AO reel 1290. It is difficult to be sure of the exact number of Cornish on board because the shipping lists show place of birth for bounty passengers only. A number of the passengers (and the Surgeon, Dr Edye) had common Cornish names and some of the steerage passengers who did not qualify as bounty emigrants may also have been Cornish, including the Edwards, Williams and Tippet families.
17. O. Bloxome, 'Journal of a Voyage to New South Wales 1838, NLA MS 236, 16 June.
18. W.S. Deloitte Esq. in 'Minutes of Evidence taken before the Committee on Immigration 17 August 1838', NSWV&P LC 1838, pp. 843–5.
19. AONSW Shipping Lists, *Florentia* 1838, AO reel 1290; 'Wesleyan Chapel Bathurst, marriage register 1839–1844', 9 May 1839. NLA MS 3290.
20. George Hawke, 'Colonial Experience: The Diary of George Hawke of Orange', unpub. ms, NLA MS 227, p. 24.
21. George Hawke, 'Colonial Experience'.
22. W.S. Deloitte Esq. in 'Minutes of Evidence taken before the Committee on Immigration 17 August 1838', NSWV&P LC 1838, p. 845.
23. *Bathurst Times*, 11 June 1917.
24. B. Mac. Smith, *Quench Not the Spirit: Merino Heritage*, Melbourne, 1972, p. 50.
25. Rogers: 1841 Census 'Rosemardine' Manaccan; Nicholls: 1851 Census, 'Treglossack' St Keverne.
26. *West Briton*, 19 July 1844.
27. Immigration Board, Sydney, 18 April 1844; (AONSW shipping list, *William Metcalfe* 1844, AO reel 2461).
28. *Sydney Morning Herald*, 14 March 1844.
29. A. Brown, *The Evans Family History*, Epping, 1987.
30. IGI, Madron, 23 October 1843.

31. AONSW Shipping Lists, AO reel 2459.
32. *British Parliamentary Papers* (BPP), 'Papers Relating to Emigration to the Australian Colonies', 1850, vol. 40, pp. 51–52.
33. BPP, 'Papers Relating to Emigration', 1851, vol. 40, p. 81.
34. V. Wearne-Frost, *Wearne of Cornwall and Australia*, Blackheath, 1981.
35. For more detail, see Patricia Lay, 'Clotted Cream and Chapel: The Mullis Family in Cornwall and New South Wales', Dip.FHS., Society of Australian Genealogists, Sydney, 1988.
36. *The Emigrant's Penny Magazine, 1850–51*, p. 71.
37. *New South Wales Government Gazette*, 28 August 1850.
38. W. and F. Ford, *Sydney Commercial Directory for the Year 1851*, Sydney, 1851.
39. IGI, St Ervan 1827.
40. *West Briton*, 7 November 1851.
41. AONSW Shipping Lists, *Lady Ann* 1854, AO reel 2466.
42. CWD, 16 July 1985.
43. A.J. Greenhalgh, *Time's Subjects: The Story of Goorangoola, a Small Community in the Hunter Valley of New South Wales, 1939–1979*, Roseville, 1982, pp. 89–91, p. 113.
44. AONSW Immigration 55/3954 28 August 1855.
45. One Cornishman, Christopher Bottrell, was singled out for special comment as 'sickly looking' (AONSW Shipping Lists, *Lord Hungerford* 1855, AO reel 2470).
46. AONSW Ship's Papers 4/4697, Reel 2853, p. 81, no.55/19 *Lord Hungerford* 1855.
47. IGI, Thomas Over, baptised Mevagissey 2 January 1837, son of Mary and Samuel.
48. AONSW Ship's Papers, *Fitzjames* 1857, AO reel 404.
49. AONSW 9/6212, Matron's Diary, *Fitzjames* 1857.
50. AONSW 9/6212, *Fitzjames* Diary, 24 December 1856.
51. AONSW 9/6212, 29 December 1856.
52. AONSW 9/6212, 19 January 1857.
53. AONSW 9/6212, 15 March 1857.
54. AONSW 9/6212, 27 April 1857.
55. Although there are no easily confirmed cases of misrepresentation of identities in the sample ships, one blatant example that was exposed at the time was that of a Cornish woman named Ellen Coad (alias Diana James). Coad had emigrated as an assisted immigrant in the *Julindar* in 1849. She subsequently returned to Cornwall but attempted to emigrate again under the assisted passage arrangements in 1853 in *Ellensborough*, using the assumed name Diana James (see AONSW Shipping Lists, *Ellensborough* 1853, AO reel 2464).

CORNISH EMIGRATION IN RESPONSE TO CHANGES IN THE INTERNATIONAL COPPER MARKET IN THE 1860s

Philip Payton

INTRODUCTION

Although Cornwall's nineteenth-century 'Great Emigration' has attracted the attention of a number of historians, the principal concern has been to chart the influence and experience of Cornish emigrants in their new lands (particularly the United States and Australia), with detailed consideration of their impact overseas in areas such as mining practices, economic activity, cultural formation, and religious and political movements.[1] This has sometimes been at the expense of full examination of the emigration process itself, and has not allowed the development of a 'Cornu-centric' overview in which the changing nature of emigration over time could be seen in proper perspective.[2] This article, then, is an initial step towards redressing the balance, for while it is not possible here to achieve that full overview, there is the opportunity to establish a new approach and to set an agenda which might emphasise synthesis (the drawing together of hitherto compartmentalised strands) as well as identifying specific socio-economic phenomena such as 'emigration culture', 'emigration trade', and 'dependency culture'.

The focus of this discussion is on the 1860s, for that decade was in many ways a watershed for Cornwall, witnessing not only a quickening in the pace of emigration but also the onset of de-industrialisation, with the demise (almost) of Cornish copper, the faltering of Cornish tin, and the first signs of the consequent fall from grace of Cornish engineering (not least the Cornish beam-engine). The several narrative histories of the Cornish mining industry have described this decline,[3] while more recently there have been renewed attempts to analyse the experience of Cornwall in the last century, explaining that despite Cornwall's early place in the forefront of technological advance (and despite the emergence of a new assertive Cornish sense of identity derived from this industrial prowess), Cornish industrialisation was in fact imperfect, over-specialised and incomplete.[4] It was this flawed industrial base that led, it has been argued, to early industrial collapse—one consequence of which was the perpetuation and growth of the 'Great Emigration'. Contemporary Cornish opinion saw this emigration as the ultimate triumph of Cornish genius, with the might and glory of Cornwall writ large across the world as 'Cousin Jacks' facilitated the mining development of America, Australia, South Africa and elsewhere,[5] but the reality was quite different. The 'Great Emigration' was a function of the distinctive and in some respects unique characteristics of the Cornish industrial experience.

Indeed, Cornwall never recovered from the blows of the 1860s, and Baines has calculated that between 1861 and 1900 Cornwall lost no less than 10.5 per cent of its male population overseas and 7.0 per cent to other counties (far and away the greatest percentage loss of any county), with a corresponding loss of 5.3 per cent of the female population overseas and 7.1 per cent to other counties. Incredibly, over the same period 44.8 per cent of the Cornish male population aged fifteen to twenty-four left for overseas, with a further 29.7 per cent leaving for other counties. Of females in the same age group, 26.2 per cent went abroad while 35.5 per cent went to other counties. In all, some 118,500 people left Cornwall between 1861 and 1900.[6] As Baines has reflected,

> This is not as high as from the famous regions of Italy . . . but it must be remembered that mass emigration from Italy lasted not much more than twenty years. Cornwall was probably an emigration region comparable with any in Europe.[7]

EMIGRATION: 'CULTURE', 'TRADE' AND METAL MARKETS

By the 1850s emigration had become already a significant feature of Cornish life. Rural poverty in the 1830s had been followed by the 'Hungry Forties' (both 'push' factors), while the discovery of copper in South Australia in the mid-1840s (at Kapunda and then Burra Burra) complemented similar activity in the 'Lakes' copper-belt at Keweenaw in Upper Michigan (i.e., the 'pull' factors). The Wisconsin lead mines also attracted many Cornish folk (by 1850 there were perhaps as many as 9,000 Cornish folk at Mineral Point in that State),[8] while others in the 1840s went to the silver mines of Real Del Monte in Mexico. In 1849 the excitement of gold discoveries in California precipitated yet further Cornish emigration, as did the opening-up of the Australian goldfields in New South Wales and Victoria after 1851.

An important 'emigration culture' had been thus established within Cornwall, with emigration viewed as a legitimate escape route from hard-times at home, a perspective much encouraged by the Cornish Methodist 'self-help' and 'mutual improvement' ethos.[9] Mineral bonanzas overseas were identified as likely destinations not only for the desperate or the adventurous but for the prudent seeking to make the best of their skills and the opportunities offered abroad. The myth of 'Cousin Jack', where mining expertise and ethnic identity became inextricably linked in the mining camps of America or Australia, was carefully cultivated by the Cornish and was central to the fabric of the emigration culture.[10] But this culture did not exist in isolation, and a symbiotic relationship was developed between it and the 'emigration trade' that grew-up in Cornwall over the same years. To a certain degree this trade was focused outside of Cornwall in the port of Plymouth, from which the overwhelming majority of emigrant ships in South West Britain sailed and where the redoubtable J. B. Wilcocks had established himself as a senior emigration agent developing, for example, an intimate relationship with the South Australian Mining Association which ran the Burra Burra copper mine.[11]

But the 'emigration trade' was also active within Cornwall itself, with a string of agents established as early as the late 1830s in strategic towns such as Penzance, Truro, Falmouth, Helston and Launceston, the most notable of whom was Isaac Latimer—a reporter on the staff of the *West Briton* who for many years acted as Agent for South Australia, Van Diemen's Land, New Zealand and elsewhere, working closely with their colonial governments' 'free' or 'assisted' emigration programmes.[12] Similarly, Cornish ports—especially Padstow, which in the 1840s was more important than Plymouth as a point of departure for Cornish emigrants[13]—were themselves active in the trade, with emigrants sailing from harbours large and small such as Fowey and Gweek.

To the distinctive characteristics of the Cornish industrial experience and its 'emigration culture' and 'emigration trade' was added the changing nature of the international metal markets. Specifically, as Newell has noted, 'By the 1860s a number of important changes were taking place which were altering the patterns of international trade in copper and ore'.[14] From the late 1820s, Swansea had become the focus for the international copper trade, not only monopolising the smelting of British-produced ore but also encouraging and tapping the increasing supply of copper from overseas. It was natural and inevitable, perhaps, that the produce of Kapunda and Burra Burra should find itself directed towards the Swansea 'ticketings',[15] but British influence in the United States (aided by British relaxation of trade regulations) and the impact of British informal imperialism in Latin America also dictated that foreign ores too should head for South Wales for processing. In Wales, by the early 1840s four companies accounted for the overwhelming bulk of ore purchases, a position that was defended in typically oligopolistic manner by the creation (in 1844) of a 'secret' cartel—the Copper Trade Association.[16] In Cornwall, this concentration of activity was evidence that the Cornish near-monopoly of copper production had been rapidly undermined, despite the early reluctance of Cornish adventurers to take seriously the threat of overseas competition.

By the early 1860s, then, the established positions of both Wales and Cornwall were already under attack, the Welsh smelting industry increasingly challenged by the emergence of overseas processing (even in South Australia), and Cornish primary production challenged at home by the continuing arrival at Swansea of foreign produce (including Chilean 'regulus' or partially refined copper ore) and on the world stage by the new multiplicity of both producers and processors. The United States, in particular, had already opted for a policy of copper self-sufficiency, while Chilean production had trebled between 1851 and 1860 (and was to double again in the following decade): as early as 1830 Chile was producing 20 per cent of the world's copper.[17] A further source of overseas competition was the resurgence of the South Australian copper industry, for although the Victorian Gold Rush had in the early 1850s (by 'poaching' workers) caused serious operational problems for Kapunda and Burra Burra, the end of the decade had witnessed not only the dwindling attraction of Victoria but also the significant discovery (in 1859) of rich copper deposits at Wallaroo on York Peninsula. This was followed in 1861 by a second and equally important find at neighbouring Moonta. As the Kapunda *Northern Star* put it in July 1861, South Australia was now 'out-Cornwalling Cornwall altogether'.[18]

LULL BEFORE THE STORM

Despite their huge long-term consequences, these various changes in the international copper market were not felt immediately in Cornwall in terms of changes in the rate and nature of emigration. Indeed, in August 1862 the *West Briton* newspaper could note that in the West Cornish mining town of Redruth there was actually a housing shortage, caused by 'the almost total cessation of emigration to our colonies, as well as the return of many persons from America and elsewhere'.[19] To some extent this was because the United States, despite the rapid development of its indigenous copper industry and despite its firmly established reputation as a destination for the emigrant Cornish miner, was by the early 1860s embroiled in a Civil War (1861–65) which wrought massive destruction and widespread social and economic dislocation.

In such conditions the States became less attractive as a potential destination, and indeed as early as October 1861 there were reports that Cornish settlers in North America were anxious to return home because of the deteriorating situation.[20] Cornish opinion was divided between those who (in good Liberal-Methodist anti-slavery tradition) opposed the 'slave-polluted territory'[21] of the Confederacy and those who (with equally sound Liberal-Methodist sensibilities) criticised the expansionist territorial imperialism of the Unionist North, but Cousin Jacks combined to agree that this was not a good time to be in America. Some Cornish left the Union States (such as Michigan) to participate in the opening-up of new mining frontiers beyond the conflict (Montana, Arizona), while those already out in California saw that the war was having an adverse effect on the local economy and advised those still at home in Cornwall not to come. The falling value of the dollar in this period meant that monies earned in America and sent home to Cornwall were in real terms of diminishing value, a further disincentive to emigration.[22]

At the same time that the American Civil War was discouraging emigration from Cornwall to the United States, so there was a temporary lull in emigration—for internal economic and political reasons— to South Australia. Over 2,000 Cornish people had emigrated to South Australia in the late 1830s and early 1840s, and between 1846 and 1850 some 6,277 'government emigrants' had sailed from Cornwall to Australia.[23] Of these, no fewer than 4,775 had gone to South Australia. In other words, between 1846 and 1850 71 per cent of all Cornish emigrants to the Australian colonies went to South Australia, while 27 per cent of all government emigrants to South Australia were from Cornwall. Similarly, between 1851 and 1860 some 48,509 immigrants were recorded in the colony's shipping passenger lists, of whom 5,177 (or 10.7 per cent) were from Cornwall, further establishing South Australia as a principal destination for emigrant Cornish folk.[24]

When, in 1859–61, there was a break in this pattern of emigration and the suspension of government-sponsored 'assisted passage' schemes, there was much debate in South Australia over the wisdom of this policy. In particular, the rapid development of the newly-discovered copper deposits at Wallarro and Moonta, along with the excellent wheat harvest in the colony in 1861, led to calls for renewed immigration, prompting a string of pleading petitions to the colonial government in Adelaide, one originating in Kapunda demanding the recruitment of a 'thousand miners'.[25] The government responded by allocating an immediate £25,000 to its immigration fund, and at the end of 1862 the so-called 'Sutherland Act' (officially the Waste Lands Sales Act) revived the policy of selling hitherto unimproved Crown lands to finance assisted immigration, with one-third of annual land-sales revenues allocated to the fund.[26] Responding as it was to a rapidly increasing demand for labour in South Australia (in part a function of the resurgence of the copper industry), this new policy had the effect of stimulating a new wave of immigration, not least from Cornwall.

In Cornwall itself the apparent lull in emigration in the very early 1860s may have been assisted (albeit indirectly, through the impact on the international copper market) by the Spanish blockade of Chile.[27] Any effect, however, was transitory, a renewal of Cornish emigration being not only a response to increased demand from South Australia but also a function of declining performance in the Cornish economy. By October 1863 the *West Briton* was reporting that 'Large numbers of the mining population are emigrating to Australia, Chili (sic), California, New Zealand, Queensland',[28] many from the districts of St Just-in-Penwith, Camborne, St Agnes, and St Blazey, where their wholesale departure was leading—it was alleged—to a scarcity of skilled labour. The newspaper also noted the importance of financial remittances received from Cornish emigrants overseas, an acknowledgement that the 'dependency culture' that would come to characterise Cornwall was already in the making. Slate-quarrymen from the neighbourhood of Delabole were also joining the ranks of departing miners,[29] and in June 1863 W. Wade—an emigration agent in Redruth—advertised that there were opportunities for assisted passages to New Zealand for miners 'with grown-up daughters',[30] farm labourers, shepherds, smiths, masons and carpenters. Things moved from bad to worse during 1864 and 1865, the *West Briton* noting in September 1865 that during the previous three months there had been a marked deterioration in the situation of the mining population: 'Employment is more difficult to obtain, emigration is going on upon a scale hitherto unprecedented, many of the small (mining) undertakings are being wound up, and the large ones becoming unprofitable.'[31]

AUSTRALIA'S COPPER MAGNETS

With the South Australian flood-gates open once again, much of this rush of Cornish emigration in 1863–65 was to that colony. Indeed, between 1860 and 1867 3,651 'government emigrants' sailed from Cornwall to South Australia, some 25 per cent of all emigrants to the colony in that period.[32] In 1863 four shiploads of immigrants arrived at Port Adelaide, each with Cornish contingents, and all but one sailing from Plymouth—which was by now firmly established as not only the principal point of departure for Cornish emigrants but also the principal embarkation point for ships bound for the Antipodes. In 1864 there were seven arrivals at Port Adelaide, each one from Plymouth and again each ship sporting its Cornish contingent, while during 1865 there were no fewer than fourteen arrivals from Plymouth—this time with a massive Cornish presence: 211 out of 315 passengers in the *Queen Bee*, 207 out of 383 in the *Clara*, 99 out of 295 in the *Coldstream*, 128 out of 422 in the *Electric*, 242 out of 388 in the *Gosforth*, and so on.[33]

During 1864 over 16 per cent of all South Australian immigrants were from Cornwall, while in 1865 the figure rose to an extraordinary 42.5 per cent.[34] Not surprisingly, many of these Cornish emigrants found work in the Wallaroo and Moonta copper mines (their families becoming integral parts of the 'Little Cornwall' community that was already forming on Yorke Peninsula), and the activities of the mining companies complemented the immigration policies of the colonial government. Building upon the Cornish practices already established at Kapunda, Burra Burra and other mines in the colony, the Wallaroo and Moonta companies determined to work their mines true Cornish-style, adopting Cornish employment methods, Cornish terminology and technology, and importing both machinery and men from Cornwall. Although there was sometimes criticism of the 'unscientific' methods of the Cornish (which contrasted, it was alleged, with that of German miners), and although in the aftermath of the 'Great Strike' in 1874 the Moonta and Wallaroo directors thought briefly to obtain '200 Miners or Pitsinkers of other than Cornish nationality',[35] South Australian mining entrepreneurs remained convinced that Cornwall was the foremost repository of mining skills and actively recruited Cornish miners in preference to all others throughout the last century.[36] In South Australia, the myth of Cousin Jack was triumphant.

In acquiring their Cornish work force, the Moonta and Wallaroo companies sought first of all (especially during the immigration lull of 1859–61) to recruit from Kapunda, Burra Burra, the plethora of smaller South Australian mines, and from the Victorian diggings. But none of these sources was large enough or consistent enough, and in 1864 the Moonta company was shocked when a brief but bitter strike demonstrated how short was the supply of skilled labour in the colony. Accordingly, in April 1864 the Moonta Mining Company wrote to its

London Agents (Messes. A. L. Elders), instructing them to recruit miners in Cornwall. The company secretary, T. F. McCoull, wrote that,

> You will learn from the Adelaide papers that the miners at Moonta and Wallaroo Mines are now out on Strike—this circumstance coupled with the fact that considerable difficulty has been experienced hitherto in getting really good hands, has induced the Directors to send to Cornwall through you for fifty men to be brought out under the Assisted Passage Regulations of the Government.[37]

Not long after, on the advice of its general manager, Captain Henry Hancock, the Moonta company asked A. L. Elders to send out an additional 200 miners, and although none of these 'New Chums' was used in strike-breaking activities, they none the less proved an important asset to the Peninsula mines during their formative years.

In an attempt to breath new life into its faltering Burra Burra mine (whose 'eyes' had been 'picked out' during the heady days of the 1840s for quick profit maximisation), the South Australian Mining Association continued to lobby J. B. Wilcocks in Plymouth,[38] complaining to the colonial government that 'the supply of miners arriving in the Colony is very far from being equal to the demand'.[39] Like its Moonta counterparts, the Wallaroo Mining Company also determined to recruit from Cornwall. By the end of 1864 a party of men had arrived in the *Tarquin*, with a further body of smelters (recruited from Swansea, part of a South Australian plan to defeat the 'Welsh monopoly') and Cornish miners preparing to come out with Captain Paul Roach—a mine manager recently engaged in Cornwall. Other Cousin Jacks earmarked for Wallaroo Mines arrived in the *Queen Bee* in 1865.[40]

THE 'GREAT CRASH'

1866 was the ultimate year of reckoning for the Cornish copper mining industry. As Rowe has explained, already 'the copper mines of Cornwall had been largely worked out; the best ones were exhausted, what remained were too poor to warrant working'.[41] And as Newell adds:

> The problem was not a cyclical fluctuation or short-term market shock but was deep-seated in the changing nature of the market: the world supply of the metal was increasing despite falling prices—to depress still further the price of ore in the unprotected British market.[42]

The end of the Civil War had signalled the full return of America to the international market, while the viability of the Cornish industry was undermined by increasing overseas competition (from countries with vast, high-grade deposits and relatively low operating costs), the continually falling price of copper, and the increasing impoverishment of reserves at home. This latter factor was sometimes exacerbated by poor managerial methods in Cornwall, the 'eyes' having been 'picked out' of mines in the days of high prices without thoughts of ore conservation for the future, while short-cut methods such as the sinking of crooked shafts to facilitate early access to deposits led to longer-term operational inefficiency. In addition, the 'cost-book' system of financing the mines had led, it has been argued, to the early dispersal of profits instead of planning and investment for the future. On top of all this was the depressing effect of the calamitous financial crash in Britain in 1866, resulting from the failure of the Overund-Guerney bank.[43]

Specifically, the problems facing the Cornish industry were reflected in the falling prices realised at the Swansea 'ticketings' for what the Cornish termed 'ore copper'—i.e. 'as much ore as will make a ton of fine copper'. In January 1860 the price had stood at £102.18s. A year later it had fallen to £86.2s, while in 1862 it fell to £84.5s and in 1863 to £79.10s. In 1864 there was an encouraging if temporary rally, the price climbing to £94.19s, but in 1865 and 1866 there was a fall to £80.14s and £80.18s respectively.[44] By January 1867 the price had slumped to a disastrous £71.16s, at which no Cornish mine could hope to operate at a profit, the *West Briton* lamenting that 'very large shipments are reported from Chili'.[45] Indeed, the awful truth was beginning to dawn that: 'the price of 1860 will not be realised again, the production of Chili and Australia . . . being now so very large that the decreasing yield of the Cornish mines makes very little difference to prices'.[46]

As the *West Briton* intimated, the fall in copper prices had been accompanied by the diminishing output of the Cornish industry. The peak of Cornish production had been in 1855–56, but this had been due to the output of the recently-discovered East Cornwall and Tamar Valley mines, disguising the fact that many of the older workings of Camborne, Redruth and Gwennap were already failing. From the peak of 1855–56, Cornish copper production had fallen by as much as a third by June 1866, and between 1865 and 1870 production fell still further from 160,000 tons to 80,000 tons per annum. This was reflected in the wholesale closure of Cornish mines, first of all in the ancient mining district of Gwennap but—after the crash of 1866—in other areas too, the 'knacked bals' including those such as Crenver and Wheal Abraham near Crowan, Perran Great St George at Perranporth, and Fowey

Consols. A number of former copper-producers in the Camborne-Redruth district (Dolcoath, South Crofty, Tincroft, Cooks Kitchen, and other famous names) were able to survive as tin mines (having fortuitously struck tin lodes at depth when the price of tin was relatively high), but tin prices had fallen from £71.11s per ton in 1860 to only £45 in 1866, and several tin mines were also abandoned in that fateful year.[47]

These reverses were of course a serious blow to Cornwall. They challenged the very *raison d'etre* of Cornwall and the Cornish, undermining a hitherto confident and assertive identity born of industrial prowess, and precipitated widespread social and economic dislocation in a land where a third of the working population (some 50,000 people) had in 1862 been employed directly in mining. In July 1866 one observer recorded that 'a settled anxiety dwells upon the countenance of almost every decent person you meet; and the general conversation is upon the great question of mining',[48] the *West Briton* in January 1867 reviewing the events of the preceding year in sombre mood:

> The year now ended is one of the most disastrous for the mining interests of Cornwall during the present century. Certain indirect prejudicial influences have tended to paralyse nearly all our industrial resources, such as the failure of banks and public companies, leading to panic, distrust, an absence of speculation, and leading further to high rates of discount which locked up money . . . all the miseries and privations have fallen upon us which await crushed speculators, a partially-employed working class, and a general langour and depression in trade.[49]

DISTRESS . . . RELIEF . . . ?

The unusually severe winter of 1866–67 caused further distress,[50] and at St Ives the difficulties arising from the closure of local mines were compounded by 'great distress among the fishermen's families, the late pilchard season having proved a failure'.[51] At Callington in East Cornwall 'In consequence of the stoppage of mines . . . there is a great distress among the poor and labouring classes'.[52] In the Helston district, the closure of mines 'has thrown hundreds of men and children out of employment, producing a state of things which it is only possible to conceive of on actual inspection',[53] the village of Ashton being 'a concentration of poverty' (there being, it was noted, no local landowner to help out). By early 1867 a 'Truro Coal, Bread and Soap Fund' had been set-up, with similar funds emerging in Falmouth, Helston,

Redruth, Camborne, Chacewater, St Austell, Bodmin, Tywardreath, St Blazey, St Columb, Liskeard, Launceston, Penryn, Penzance, and St Ives, with the need for further relief being recognised in districts as disparate and diverse as Breage and Sithney, Carharrack, Fowey, Looe, Lanreath, Lostwithiel, and Boscastle.[54]

These individual efforts were co-ordinated into a 'Cornwall Distress Fund', Queen Victoria herself donating £10 to the cause.[55] Sir William Williams, the Scorrier mining magnate, lent his financial support to the propping-up of Poldice (or St Day United, as it had become), and so through the 'liberal manner in which he dispenses his boundless wealth (he) . . . prevented a large number of families being deprived of employment'.[56] Modest support came from other sources in Cornwall, such as the £4.3s.7d 'proceeds of musical entertainments and readings at Duloe',[57] the £5.7s.6d raised by the church choir at Pelynt, and the £10 sent by Mr Deeble Boger of Wolsden, Antony, near Torpoint. The Fund was hardly equal to its task, however, it being noted in January 1868 that the average earnings of 1,000 persons of all ages at Chacewater was only 1s.6d per week, the situation little better in St Just and St Agnes, and with Penzance Union workhouse brimming with its 312 inmates—the largest number 'for many years'.[58] At Helston £50 was voted to assist 197 families in Sithney, Breage, Germoe, Godolphin, and Carnmenellis, and likewise £100 was voted for St Just-in-Penwith, £50 for Lelant, £50 for East Penwith (i.e. Camborne and Redruth), £60 for Tywardreath, and £30 for Callington.

Cornish communities overseas also responded to the call for assistance and, heralding the part that were soon to play in the creation of a 'dependency culture', organised collections of monies to be sent home to Cornwall. In 1868 Cornish folk on the Oven River diggings in Victoria, Australia, sent home £71 to support the relief fund and later the Sandhurst district in the same colony raised £500 for the distressed in Cornwall.[59] Later still, in 1880, it was reported that recent efforts on behalf of Cornwall had raised some £3,179 in Australia—£1,050 in South Australia and the rest in Victoria.[60]

At Kapunda in South Australia there was a strong sense of ethnic solidarity with kinfolk in Cornwall, an indicator of the strength and significance of the international Cornish identity that had by now emerged. At a public meeting in the town correspondence describing Cornish conditions was read from contacts in Marazion, Penzance, Helston, Redruth and Truro. The Mayor of Kapunda, J. Rowett (from St Austell) thanked 'God his father brought him from Cornwall when he was young' and Henry Wheare—who had emigrated from Marazion in 1847—felt that 'South Australians should support the Cornish miners in their distress, for to the energy of some of them in opening up the mines, the colony owed its prosperity'.[61] These assertions of Cornish identity evidently caused some discomfort for the non-Cornish, however, one complaining that 'He should be sorry to see it made altogether a Cornish question,' another arguing the relief effort 'must not be considered a Methodist movement'.[62] Nonetheless some £31 guineas were raised, and it was said that when the 'English Mail' sailed from Port Adelaide in June 1879 it carried contributions for Cornwall from South Australia to the tune of £4000—£300 of which had been raised in Kapunda.[63]

In Cornwall itself there were occasional glimmers of hope, as in February 1868 when it was reported that 430 families in the Helston area were receiving adequate relief support, as were 238 at St Just-in-Penwith and eight-one at Tywardreath, with Callington and Calstock 'sufficiently relieved', and with the optimistic news that 'In Liskeard there is no distress'.[64] Similarly, there were occasional moments of optimism in the Cornish mining industry, such as the announcement in 1868 that West Caradon mine near St Cleer (one of the newer East Cornwall workings) was about to be extended. Captain Richard Boyns was also positive about prospects in the far West, publishing cautious but sanguine estimates of the likely future survival of Bosweddan and Wheal Castle.[65] But the reality was that the situation was unlikely to improve, at least in the short-term, and there were threats of civil disturbances and a return to the 'bread riots' that had characterised Cornwall in the eighteenth and early nineteenth centuries. In 1868 one provision dealer in St Austell was warned that 'You had better keep your (flour) prices down, or we are determined to burn you down. We are fifty . . . We have Greek fire'.[66] As a precaution, 130 Special Constables were sworn in, an echo of the events two years earlier when strikes in the East Cornwall and Tamar Valley mines had also prompted the mobilisation of the constabulary as half-forgotten fears of the lawless miner were rekindled in an anxious establishment.

Against the background of continuing distress, the 'Cornwall Distress Fund' (and the 'Cornwall Central Relief Committee' which ran it) turned increasingly to emigration as the means of 'improvement', a close relationship developing between the Fund and the emigration agents (the practitioners of the 'emigration trade'). As well as promoting the cause of emigration and helping to publicise the work of the agents, the Fund was also on occasions prepared to pay the passage for deserving would-be emigrants, as in January 1868 when it arranged for several miners' families in the East Penwith and St Austell areas to join husbands already overseas.[67] Not surprisingly, the 'emigration trade' itself was not slow in rising to the challenge of the great crash of 1866. There continued to be internal movement within Cornwall, the china clay industry around St Austell and the East Cornwall mines engaging skilled men thrown out of work in the West (though the Caradon strikes of 1866 prompted a flurry of emigration from St Cleer),[68] and there was also migration to other parts of the United Kingdom. In October 1865, for example, Samuel Abbott of Redruth advertised to the effect that he was acting as Agent for the Esk Valley Iron Company which planned to recruit Cornish miners to work its ironstone deposits at Grosmont, Yorkshire. In August 1866 St Ives, St Just and Calstock men were noted mining in South Wales, while in the November 300 Cornish miners were contracted for Scottish coal and iron mines.[69] During 1867 'several widows with their families'[70] in the neighbourhood of Camborne and Redruth were recruited for the cotton mills of Lancashire.

THE DIASPORA

The main thrust of the dispersal continued to be overseas, however, the emigration agents busy advancing the rival claims of the several potential destinations. 'Look Here—Friend to Miners' advertised one William Fairburn—a 'Licensed Emigration Agent' of Liverpool—who promised 'cheap passage to America and Australia', and who offered to meet emigrants at Liverpool from the boat or the train and (prior to their departure overseas) 'take them into his house free of charge, and protect them from being imposed upon'.[71] More material were the incentives offered by B. J. Nott, Emigration Agent, St Austell, who advertised assisted passages to Otago, New Zealand, for single female domestic servants, farm servants, labourers, and shepherds, em-phasising that wages there were 'higher than in other provinces':[72] shepherds might earn up to £70 per annum, while skilled artizans could make 10s-15s a day.

J. B. Wilcocks continued to play a central role (now operating as 'Messrs Wilcocks and Weekes'), in January 1867 (and in subsequent weeks and months) advertising details of the 'Government Emigration and General Passenger Service'.[73] Ships for Melbourne were to sail each month on the 7th and 21st from London, on three other occasions from Liverpool, and on the 27th from Plymouth—fares were £14 pounds and upwards. Sailings for Adelaide and Sydney were monthly from London and Plymouth, at a cost of £20 and upwards. There were similar details of passages to Queensland, New Zealand, and Canada, together with news of a free emigration scheme for Melbourne applicable to single female domestic servants and married agricultural labourers with no more than two children under twelve years of age. A year later, Wilcocks was able to offer assisted emigration to

Canterbury, New Zealand, and to Melbourne for married couples 'of the right classes'. There was also the possibility of free emigration to Adelaide for agricultural labourers and female domestic servants. Other agents advertised passages to South America ('Falmouth direct to Brazil and River Plate') and New York.[74] In particular, the National Steam Ship Co Ltd. advertised weekly sailings to New York in its 'new full-powered British Iron Screw Steamships'.[75] The company detailed agents in Camborne, Redruth and Hayle, but also published its intention to seek further assistance: 'Agents wanted in the principal towns in Cornwall.'[76] In 1868, as Cornish interest in South Africa began to grow, the Colony of Natal announced grants of land for suitable intending emigrants.[77]

Needless to say, the efforts of the emigration agents bore fruit, the *West Briton* in June 1866 recording 'The unprecedented exodus of the bone and sinew of the working population of our county',[78] adding in May 1867 that in the previous twelve months no fewer than 7,380 miners had left Cornwall. Of these, it was claimed, 1,155 had gone to the United States, 450 to California, 670 to Australia and New Zealand, and 1,090 to Scotland and the North of England. Similarly, the newspaper commented that of these 1,390 had left Camborne-Redruth, 880 had come from Gwennap and environs, with a further 1,390 from Lelant and St Just, 80 from Wendron, 205 from St Agnes and Perranzabuloe, 220 from St Austell, and 1,200 from Liskeard and Callington.[79] Just over six months later it was observed that although the collapse of the Copper Trade Association (through desperate members breaking ranks) in May 1867 had been perceived as advantageous for Cornwall, nonetheless the period since then had witnessed the closure of some 300 copper mines in Cornwall and West Devon, precipitating the further emigration of some 4–5,000 miners, many with their families.[80] In January 1868 the *Royal Cornwall Gazette* reported that 'Eight thousand miners have recently left Cornwall'.[81]

This exodus was perpetuated into the 1870s (so much so that the brief up-turn in the tin industry in the early '70s revealed an acute shortage of skilled labour), the closure of Clifford Amalgamated mines in April 1870 marking the end of copper mining in its former Gwennap heartland. In May 1871 'The tide of emigration has again set in in the mining districts',[82] while

In the Redruth district, although tin is high, and times should be better, there appears to be a feeling of general depression among the labouring classes—a longing to be off somewhere, anywhere, in fact, to escape the grinding process now being brought to bear upon mine labour.[83]

Even in the relatively successful (for tin) year of 1872, the pace of emigration continued, several hundred miners—for example—being engaged to work at the Peak Downs copper mine in Queensland.[84] 1873 brought falling tin prices. In April 1874 'There is quite a panic in the West Cornish mines',[85] with closure of major producers such as Balleswidden, Wheal Owles, North Roskear, and Wheal Seton, together with the partial abandonment of Botallack. In January 1875 came the gloomy reflection that 'In the history of mining in Cornwall it has known no such disastrous year as that of 1874.'[86]

INTERNATIONAL COPPER POWER

Of course, the declining copper prices of the 1860s and the crash of 1866 affected overseas producers as well, but these foreign and colonial competitors did not suffer the inherent disadvantages of the Cornish mines and, by and large, could still sport large, rich and easily accessible deposits. In South Australia the relatively old (by colonial standards) mines of Burra Burra and Kapunda did feel the pinch, the South Australian Mining Association secretary writing in August 1866 that news of the international copper market continued to be 'of a discouraging nature',[87] Burra Burra by February 1867 losing up to £100 a day. Nonetheless, a series of economies and innovations allowed the mine to remain in production until its final abandonment at the end of 1877, with Kapunda surviving for a further year.[88]

Wallaroo and Moonta were even better-equipped to weather the 1860s, the early years of the decade witnessing the rapid exploitation of exceptionally rich deposits at hardly any depth, with capital investment ensuring longer-term efficiency and viability. In practice, the two mine companies worked in close co-operation, moving finally to amalgamation in 1888–89, their position strengthened by the construction of a large smelting works at Wallaroo itself. Wallaroo's most productive years were 1866–75 (the same years that saw the virtual extinction of copper mining in Cornwall), with 25,000 tons of ore being raised per annum. Moonta proved the more productive of the mines in the years before amalgamation, production for the entire period 1862–89 averaging 19,000 tons per annum.[89]

Together, Wallaroo and Moonta acquired an air of quiet superiority—in South Australia but also on the world stage. The *Wallaroo Times* newspaper in August 1868 spoke of 'Cornish mines, poor and low as colonial miners regard them',[90] and in 1875 it was alleged in the *Yorke's Peninsula Advertiser* that the production of the Moonta alone had already outstripped the performance of even the mightiest of the once-great Cornish copper mines. In the period

October 1861 to July 1875, Moonta had raised 236,160 tons of ore worth £4,000,000, while the Consolidated Mines (in Cornwall) had between 1815 and 1856 raised only 230,296 tons of ore worth £2,893,482, with Dolcoath, Fowey Consols and even mighty Devon Great Consols all similarly falling short of the Moonta performance.[91]

Given the continued strength of the South Australian mining industry (and, in the 1870s, the rapid development of deep quartz mining in the Victorian goldfields), it was inevitable that many of the Cornish emigrants of 1866 and subsequent years should find their ways to the Antipodes. Arrivals at Port Adelaide during 1866 itself included sizeable Cornish contingents, such as the 103 in the *Trevelyan*, the 162 in the *Salamanca*, and the 51 in the *Atlanta*, page after page of the shipping passenger lists revealing the tell-tale Cornish surnames: James Berryman (miner), Fanny Pascoe (servant), John Angove (copper miner), Joshua Treloar (labourer), Samuel Williams (quarryman), William Roskelly (labourer), William Trembath (miner), and so on.[92] Although a more restrictive immigration policy from 1867 to 1871 served to prevent a mass exodus from Cornwall to South Australia, individual groups continued to find their way to Wallaroo and Moonta. In 1872 the Adelaide Parliament passed a new and more liberal Immigration Act, the continuing decline of Cornish copper and the emerging tin crisis ensuring a renewed stream of Cornish immigration. In September 1872 the Moonta directors suggested that 5,000 miners be recruited directly from Cornwall at the expense of all the dividend-paying mines in the colony (but the plan was dropped when it was pointed-out that almost all the expense would fall on Wallaroo and Moonta), and even the faltering Burra Burra took steps to attract Cornish immigrants.[93] To this was added the colonial government's anxiety to attract new settlers to help advance the renewed expansion of the South Australian agricultural frontier (a policy associated with Cornish-born Premier, James Penn Boucaut), so that between 1872 and 1879 approximately 7 per cent of the 24,000 or so immigrants recorded in the passenger list were Cornish.[94]

The ability of the South Australian copper mines to weather the difficult decade of the 1860s was matched by the similar performance of those in the United States, especially in the relatively long-established Keweenaw 'Lakes' area of Upper Michigan with its already significant Cornish population. First opened in the boom times well before the Civil War, early development had been haphazard and management poor (profits were so vast it did not really matter), but the impact of the War and then the price collapse in the 1860s brought new problems. However, the Calumet and Hecla mines (the two most important Lakes workings) responded with new developmental work and striking new, rich lodes, applying too new technology to improve efficiency. Even so, it was not until 1868 that Michigan production exceeded that of Cornwall, and it was not until 1868-69 that Calumet and Hecla was producing copper at a cost which could allow it to compete successfully on the international market.[95]

Thereafter there was much improvement—within four or five years Calumet and Hecla had combined to form one giant conglomerate (anticipating the later merger of Wallaroo and Moonta), with the Lakes once again a significant attraction for emigrant Cornish folk: as always, many are identified by their distinctive Cornish names, Chynoweth, Gribble, Bawden, Trevethan, Rosemergy, Lobb, Penhallegon, Polglase. At its height Calumet and Hecla employed 16,000 people, and it is said that by the late 1870s 'there were more Cornishmen working at Calumet and Hecla mines in Michigan than there were at any other copper mine in the world'.[96] Certainly, superintendents, captains, shift bosses and others in positions of responsibility were almost always Cornish.

RELIEF ... DEPENDENCY ... ?
The initial reaction of the Cornwall Distress Fund, and indeed of Cornish opinion generally, to this continuing emigration was one of relief. In June 1866 the *West Briton* wrote that the exodus was 'relieving us to a very beneficial extent of the surplus population of our mining districts'.[97] There was even a certain pride in the achievement, in the knowledge that the fame of Wallaroo and Moonta or Calumet and Hecla was in large measure the result of Cornish labours, and there was satisfaction that—despite the decline of mining at home—there were still opportunities to put specialist Cornish skills to good use. However, there was a negative side to all this, recognised but slowly in Cornwall. As Rowe has written,

> The success and prowess of these Cousin Jack mine captains
> on the Lakes encouraged others to emigrate in their wake,
> especially when Cornish mining was in an economic position
> that held but poor prospects of promotion; this meant that
> emigration to Michigan and elsewhere was denuding Cornwall
> of its most enterprising and ambitious practical men.[98]

Cornwall was thus also robbed of its younger and more energetic folk and, although whole families often emigrated together (particularly to the Antipodes), sometimes the menfolk went overseas alone (especially to the United States), leaving wives, children, parents behind. In this way, the development of Cornwall's 'dependency culture' continued apace after 1866 (reaching its apogee at the end of the century, with the widespread dependence on South Africa). In August 1869, for example, it was estimated that Camborne men in the California and Nevada goldfields were sending home between £15,000 and £19,000 a year,[99] while in the St Just and Marazion districts 'numbers of able-bodied men have gone, leaving wives and families, the labouring classes in some localities consisting chiefly of old men, women and children'.[100] A decade later, things had not changed. Although the *West Briton* complained that 'the real men' had emigrated, 'and those whom the excellent vicar of St Just accurately designates the "half men" remain to perpetuate the race of the weak, the sickly, the mentally and physically good for little', the families left behind by the intinerant miner were generally supported by monies sent home from abroad and were not left 'on the parish, be it said to his honour'.[101]

But if, for some reason, the able-bodied were unable to send home remittances, then the effect of emigration was exactly the reverse of that anticipated by the Distress Fund—'contributing to the distressed conditions of large numbers in the mining districts'.[102] In 1868 one William Rowse wrote to the local press, detailing such conditions. He drew attention, for example, to the case of a certain 'M. W.', a woman with three children who earned just 5s a week. Her husband had left for America three years before, but had not been heard from since. 'S. N.' was a widow with four children—her husband had gone to America two years before but was 'soon after drowned crossing a river'.[103]

Sometimes there are glimpses of pathetic individual cases, such as that of Mrs S. Sleep who in 1869 wrote in desperation to the Moonta directors, asking whether her husband was working out there—the directors could only pass on the letter to Captain Hancock, asking him to investigate.[104] On another occasion the captain of Wheal Basset, in Illogan, wrote to Captain Hancock on behalf of one distraught woman in Carnkie whose husband had disappeared in Australia, leaving her and her two young children without support. The poor woman related later that her husband was indeed found at Moonta but that Captain Hancock 'could not do anything, but asked him to write to me. Captain Hancock's daughter sent me £1'.[105] More tragi-comic in nature was the experience of Lavinia Allen and George Lory, both of Helston, who had married in the early 1860s. After some 'unpleasantness' between the two, Lory left for the Australias. Thinking that was the last she would see of him, Allen formed a relationship with one James Colenso Arthur, these two living together as man and wife and rearing a family. Years later, some property was left to Lory and, following extensive advertising in the American and colonial press, he was finally tracked down in Victoria—at which point he announced his intention of returning to Cornwall and (being repentant) of seeking a reunion with his wife![106]

Such intricate personal problems, with all the attendant complex issues of difficult communications and possible legal activity, led to a new twist in the 'emigration trade' in Cornwall. One advertisement said it all:

> Missing Friends in South Australia. S. Morcom wishes to state, that from the numerous correspondence entailed upon him, he must henceforth receive the usual fee of 2s 6d or 5s if from abroad to ensure a reply. As he possesses the best facilities to ascertain the whereabouts of any said person, parties applying may rely almost with a certainty, of a successful result. In case of death, a certificate properly attested, can be furnished, or where property is left, the same will be recovered. When special advertisements are desired an additional fee of 5s (in postage stamps or Post Office Order) will be requisite.[107]

CONCLUSION

Taken together, the events of the 1860s and their aftermath present an extraordinary picture. The profound changes wrought in the international copper market led to increased production (much of this facilitated, ironically, by Cornish emigration to areas such as Michigan and South Australia) at a time of falling prices. Cornwall was unable to stand these changes, her copper mining industry plunged into swift decline, but the overseas competitors proved more robust and survived the lean years, attracting increased international investment at a time when investment in Cornwall was collapsing. Consequently, Cornish emigrants anxious to escape distress at home were attracted in their thousands to these competitors, the already long-established 'emigration culture' and 'emigration trade' in Cornwall assisting this exodus and in the process becoming even further entrenched as features of Cornish life. But although this emigration did indeed stave-off the worst potential consequences of the crisis, in the longer term it contributed to Cornwall's blighted character of de-industrialisation, dereliction and depopulation, with its creeping 'dependency culture', as the cream of Cornish youth and the reservoir of Cornish skill were lost.

NOTES AND REFERENCES

1. Principal contributions are: A. C. Todd, *The Cornish Miner in America*, Truro, 1969; A. L. Rowse, *The Cornish in America*, London, 1969, repub. Redruth, 1991; John Rowe, *The Hard-Rock Men: Cornish Immigrants and the North American Mining Frontier*, Liverpool, 1974; A. C. Todd, *The Search For Silver: Cornish Miners in Mexico 1824–1947*, Padstow, 1977; Philip Payton, 'The Cornish in South Australia: Their Influence and Experience from Immigration to Assimilation, 1836–1936', unpub. PhD., University of Adelaide, 1978; Philip Payton, *The Cornish Miner in Australia: Cousin Jack Down Under*, Redruth, 1984; Philip Payton, *The Cornish Farmer in Australia*, Redruth, 1987; Philip Payton, 'The Cornish', in J. Jupp (ed.), *The Australian People*, Sydney, 1988; Jim Faull, *The Cornish in Australia*, Melbourne, 1983; Ruth Hopkins, *Where Now Cousin Jack?*, Bendigo, 1988; Ruth Hopkins, *Cousin Jack: Man for The Times*, Bendigo, 1994; Ann Colman, 'Colonial Cornish: Cornish Immigrants in Victoria, 1865–1880', unpub. MA, University of Melbourne, 1985; Patricia Lay, 'One and All: The Cornish in Nineteenth-Century New South Wales', unpub. MA, Australian National University, 1992; Graham B. Dickason, *Cornish Immigrants to South Africa*, Cape Town, 1978; Richard D. Dawe, 'The Role and Influence of the Cornish Miners in South Africa, 1886–1925', unpub. MA, CNAA (Middlesex Polytechnic), 1986.

2. One useful attempt at achieving an overview is Gillian Burke, 'The Cornish Diaspora of the Nineteenth Century', in Shula Marks and Peter Richardson (eds), *International Labour Migration: Historical Perspectives*, London, 1984.

3. D. B. Barton, *A History of Copper Mining in Cornwall and Devon*, Truro, 1961, revised edn 1968; D. B. Barton, *The Cornish Beam Engine*, Truro, 1965, repub. Exeter, 1989; D. B. Barton, *A History of Tin Mining and Smelting in Cornwall*, Truro, 1967, repub. Exeter, 1989.

4. Philip Payton, 'Modern Cornwall: The Changing Nature of Peripherality', unpub. PhD., CNAA (Polytechnic South West), 1989; Philip Payton, *The Making of Modern Cornwall: Historical Experience and the Persistence of 'Difference'*, Redruth, 1992.

5. Payton, 1989, pp. 207–208.

6. Dudley Baines, *Migration in a Mature Economy: Emigration and Internal Migration in England and Wales, 1861–1900*, Cambridge, 1985, pp. 230–232.

7. Baines, 1985, pp. 157–159.

8. Rowe, 1974, pp. 42–44.

9. Todd, 1967, p. 24.

10. Ronald M. James, 'Defining the Group: Nineteenth-Century Cornish on the North American Mining Frontier', *Cornish Studies: Two*, 1994; Philip Payton, 'From Cousin Jack to Map Kernow', *Australian Studies*, forthcoming.

11. Payton, 1978, p. 97, pp. 103–109; see also Mark Brayshay, 'The

Emigration Trade in Nineteenth-Century Devon', in Michael Duffy, Stephen Fisher, Basil Greenhill, David J. Starkey and Joyce Youings (eds), *The New Maritime History of Devon, Vol. II*, London, 1994.

12. Payton, 1978, pp.52-62.
13. Margaret James-Korany, ' "Blue Books" as Sources for Cornish Emigration History', *Cornish Studies: One*, 1993.
14. Edmund Newell, ' "Copperopolis": The Rise and Fall of the Copper Industry in the Swansea District, 1826-1921', *Business History*, Vol. 32, No. 3, July 1990.
15. Mel Davies, 'The South Australian Mining Association and the Marketing of Copper and Copper Ores, 1845–77', unpub. MA, University of Adelaide, 1977.
16. Newell, 1990.
17. Rowse, 1969 and 1991, p. 162.
18. *Northern Star* (Kapunda), 20 July 1867.
19. *West Briton*, 8 August 1862.
20. *Royal Cornwall Gazette*, 4 October 1861.
21. *West Briton*, 20 February 1863.
22. Rowe, 1974, pp. 146–151.
23. See F. K. Crowley, 'British Migration to Australia', unpub. D.Phil, Oxford, 1951.
24. Payton, 1978, pp 46–52, p 110.
25. *Northern Star*, 27 July 1867.
26. *South Australian Parliamentary Debates*, 1862, p. 588.
27. Rowe, 1974, p. 154.
28. *West Briton*, 23 October 1863.
29. *West Briton*, 18 March 1864.
30. *West Briton*, 19 June 1863.
31. *West Briton*, 22 September 1865.
32. Crowley, 1951.
33. Payton, 1978, pp. 115–116.
34. Payton, 1978, pp. 115–116; see also South Australian Archives (hereafter SAA) 313 *Passenger Lists*.
35. SAA BRG 40/543, *Moonta Mine Proprieters, Minute Books, 1861–91*, 3 May 1875, 7 February 1876.
36. Payton, 1978, pp. 208–216.
37. SAA BRG 40/538, *Moonta Mine Proprieters, Out-Letter Books, 1863–69*, McCoull to A. L. Elders, 26 April 1864; McCoull to Young, 26 April 1864; SAA BRG 40/543, 24 April 1864, 29 August 1864.
38. SAA BRG 22/960, *South Australian Mining Association, Director's Letter Books*, Ayers to Wilcocks, 19 July 1859.
39. SAA BRG 22/60, Phillips to Duncan, 21 December 1864.
40. Payton, 1978, pp. 117–118.
41. Rowe, 1974, p. 158.
42. Newell, 1990.
43. Barton, 1968, pp. 75–90.

44. *West Briton*, 25 January 1867.
45. *West Briton*, 25 January 1867.
46. *West Briton*, 25 January 1867.
47. Barton, 1968, pp. 75–90; Rowe, 1974, pp. 157–158.
48. *West Briton*, 20 July 1866.
49. *West Briton*, 4 January 1867.
50. *West Briton*, 18 June 1867.
51. *West Briton*, 25 January 1867.
52. *West Briton*, 25 January 1867.
53. *West Briton*, 1 March 1867.
54. *West Briton*, 25 January 1867, 1 February 1867.
55. *West Briton*, 23 January 1868.
56. *West Briton*, 2 January 1868.
57. *West Briton*, 2 January 1868.
58. *West Briton*, 2 January 1868.
59. *West Briton*, 7 May 1868.
60. Hopkins, 1988, pp. 122–123.
61. *Kapunda Herald*, 13 May 1879.
62. *Kapunda Herald*, 13 May 1879.
63. *Kapunda Herald*, 24 June 1879; 11 July 1879.
64. *West Briton*, 20 February 1868.
65. *West Briton*, 2 February 1868.
66. *West Briton*, 30 January 1868.
67. *West Briton*, 23 January 1868.
68. Bernard Deacon, 'Attempts at Unionism by Cornish Metal Miners in 1866', in *Cornish Studies*, 10, 1982.
69. *West Briton*, 6 October 1865, 31 August 1866.
70. *West Briton*, 25 January 1867.
71. *West Briton*, 4 January 1867.
72. *West Briton*, 4 January 1867.
73. *West Briton*, 4 January 1867.
74. *West Briton*, 9 January 1868, 16 January 1868.
75. *West Briton*, 16 January 1868.
76. *West Briton*, 16 January 1868.
77. *West Briton*, 23 January 1868.
78. *West Briton*, 15 June 1866.
79. *West Briton*, 17 May 1867.
80. *West Briton*, 2 January 1868.
81. *Royal Cornwall Gazette*, 2 January 1868.
82. *West Briton*, 16 May 1871.
83. *West Briton*, 16 May 1871.
84. *West Briton*, 11 April 1872.
85. *West Briton*, 13 April 1874.
86. *West Briton*, 7 January 1875.
87. SAA BRG22/961, *South Australian Mining Association, Letters to Burra*

Mine Officials (Superintendent's Letter Books), Ayers to Roach, 12 August 1866.
88. Payton, 1978, pp. 175–181.
89. Payton, 1978, pp. 193–195.
90. *Wallaroo Times*, 5 August 1868.
91. *Yorke's Peninsula Advertiser*, 6 August 1875.
92. SAA 313.
93. SAA BRG40/543, 23 September 1872; SAA BRG22/961, Ayers to Sanders, 23 December 1873, 2 January 1874, 14 December 1875; *Northern Mail* (Burra), 14 July 1876.
94. Payton, 1987.
95. Todd, 1967, p. 132; Rowse, 1969 and 1990, pp. 182–183; Rowe, 1974, p. 172.
96. Cited in Rowse, 1969 and 1990, p. 166.
97. *West Briton*, 15 June 1866.
98. Rowe, 1974, p. 172.
99. *West Briton*, 12 August 1869.
100. *West Briton*, 23 January 1868.
101. *West Briton*, 23 January 1879.
102. *West Briton*, 23 January 1868.
103. *West Briton*, 9 January 1868.
104. SAA BRG40/543, 2 August 1869.
105. *People's Weekly* (Moonta), 24 May 1924.
106. *Yorke's Peninsula Advertiser*, 3 March 1882.
107. *West Briton*, January 1864.

THE GREAT WESTERN RAILWAY AND THE CORNISH-CELTIC REVIVAL

Philip Payton and Paul Thornton

INTRODUCTION

In Cornwall, serious analysis and discussion of the tourist industry has been generally socio-economic in character, its apologists pointing to the alleged central role of tourism in supporting an otherwise ailing Cornish economy, detractors highlighting its apparent deleterious features such as low wages, seasonal unemployment and problems of long-term unsustainability.[1] Of late, however, observers have begun to focus on the cultural impact of Cornish tourism. Echoing the work of Urry on the 'tourist gaze',[2] Deacon, Lowerson, Payton, Thornton and others have sought to explore the 'invention' of a 'guide-book' view of Cornish culture, showing why Cornish 'difference' has been emphasised as a touristic device and how this has both reflected and been accommodated within culture change in the wider Cornwall.[3]

This new focus, however, has raised new problems for students of modern Cornwall, not least with regard to the relationship between the 'guide-book' view (with its vivid repertoire of Cornish symbolism) and the potent images of Cornwall constructed by the Cornish-Celtic Revival movement. This article seeks to explore this relationship, hypothesising that the 'coming of the railway' and—in particular— almost half a century of sustained Great Western Railway propaganda produced an array of symbols and images (tangible and conceptual) which both borrowed from and helped to inform the cultural constructions of the Revivalists. This is a hypothesis which echoes Chapman's recent deconstruction of modern 'Celtic' identities, where it is argued that the image of 'the Celt' as 'Other' is a romanticised invention of (principally English) 'outsiders'.[4] But it also offers a corrective to Chapman's analysis in that it is contended here that the reconstruction of 'Celtic Cornwall' was in fact a collaborative effort by both 'outsiders' and 'insiders', albeit that for the most part these 'insiders' were middle-class activists remote from popular, working-class Cornish culture.

CONVENTIONAL WISDOMS

As has been argued elsewhere,[5] there was something of a symbiotic relationship between tourism and the Cornish-Celtic Revival, both emerging in the aftermath of Cornwall's catastrophic experiences of de-industrialisation, both appealing to images of a pre-industrial Celtic-Catholic Cornwall, the former attempting to construct a post-industrial economy and the latter striving to revive a pre-industrial culture. This is, however, a controversial assessment, one which not only goes against the grain of opinion in the contemporary 'Cornish movement' but also challenges the assumptions of others working in the broader field of tourism and culture. Young has posed the critical question *Tourism: Blessing or Blight?*[6] and even those who accept the 'tourist gaze' thesis may see the promotion of 'difference' as merely the cynical exploitation of cultural identity by external forces, a kind of prostitution (as Laity argued in the Cornish context[7]) in which the host culture is inevitably debased. Moreover Smith, in his *Hosts and Guests: The Anthropology of Tourism*[8] has successfully illustrated the causes of conflict between a host community and the visiting tourist population, and has warned of the potential role of tourism in destroying local cultures. In Smith's analysis tourism is the vehicle of homogenisation, rather than the perpetuator of 'difference'.

In Cornwall itself, as noted above, the conventional wisdom suggests a deep and unbridgeable chasm between tourism (with its 'guide book' view of Cornish culture) and the perspectives of many Cornish people, particularly the 'Cornish movement'. In 1964 Moorhouse considered that even those indigenous Cornish involved in the tourist industry exhibited hard-headed resignation rather than affectionate commitment to their occupation: 'Those with a stake in the tourist trade make hay while the sun shines, but look forward to rainy days.'[9] The activists of the Cornish movement, meanwhile, 'take a dim view of the romantic image of Cornwall put about by the likes of Daphne du Maurier. And they have a huge contempt for the purveyors of piskies in Polperro and elsewhere'.[10] Nearly twenty years later, in 1983, things apparently had not changed, Paul Theroux noting in his celebrated literary tour of Britain that 'The loathing for tourists and outsiders in Cornwall was undisguised. I had a feeling that it was the tourists who made the Cornish nationalistic.'[11]

In 1988 *Cornwall at the Crossroads* was published, a provocative assessment of the condition of modern Cornwall in which, amongst other things, the role of tourism in constructing an 'inauthentic' 'guide book' view of the 'Land of Legend and Laughter' was criticised. Significantly, the authors pointed the finger of blame at 'the media men of the old Great Western Railway' who were responsible for 'a heady concoction of Celtic Remains, Merlin's Magic Land, tales of smugglers and wreckers, ruined tin mines, pasties, pixies and cream'.[12] But for other observers the intrusion of the railway across the Tamar in 1859 was a mechanism of 'incorporation' (as Robbins termed it[13]) into England in which Cornish 'difference' was not re-invented but submerged. The Royal Albert Bridge at Saltash had facilitated this intrusion, David St John Thomas arguing that: 'The bridge was supposed to let in the Devil. What in fact trickled in were all kinds of national unifying influences—to the true Cornishman, of course, these were the very Devil.'[14]

This article, then, challenges a number of conventional wisdoms and seeks to probe more extensively into the role of tourism and the railway in 're-inventing' Cornwall. It will be argued (in contradiction of Thomas) that this role promoted diversity rather than homogeneity, and (taking issue with *Cornwall at the Crossroads*) it will be further argued that the images it formed were not an 'inauthentic' imposition but were part of a wider process of cultural change in Cornwall aimed at re-defining the Cornish identity in the aftermath of industrial collapse. In short, it will be postulated that there was a high degree of collaboration, sometimes overt, between the Great Western Railway and the Cornish-Celtic Revival in which a significant section of Cornish society colluded in the creation of touristic images of Cornwall.

THE CORNISH REVIVAL

The so-called 'Cornish Revival' was part of a wider 'Celtic Revival', allied in turn to the Romantic movement, which had had already a profound effect on culture change in the 'Celtic lands', notably Ireland and Scotland. It is not the place of this article to chart the Cornish-Celtic Revival in detail but it is important to recall its salient features and preoccupations, as well as to rehearse its ideological imperatives. The latter, put simply, were to respond to the cultural crisis engendered by rapid de-industrialisation in the late nineteenth century (which made untenable the notion of a Cornish identity based on industrial prowess) by reaching out across the debris of the industrial era to a time when Cornwall was more 'purely Cornish'.[15] This was the era of Celtic-Catholic Cornwall, its origins shrouded in the mysteries of Arthur and the Saints, which was plunged into swift decline after the Cornish Prayer Book Rebellion of 1549 when the intrusion of the English State became more insistent, leading not only to the decline of the Cornish language and the abandonment of the Miracle Plays but—in time—to the growth of Methodism and its desire to stamp out Cornish folk-customs in an increasingly semi-urban industrialising society.

Although we may seek to trace the origins of the Revival as far back as Hawker of Morwenstow, with his Anglo-Catholic and anti-industrial sentiments and his enthusiasm for things Celtic and Arthurian, it is Henry Jenner who has rightly been called 'The Father of the Cornish Revival'.[16] In 1901 he formed the Cowethas Kelto-Kernuak (the Cornish-Celtic Society), and in 1904 in Brittany he secured Cornwall's membership of the Celtic Congress. His *A Handbook of the Cornish Language*[17] was published in the same year, a text designed as both an introduction to the language and an aid to learning it. The First World War interrupted the work of the Revivalists but in 1920 the first Old Cornwall Society was formed at St Ives, the precursor of the Federation of Old Cornwall Societies which was established in 1924 to further the work of the Revival and to draw together the many Old Cornwall societies that were then springing up. Jenner had by now been joined in his efforts by other notable activists, not least Robert Morton Nance who was to play a key role in the development of a 'Unified' spelling of Cornish based on the medieval texts of the Miracle Plays. One early and tangible success of the Old Cornwall movement was the foundation of a journal, itself called *Old Cornwall*, which was to become an important vehicle for the dissemination of Revivalist ideas. An enduring aim of the early Revivalists had been the establishment of a Cornish Gorsedd (Gorseth Kernow), based on the revived Gorseddau of Wales and Brittany, and this too was achieved in 1928. As Nance commented, 'With peace it became possible for the idea of Cornish nationality to rise again, and starting inconspicuously the Old Cornwall movement and the Cornish Revival as a whole began'.[18]

The journal *Old Cornwall* in this early period is for us an important window into the motives of the Revivalists. A concern to establish the 'Celticity' of Cornwall was evident everywhere. When the Celtic Congress visited Cornwall in 1932 Jenner spoke on the 'Awakening of Celtic Cornwall', with one observer deciding that 'no intelligent Cornish person can remain utterly ignorant of his or her Celtic nationality'.[19] The Cornish language was seen as perhaps the central feature of this Celticity with W. D. Watson writing in 1926 in the third edition of *Old Cornwall*, that 'Today a great renewal of Celtic thought and feeling is taking place, and although we Cornish have but relics of our language, and are small in numbers, yet we have our part to play in the movement.'[20] Five years later such assertions displayed even greater confidence, one contributor insisting that 'The Cornish language is more and more taking its place as the chief token of Celtic nationality in Cornwall',[21] and in 1932 it was claimed that 'the most Celtic thing in Cornwall is the Kernewek'.[22] When Tyr ha Tavas (Land and Language), a movement aimed at mobilising Cornish youth, was launched in 1933, a principal objective was 'to further Cornish ideals and to build up a better and greater Cornwall'.[23] Equally important, however, was the desire 'to utilise the Cornish Language, both as an outward and visible sign of nationality and as a means of helping Cornish people to realise their essential kinship with other Celtic Races'.[24]

Other preoccupations were 'the mystic Celtic temperment'[25] and 'the Celtic Church, which survived and flourished in Wales and Cornwall when most of Britain had relapsed into paganism'.[26] Folklore, customs and superstitions were seen as a direct link between modern Cornwall and more ancient Celtic times with F. W. Johns claiming in 1931 that 'There are still parts of Cornwall where one may find ample remains, in the folklore of the people, of the past history of the Cornish race',[27] and L. J. Dickinson agreeing that 'Those who have lived in Cornwall for many years, and are in touch with country folk, often come across old practices of witchcraft that they formerly thought of as exploded superstitions.'[28] William H. Paynter, the Recorder for Callington Old Cornwall Society, in 1929 mused on 'how widespread was the belief only a few years ago in charms and charmers and all other superstitions' and went on to recount some of 'the many witch tales I have collected during the past six months'.[29] In the following year Paynter recalled that 'There once lived near Launceston, an old man tells me, an old dame who had a piskey who appeared in her house in the form of a little boy', adding that 'Still another old women living in this district was fully persuaded that her only child had been carried away, and a piskey substituted'.[30]

The work of nineteenth-century antiquarians, in particular, was seen as important in establishing the links between pre-industrial and post-industrial Cornwall, J. Hambly Rowe (a founder of the Arthurian Congress) writing in 1929 that the folklore collections of the 'old Celt' William Bottrell (published in the 1870s and 1880s) have 'taken us back in fancy to a Cornwall before railways, an intensely Cornish Cornwall, in which we . . . can hear the Celtic rise and fall of their voices as they utter the old familiar words and phrases'.[31] Similarly, Davies Gilbert's claim in 1826 that a white cross on a black background was formerly the banner of St Piran and the standard of Cornwall was remembered enthusiastically in *Old Cornwall* in 1936, the journal opining that: 'If we took to this old cross-banner of Cornwall . . . we should probably have Cornwall more in evidence on occasions when the flags of all nations decorate Cornish streets.'[32]

This concern for Celtic symbolism was commonplace. In the dark days of 1942 C. S. Murrish noted with relish the words of Scott's *Redgauntlet* at the Jacobite Council: 'Pengwinion, you Cornish Chough, has the good wind blown you north?'[33] Not recognising that 'Cornish Chough' was once a pejorative term (as Richard Carew knew, and as the Roundhead pamphleteers remembered in the Civil War), and not guessing that 'Pengwinion' and 'Chough' might be an obscure play on words, Murrish exclaimed that 'I was so delighted with Scott for this last reference to our National Emblem, the very essence of all that Arthur and his legends stand for, written more than one hundred years before the revival of our Cornish Gorsedd'.[34]

In June 1927, the year before the 'revived' Gorsedd was set-up, Henry Jenner addressed the Federation of Old Cornwall Societies on 'The Gorsedd of Boscawen-Un', claiming that 'The circle of Boscawen-Un is the most noteworthy stone circle in Cornwall'[35] for it was none other than the 'Beisgawen' mentioned in the ancient Welsh Triads as one of the three traditional 'Gorsedd' meeting places in the Isles of Britain. Combining in his lecture allusions to pre-Celtic archaeology, Druidism, Arthurianism, Celtic Christianity, Breton Bards and medieval Welsh and Irish literature, Jenner succeeded in producing a powerful synthesis of Revivalist imagery, an exemplar of the whole process of Revival and the Cornish-Celtic movement.

EARLY CORNISH TOURISM

Just we as we may look into the nineteenth century to find the first stirrings of the Cornish Revival, so too we must glance back to seek the early origins of tourism in Cornwall. Walvin has proposed that two major influences can be identified in the encouragement of early tourism developments in Britain: contemporary medical opinion and Royal example, both of which drew attention to the efficacy of sea-bathing.[36] The earliest response to this demand in Cornwall was at Penzance, which offered itself as a health resort. Bennett argues that Penzance grew beyond purely local significance when the Napoleonic Wars restricted access to Mediteranean health resorts, forcing affluent British health tourists to look closer to home for substitutes.[37]

Cornwall as a surrogate Mediteranean destination was a theme developed extensively in later years, with Penzance and later other resorts such as Newquay and Bude making much of their 'mild', beneficial climates. For example, the 1890 *Guide to Penzance* noted that the town was 'climatically extremely mild and suitable for invalids; the situation of the town is delightful and the sanitary conditions perfect'.[38] However, outside the immediate hinterlands of these Cornish resorts, the social, economic and cultural impact of tourism was still limited at the end of the nineteenth century. Visitor numbers were small and local transport limited to cabs and carriages. While cabmen were described as 'intelligent and obliging, and will point out en route, places of interest',[39] a trip from Penzance to nearby St Michael's Mount was considered a serious excursion. Penzance and the few other Cornish resorts in 1900 were in what Butler has termed the 'exploration stage'[40] of touristic development, a precursor of the dramatic events to come.

However, by this time copper mining had all but ceased to exist in Cornwall, with tin in serious trouble and other economic activities in decline, and informed opinion in Cornwall was aleady looking to tourism as a possible growth area for the future. Amongst tourism's early enthusiasts was Silvanus Trevail, the noted Cornish architect who was himself responsible for the construction of tourist infrastructure such as King Arthur's Castle Hotel at Tintagel (1899) and the Headland Hotel at Newquay (1900).[41] A more cautious and considered response was that of Q., Sir Arthur Quiller Couch, the distinguished Cornish literary figure. Q. also became an adherent of the Cornish Revival, joining the Cowethas Kelto-Kernuak at its foundation, although he was sceptical about some of its more idealistic ambitions (such as the desire to resurrect the Miracle Plays in the Cornish language). But like the other Revivalists, Q. was prepared to look back beyond the industrial period to Celtic-Catholic Cornwall for his models for the future, and he saw that this had economic as well as cultural consequences. Q. encouraged debate in his *Cornish Magazine* on the advantages or otherwise of tourism and in 1898 expressed his now oft-quoted own views on the subject:

> The suggestion is that Cornwall should turn her natural beauty to account, and by making it more widely known, at once benefit thousands and honestly enrich herself . . . Were it within human capacity to decide between a revival of our ancient industries, mining and fishing, and the development of this new business, our decision would be prompt enough. But it is not . . . Well then, since we must cater for the stranger, let us do it well and honestly. Let us respect him and our native land as well.[42]

The question, however, was how to turn the trickle of tourist visitors into the flood that would be necessary if tourism were to become the main plank of a post-industrial economy in Cornwall. Cornwall's geographical peripherality was clearly a logistical problem (although in other respects 'remoteness' was to be an asset), and even at the end of the nineteenth century Cornwall's most effective transport links continued to be maritime. The opening of the Royal Albert Bridge in 1859 had connected Cornwall's railways with the rest of Britain but the development of what was then the Cornwall Railway was lacklustre, the connection having come too late to play a major role in Cornwall's already declining industrial economy. However, one particularly astute gentleman, R. D. Boase, wrote to Q. in 1898 suggesting 'our first requisite is accessibility. For this we require, and ought to receive, special favour from the Great Western Railway Company'.[43]

THE GREAT WESTERN AND THE CORNISH RIVIERA

Boase's words must have echoed through the corridors of power at Paddington, for by 1904 the Great Western Railway had risen to the challenge of Cornish tourism. It did so in a manner that reflected considerable foresight and sophistication, clearly identifying those tourism strengths that Cornwall had already developed but also anticipating (and helping to shape) the nature of both economic and cultural change in Cornwall, at the same time carving-out a new role for its railway assets west of the Tamar.

Significantly, railway companies in Scotland had already demonstrated successfully the potential of such a strategy. There a 'Celtic Revival', aimed at 'rehabilitating' the post-'Forty-Five' Highlands and bridging the Lowlands-Highlands gap through the construction of a 'Celtic Scotland' identity, had attracted Royal patronage (first through George IV, and later Queen Victoria) and both literary and popular enthusiasts. Before the turn of the century the Highland Railway had introduced special trains to take tourists to savour the melancholy Jacobite atmosphere of Culloden Moor. On the West Highland the expansion of tourist traffic in the 1890s surpassed even the optimistic expectations of the railway's directors, while in the Border country unashamed exploitation of the geographic link with Sir Walter Scott led (for example) to the opening of a 'Waverley Route' and the naming of Edinburgh's principal station as 'Waverley'.[44]

In Cornwall tourist resorts in the 1890s had actually been busier in winter rather than summer,[45] such was the success of the 'mild climate', but the Great Western soon recognised that 'Mediteranean' allusions could be used to even greater effect. Not only might tourists be attracted to 'Mediteranean' summers as well, but attendant connotations of an 'exotic' and 'foreign' culture might also be exploited —particularly as these were notions being promoted by the emerging Cornish-Celtic Revival. Thus in posters and promotional literature the Great Western was able to hint at the visual images of Cornwall portrayed already by Stanhope Forbes and the Newlyn School of painters, directly intimating the exotic and the foreign, and both implicitly and explicity drawing comparisons with Brittany as a sister Celtic country. Paradoxically, at the same time as it emphasised this Cornish 'difference' the Great Western, through infrastructural and timetabling improvements (the conversion to standard gauge in 1892, the opening of the Westbury 'cut-off' in 1906), actually made it easier and quicker for tourists to travel to Cornwall. As Robbins has noted, for the development of commercial tourism Cornwall 'had to remain remote yet also become accessible in its remoteness'[46]—a sleight of hand that the Great Western Railway was able to perform.

As Simmons has argued,[47] the change from broad to standard gauge in 1892 prompted a new enthusiasm which permeated the entire Great Western system, not least in Cornwall. Generally, the role of railways in the development of the British mass tourism industry has been perceived as that of an enabling technology. Walton, for example, has noted the importance of railways in reducing journey times and making new destination areas available, as well as assisting the percolation of the seaside habit downwards to the middle class and (eventually) the working class. The Great Western certainly performed these roles in Cornwall but its more proactive involvement extended to the enhancement of the external tourist infrastructure, such as the acquisition and rebuilding of the Tregenna Castle Hotel at St Ives. However, the key to the Great Western's success in Cornwall was not its investment in infrastructure but its marketing strategy.

In 1886 the Great Western Railway had set-up its advertising department, the first step in the development of an unrivalled railway propaganda machine that survived until nationalisation in 1948 (the Great Western alone of railway companies had survived the Grouping of 1923), a publicity organisation whose outpourings have been carefully chronicled by R. Burdett Wilson.[48] In 1904, the same year that Jenner published his book on the Cornish language and secured Cornwall's membership of the Celtic Congress, the Great Western published its own book, *The Cornish Riviera*, costing one penny and written by the prolific topographical author A. M. Broadley. The first edition sold a quarter of a million copies, followed by a further four editions.[49] Also in 1904 passenger receipts at Penzance increased by an impressive 68.4 per cent,[50] and in that year the unofficially-named

Cornishman train ran the 245.25 miles from Paddington to Plymouth non-stop—a world record. The Great Western decided that such a prestigious service should have an official name, and it ran a competition in association with the *Railway Magazine* to determine what that should be. The choice was the *Cornish Riviera Express*, introduced formally in 1905 as the *Cornish Riviera Limited*. Thirty years later the 10.30 am from Paddington was still the *Limited*, running in the summer with reserved seats only and serving Truro, Falmouth and St Ives, and by the summer of 1939 the train consisted of eight portions with through coaches for Penzance, St Ives, Falmouth and Newquay, together with other destinations in Devon and Dorset. The Great Western could boast: 'it is doubtful if ever any train has attained more world fame than the *Cornish Riviera Limited* . . . this "aristocrat of trains" '.[51]

The concept of the 'Cornish Riviera' was a stroke of marketing genius, heralding the start of a concerted campaign that would change the face of tourism in Cornwall. It helped capture the middle-class holiday-makers who were increasing in numbers in the years before 1914 (accommodated in such trains as the *Devon and Cornwall Special*, with its 3rd class-only restaurant car) and after 1918 helped create the dramatic rise in Great Western holiday traffic. The 'Cornish Riviera' perpetuated comparisons with the Mediterannean and with Brittany, and continued to foster images of the exotic and the foreign. It was also imbued with a particular 'Cornishness', emphasising Cornwall's Celtic identity and drawing a distinction between Cornwall and England. Extraordinarily, the Great Western was able to equate its own identity with that of Cornwall (and other places too, such as 'Smiling Somerset' and 'Glorious Devon'), and in surviving the Grouping it 'combined the appeals of permanency and nostalgia with fast innovation'.[52]

In 1924, in the aftermath of the Grouping, the advertising department was renamed the publicity department, with William Henry Fraser (a Great Western man since 1892!) appointed Publicity Agent.[53] Fraser's recipe was 'more of the same', and a vast outpouring of jig-saws, train-spotting booklets, children's painting books, books 'For Boys of All Ages' (including *The 10.30 Limited*), postcards, essay competitions for girls and boys, a *Great Western Magazine*, and (in the 1930s) a quarter of a million full-size posters, joined existing publications such as *Holiday Haunts* and A. M. Broadley's *Beautiful Brittany*. All this was conducted with a keen sense of propriety, so that (as T. W. E. Roche pointed out[54]) when Sir Charles Oman, then Chichele Professor of Modern History at Oxford and perhaps the foremost military historian of his day, was commissioned by the Great Western to write a survey of castles in Great Western territory he studiously avoided mention of Tregenna on the grounds that it was not a 'real' castle![55] As Sir Charles himself admitted, deferring to the enthusiasts of the Cornish Revival, 'Visitors betake themselves to the Duchy for many reasons ranging from the study of dolmens and cromlechs, and neolithic hut-circles . . . But it would be unusual to meet anyone who had journeyed towards the Land's End with the sole purpose of hunting castles.'[56]

Like other railways, the Great Western pursued a fulsome policy of locomotive naming, exhibited throughout the first half of the twentieth century, which resulted in such evocative titles as *Cornubia, Duke of Cornwall, Mount's Bay, Tintagel Castle, Pendennis Castle, Trelawney, Tre Pol and Pen, Trevithick, Chough, Tregeagle, One and All, Cornishman, City of Truro*, and so on, each one redolent of Cornwall and Cornishness and more than a few reflecting the symbolism of the Revival.[57] These were, of course, part of the campaign to present Cornwall on the basis of some carefully selected sources, particularly Celtic legend and literary images of person and place.

This approach was also reflected in the impressive series of Great Western posters, two classic early posters being those released in 1908. The first placed a map of Cornwall alongside that of Italy, separated by two young women in 'national costumes' standing in front of a flourishing orange tree. The foreign countenance of both women, together with an element of artistic license in the distortion of the Lizard to produce a more convincing mirror image of the toe of Italy, helped to reinforce the paradoxical message 'See Your Own Country First'.[58] As the poster explained ambiguously, 'There is a great similarity between Cornwall and Italy in shape, climate and natural beauties'. Cornwall as a separate country (and a Celtic nation to boot) was emphasised in the second poster of 1908, which depicted Cornwall's St Michael's Mount alongside the very similar Mont St Michel in Brittany. Here the message was: 'Another striking similarity. Beautiful Britain. Beautiful Brittany'.[59]

A second period of striking poster production occurred in the late 1920s and 1930s. 'The Cornish Riviera', produced *c.* 1925 by Louis Burleigh Bruhl, depicted Cornwall as 'the warmest place in Britain and also as a land of legend, superstition and romance, the home of the wild and imaginative,'[60] while in 1932 the artist Charles Mayo joined the publicity team, producing his own highly evocative posters. In 1931 Fraser had retired, to be replaced by Keith Grand who put even more emphasis on the poster campaign and introduced the ubiquitous *GWR* roundel. Grand was promoted two years later, and replaced in turn by J. Dewar who commissioned high quality modern poster work by

Edward McKnight Kauffer and Ronald Lampitt, including the latter's famous 'mosaic' portrayal of Newlyn. Perhaps the greatest strength of the Great Western poster campaign was its coordination with local areas. Penzance, Newquay, Looe, Newlyn and St Ives had local posters produced specifically for them, each appearing with the *GWR* roundel and presenting a unified Cornish image with local variants—albeit determined by a highly centralised publicity machine.

Great Western guide books, even more than the posters, were vehicles for Cornwall as the land of 'difference', and it is in their pages that we can trace most successfully the influence of (and on) the Cornish-Celtic Revival. For example, the well-known *Through the Window*, published in 1924, described Paddington as almost a metropolitan outpost of Cornwall itself where the '*patois* of Devon and Somerset mingles with the dialect of West Cornwall, which at times has a quaint, musical note and brings into play local words that only a Cornishman would understand'.[61] As the book explained, 'Cornwall . . . is so different from the rest of England as to be a distinct country rather than a county'.[62] Indeed:

> This holds true even if one judges only by such superficial characteristics as the names of railway stations and things seen from the carriage windows. Its truth is emphasized as one probes into history, legend and folk-lore, into the dead Cornish language and stories of the Cornish saints. Here, indeed, is a part of Britain with a culture and character peculiarly its own.[63]

A DUCHY IN EVERY RESPECT UN-ENGLISH

The classic exposition of the Great Western Railway's image of Cornwall was that elaborated in *The Cornish Riviera* by S. P. B.Mais, first published in 1924 and reprinted on several occasions in the 1920s and 1930s. Mais rehearsed the long-familiar arguments of mild winters and balmy summers ('we claim the right to describe the Duchy as the Cornish Riviera . . . We had to have a name for this Elysium'[64]) but his main preoccupation was with Cornwall as a land apart, a Celtic realm wrapped in mysticism, superstition and legend. As Mais explained,

> You may go there with the idea that you are in for a normal English holiday, and find yourself in an atmosphere of warlocks and pixies, miracle working saints and woe-working witches. One ceases from scoffing on reading in the papers of

old women being sent to gaol for exercising their craft of the
evil eye and black magic.[65]

The Cornish themselves were like the Irish, expressing a profound,
if dumb, love for their homeland: 'Your Cornishman thinks little of
Devon, and less of the rest of England. He is sufficient unto himself,
affable and hospitable, like the Welsh extremely devout, and like all
Celts extremely superstitious.'[66]

For, as Mais insisted, Cornwall is 'a Duchy which is in every respect
un-English . . . the Cornish people are not English people'.[67] Like the
Revivalists, Mais took every opportunity to stress the Celticity of the
Cornish, drawing comparisons where possible with the Bretons, Welsh
and Irish. And sharing the medievalist predelictions of the Revivalists
he all but ignored the modern history of copper, tin and china clay,
harking back to Celtic-Catholic Cornwall and beyond, for 'in the Duchy
medievalism still exists, the candle lit by the early saints still burns'.[68]
Standing stones and stone circles were singled out for particular
attention (the circle at Boscawen-Un that was to inspire Henry Jenner
even honoured with a photograph) and there was constant emphasis
on folk-tale and legend—not least that of the infamous folk-figure
Tregeagle: 'Tregeagle's Cornwall is Cornwall at its truest'.[69]

Other Revivalist themes grace the pages of Mais's book. We learn,
for example, that North Cornwall is 'The country sacred to King
Arthur',[70] and that 'The musical placenames make etymologists of us
all . . . (they) are not to be passed without enquiry into the language
that gave them birth.'[71] The separate nationality of Cornwall and the
Cornish was something that would enchant both the *afficianado* ('You
may go to the Duchy to re-establish contact with the Arthurian court'[72])
and the sceptic or plain ill-informed ('You may go there intent only
on tennis, and find yourself at the end of a fortnight a devotee of holy
wells and Celtic crosses'[73]), inescapable phenomena that would arrest
every tourist who crossed the Tamar.

The Great Western's unequivocal embrace of Revivalist icono-
graphy was, of course, a great success. The Company liaised closely
with the several Cornish resorts, not least through the Great Western-
inspired 'Come to Cornwall Association', and in the inter-war period
Newquay hoteliers openly acknowledged that Newquay would not have
become Cornwall's premier holiday destination without the expert
assistance of the railway.[74] The tourists themselves were quickly
ensnared in the sense of mystery and anticipation that accompanied a
journey to Cornwall. T. W. E. Roche recalled the atmosphere of
expectation as the train left Plymouth for the West: he 'tingled with
excitement as we pulled out of North Road'.[75] Ironically, only the infant

Daphne du Maurier was disappointed: ' "There. Now we're in Cornwall", said our mother, laughing. I stared out, disenchanted. For what
was different about this?'[76] Miss du Maurier, of course, spent a life-time
repenting. Most people—hoteliers, tourists and Revivalists alike—for
their several reasons welcomed the imagery of the Great Western
Railway. As Bennett has suggested, 'If initiative and ingenuity frequently out-ran more mundane reality in presenting the delights of the
Cornish Riviera, there was little criticism, more, in fact, a willing
surrender of sorts to the seductive imagery.'[77]

Indeed, S. P. B. Mais, the foremost Great Western literary icono-
grapher, was careful to maintain contact with the personalities of the
Cornish-Celtic Revival and to listen to their advice. As he observed in
the preface to the third edition of *The Cornish Riviers*, published in
February 1934, 'Owing to the kindness of the Cornish Association, the
Rev. G. H. Doble, Vicar of Wendron, Mr. Trelawny Roberts, and
other correspondents I have been able to rectify a few inaccuracies.
Such help is invaluable, and will, I hope, be continued'.[78] The only
Revivalists to express reservations were, predictably, Sir Arthur Quiller
Couch and A.K. Hamilton Jenkin. Q., a reluctant Revivalist in any case,
complained in 1928 that 'Cornwall is *not* an improvised playground; it
is *not* a "Riviera", and the use of that word, whoever first applied it
to Cornwall was, and has been, guilty of a commercial inexactitude'.[79]
Q. had, however, coined the not disimilar term 'the Delectable Duchy'.
Hamilton Jenkin's position was more complex, for while he became an
early Bard of the Gorsedd, his emphasis on the stories of bygone
Cornwall fitting the Revivalist mould, he was at root a mining enthusiast
and knew that the recent history of industrial Cornwall had been a
powerful determinant of the condition of the inter-war period—
characterised as it was by high unemployment and desperate poverty.
As he noted, 'Though in latter years becoming known as "England's
Riviera", the charactersitics of Cornwall are in truth the reverse of
tropical luxuriance.'[80] However, while Hamilton Jenkin's misgivings
hinted at an ongoing but muted ideological contest between those who
wished to cling to the identity of industrial Cornwall and others
reaching back to Celtic-Catholic times, his objections did not prevent
the Great Western-Revivalist nexus from becoming the predominant
influence on the new cultural constructions of Cornwall that emerged
in the period before 1945.

THE SOUTHERN

While the Great Western undoubtably led the way in the promotion
of Cornwall and in the adoption of Revivalist imagery, the efforts of the

London and South Western Railway (LSWR) and its post-Grouping successor, the Southern, should not be overlooked. Although the LSWR had acquired the Bodmin and Wadebridge line earlier in the century, its principal network did not cross the Tamar until much later, reaching Bude and Padstow in 1898 and 1899 respectively. North Cornwall, with the emerging resorts of Tintagel and Boscastle, together with Bude and Padstow and more obscure spots such as Port Isaac, was King Arthur country. In the years before 1914 the LSWR produced *By the Cornish Seas and Moors: Holidays in King Arthur's Land*,[81] while both before and after the Grouping a fleet of 'King Arthur Class' locomotives was manufactured to haul the Cornish expresses westwards from Waterloo. Names such as *Merlin, Lyonesse, Excalibur, Pendragon, Iseult, Sir Cador of Cornwall* were entirely reminiscent of Arthurian-Revivalist Cornwall[82], although the fact that these engines were not permitted to work over the Meldon Viaduct and actually into Cornwall was an irritant. Rather later, however, in 1945, the Southern did introduce its named 'Westcountry Class', and whilst *Launceston, Camelford, Bodmin, Calstock, Wadebridge* and *Callington* might be more prosaic than *Sir Dodinas Le Savage* or *Sir Harry Le Fiselake*, these locomotives were able to penetrate as far as Padstow and at least their names were an accurate reflection of the railway's Cornish destinations[83].

Mindful of the important results already achieved by the Great Western, the Southern after the Grouping engaged in 1925 J. B. (later Sir John) Elliott as Public Relations Assistant. The important departures from Waterloo for Cornwall were the 10.00am, 11.00am and 12.00 noon trains. The 10.00am was soon named the *North Cornwall Express*, and the 11.00am (which had featured in LSWR timetables since 1890!) was the subject of a competition the results of which were announced in the *Southern Railway Magazine* in July 1925. The winning suggestion was the *Atlantic Coast Express* (with its attractive acronymic contraction, the *ACE*), the title first being applied on 19 July 1926.[84] No less an authority than S. P. B. Mais was engaged to capitalise on the *ACE*, leading in 1936 to his *Let's Get Out Here*, a guide to twenty-six walks from the route of the *Atlantic Coast Express*. Mais produced a further volume, simply entiled *ACE*, with evocative drawings by the noted Anna Zinkeisen depicting Celtic legends such as St Brannock and the Devil.[85] Southern propoganda insisted that

> the strangely compelling atmosphere of the Duchy begins to make itself felt almost as soon as the ATLANTIC COAST EXPRESS begins to leave the purple Tors of Dartmoor in the rear. At one moment you are in comfortable Devon with its

terra-cotta warm loam, white cottages and thickly wooded coombes, all typically English, the next you are on strange soil, suddenly thrown back five thousand years in the British region where the successive centuries have failed to efface all trace of legend and romance. There is rich haunting music in the very place names.[86]

Like Great Western propaganda, these Southern efforts produced the desired results. John Betjeman became a devotee of the North Cornwall line to Padstow, immortalising in his verse both the very Cornish-sounding stations of Egloskerry and Tresmeer and the Bible Christians who inhabited neighbouring fields, asking 'Can it really be that this same carriage came from Waterloo?'[87] T. W. E. Roche dubbed the North Cornwall route 'Betjemanland' and wrote that Launceston (where the Southern main line was joined by the terminating Great Western branch from Tavistock and Plymouth) was:

the frontier town between England and Cornwall, with a sense of division about it—here the Celtic land really began, here lush Devon was left behind and austere Cornwall lay ahead. The fact that the GWR had a terminus here accentuated this— it had reached the foreign land but could go no further.[88]

CONCLUSION

Although Roche was recalling pre-war days he was in fact writing as recently as 1967, a powerful indicator of the enduring strength of Southern Railway images of Cornwall. Great Western images were equally, if not more, powerful and enduring, nationalisation in 1948 in many respects failing to end the ethos of the old Company. The *Cornish Riviera Express* survived, to be joined by the *Royal Duchy*, and for a time the old Great Western style of poster was perpetuated by the new Western Region of British Railways. In 1953 a British Railways publicity film *Western Lands* was produced. The commentary explained that the train was 'Now across Saltash Bridge; out of Devon, out of England!' Cornwall was 'magic, mysterious . . . she remembers her Celtic heritage and calls for the blessings of her saints . . . she wears her houses with a foreign air, as if she had borrowed them from Brittany'.[89] The Westcountry Writers' Association, dominated at the time by the literary critic J. C. Trewin and other Cornish authors, passed a resolution 'Bring back our Great Western Railway'[90] (a cry that had little to do with politics and everything to do with identity). Later, G. Freeman Allen alluded wryly to the 'Great Western Region', noting that 'No writer to an editor from an address in the West Country seemed to have had anything but remarkable food, deferential service, elysium comfort and breathless speed on his every journey by the old Great Western.'[91]

In response to such sentiment, in the late 1950s the Western Region reintroduced the old Great Western livery of chocolate-and-cream for the coaching stock on the *Cornish Riviera Express* and other principal trains, while even the new diesel-hydraulic locomotives that were soon to appear on the Region sported evocative 'regional' names such as *Western Druid* and *Western Buccaneer*.[92] Lostwithiel station, with its palm trees and fading brown and cream paintwork, survived as an icon of Great Westernry until the late 1970s, cherished by railway enthusiasts and Old Cornwall devotees alike: 'Time had stood still for over 100 years.'[93] In the 1980s, in a brief experiment of managerial and marketing devolution to 'Cornish Railways', a china clay freight locomotive was given the old Great Western name *Tre Pol and Pen*.[94] In the 1990s the title 'Great Western' was itself resurrected for Inter-City services into Cornwall.

The survival of such nostalgia well into the post-war era hardly squared with the anti-tourist mood noted by Moorhouse and Theroux or the criticisms of tourist imagery made by *Cornwall at the Crossroads*. But after the war Cornwall had changed rapidly, mass tourism itself undergoing significant transformation (not least to road transport) and with other socio-economic upheavals such as mass in-migration leading to a further re-definition of Cornish identity in which Revivalst symbolism and ideology was but one part of a new synthesis which ranged in content from the politics of anti-metropolitanism to the extravaganza of 'Trelawny's Army'.[95] The Great Western could, indeed, be safely consigned to the realms of nostalgia, for the images it portrayed, based on an erstwhile alliance of 'outsider' and 'insider' agendas, were a response to a cultural imperative that had by now passed.

And yet, even if there was evidence of a re-definimg identity *within* post-war Cornwall, *outsiders'* images of Cornwall and the Cornish might still be focused firmly on 'the Celt' as Chapmanesque 'Other'—a tribute, amongst other things, to the residual power of the old Great Western in English folk-memory. As recently as 1993 one newly-published railway enthusiasts' volume could explain confidently in its opening sentences that:

A peninsula largely separated from Devon and the rest of England by the River Tamar, Cornwall is probably the most distinctive county in the country. Its isolation has helped to

foster an independent spirit among its inhabitants, not least
in their celebration of Celtic traditions and the revival of their
own language.[96]

NOTES AND REFERENCES

1. see Allan M. Williams and Gareth Shaw, 'The Age of Mass Tourism', in
   Philip Payton (ed.), *Cornwall Since the War: The Contemporary History
   of a European Region*, Redruth, 1993.
2. J. Urry, *The Tourist Gaze: Leisure and Travel in Contemporary Societies*,
   London, 1990.
3. Bernard Deacon and Philip Payton, 'Re-inventing Cornwall: Culture
   Change on the European Periphery', and Paul Thornton, 'Cornwall and
   Changes in the Tourist Gaze', both in *Cornish Studies: One*, 1993; John
   Lowerson, 'Celtic Tourism—Some Recent Magnets', *Cornish Studies: Two*,
   1994.
4. Malcolm Chapman, *The Celts: The Construction of a Myth*, London, 1992.
5. Philip Payton, *The Making of Modern Cornwall: Historical Experience and
   the Persistence of 'Difference'*, Redruth, 1992, pp. 125–129.
6. G. Young, *Tourism: Blessing or Blight?*, London, 1973.
7. Paul Laity, 'Tourism—Whorism', *An Weryn*, No. 11, 1979.
8. V. L. Smith, *Hosts and Guests: The Anthropology of Tourism*, Philadelpia,
   1989.
9. Geoffrey Moorhouse, *Britain in the Sixties: The Other England*, London,
   1964, p. 37.
10. Moorhouse, 1964, p. 41.
11. Paul Theroux, *The Kingdom By the Sea*, London, 1983, p. 117.
12. Bernard Deacon, Andrew George, Ronald Perry, *Cornwall at the Cross-
    roads: Living Communities or Leisure Zone?*, Redruth, 1988, pp. 105–106.
13. Keith Robbins, *Nineteenth-Century Britain: England, Scotland and Wales
    —The Making of a Nation*, Oxford, 1989, p. 25.
14. David St John Thomas, *A Regional History of the Railways of Great Britain,
    Vol. 1: The West Country*, Newton Abbot, 1960, 5th edn 1981, p. 135.
15. see Bernard Deacon, 'And Shall Trelawny Die? The Cornish Identity', in
    Payton (ed.), 1993.
16. P. Berresford Ellis, *The Cornish Language and Its Literature*, London,
    1974, p. 141.
17. Henry Jenner, *A Handbook of the Cornish Language*, London, 1904.
18. *Old Cornwall*, Vol. II, No. 8, Winter 1934.
19. *Old Cornwall*, Vol. II, No. 4, Winter 1932.
20. *Old Cornwall*, Vol. I, No. 3, April 1926.
21. *Old Cornwall*, Vol. II, No. 2, Winter 1931.
22. *Old Cornwall*, Vol. II, No. 4, Winter 1932.
23. *Old Cornwall*, Vol. II, No. 5, Summer 1935.
24. *Old Cornwall*, Vol. II, No. 5, Summer 1935.
25. *Old Cornwall*, Vol. II, No. 8, Winter 1934.

26. *Old Cornwall*, Vol. II, No. 10, Winter 1935.
27. *Old Cornwall*, Vol. II, No. 2, Winter 1931.
28. *Old Cornwall*, Vol. II, No. 2, Winter 1931.
29. *Old Cornwall*, Vol. I, No. 9, April 1929.
30. *Old Cornwall*, Vol. I, No. 12, Winter 1930.
31. *Old Cornwall*, Vol. I, No. 10, October 1929.
32. *Old Cornwall*, Vol. II, No. 11, Summer 1936.
33. *Old Cornwall*, Vol. III, No. 2, Summer 1942.
34. *Old Cornwall*, Vol. III, No. 2, Summer 1942.
35. *Old Cornwall*, Vol. I, No. 7, April 1928.
36. J. Walvin, *Leisure and Society*, London, 1978; J. Walvin, *Beside the Sea*, London, 1978.
37. W. Bennett, 'The Origins and Development of the Tourist Industry in Cornwall', *Annual Report of the Royal Cornwall Polytechnic Society*, 1948.
38. *Guide to Penzance*, 1890.
39. *Guide to Penzance*, 1890.
40. R. W. Butler, 'The Concept of a Tourist Area Cycle of Evolution: Implications for Management of Resources', *Canadian Geographer*, XXIV, No. 1, 1980.
41. Peter Laws, 'The Cornish Riviera—Architects and Builders Provide the Necessary Ingredient', in Joanna Mattingly and June Palmer (eds), *From Pilgrimage to Packet Tour*, Truro, 1992.
42. *Cornish Magazine*, Vol. I, 1898.
43. *Cornish Magazine*, Vol. I, 1898.
44. H. A. Vallance, *The Highland Railway*, 1938, repub. (4th edn) Newton Abbot, 1985, p. 79; John Thomas, *The West Highland Railway*, Newton Abbot, 1965, 3rd edn, 1984, p. 83; John Thomas, *A Regional History of the Railways of Great Britain: Volume 6: Scotland—The Lowlands and the Borders*, Newton Abbot, 1971, new ed. 1984, pp. 100–07; David St John Thomas and Patrick Whitehouse, *The Romance of Scotland's Railways*, London, 1993, p. 50.
45. David St John Thomas and Simon Rocksborough Smith, *Summer Saturdays in the West*, Newton Abbot, 1973, p. 13.
46. Robbins, 1989, p.25.
47. Jack Simmons, 'The Railway in Cornwall', 1835–1914', *Back Track: Recording Britain's Railway History*, Winter 1987 (first published in *Journal of the Royal Institution of Cornwall*, 1962).
48. Roger Burdett Wilson, *Go Great Western: A History of GWR Publicity*, Newton Abbot, 1970, repub. 1987.
49. Patrick Whitehouse and David St John Thomas (eds), *The Great Western Railway: 150 Glorious Years*, Newton Abbot, 1984, p. 146.
50. Simmons, 1987 (1962).
51. David St John Thomas (ed.), *GWR Engines, Names, Numbers, Types and Classes: A Reprint of the Engine Books of 1911, 1928 and 1946 with some pages from that of 1938*, Newton Abbot, 1971, pp. 88–89 (1938).
52. Whitehouse and Thomas (eds), 1984, p. 146.

53. Whitehouse and Thomas (eds), 1984, p. 147; see also Wilson, 1987, and Beverly Cole and Richard Durack, *Railway Posters 1923–1947*, London, 1992, p. 9.
54. T. W. E. Roche, *Go Great Western: Reminiscences of the GWR Main Line and Branches in Devon*, Bracknell, 1966, repub. 1984, p. 17.
55. Roche, 1966 (1984), p. 17.
56. Charles W.C. Oman, *Castles*, New York (reprint), 1978, p. 103.
57. Thomas (ed.), 1971, pp. 5, 7, 15, 17, 19, 21, 23.
58. Wilson, 1987, p. 18.
59. Ibid.
60. Cole and Durack, 1992, p. 31.
61. *Through the Window*, London, 1924, repub. Newton Abbot, 1994, p. 7.
62. Ibid.
63. Ibid.
64. S. P. B. Mais, *The Cornish Riviera*, London, 1924, 3rd edn, 1934, p. 1.
65. Mais, 1924 (1934), p. 3.
66. Mais, 1924 (1934), p. 4.
67. Mais, 1924 (1934), p. 9.
68. Mais, 1924 (1934), p. 7.
69. Mais, 1924 (1934), p. 140.
70. Mais, 1924 (1934), p. 141.
71. Mais, 1924 (1934), p. 6.
72. Mais, 1924 (1934), p. 3.
73. Mais, 1924 (1934), p. 3.
74. Whitehouse and Thomas, 1984, p. 146.
75. T. W. E. Roche, *More Great Westernry*, Bracknell, 1969, p. 51.
76. Daphne du Maurier, *Vanishing Cornwall: The Spirit and History of Cornwall*, London, 1967, repub. 1972, p. 4.
77. Alan Bennett, *Images of Cornwall*, Cheltenham, 1992, p. 43; see especially Bennett's chapters 'Tourism and Railways—The Twentieth Century' and 'The GWR and Newquay'.
78. Mais, 1934, p. 7.
79. Cited in Laws, 1992, p. 11.
80. A. K. Hamilton Jenkin, *Cornwall and its People*, London, 1945, repub. Newton Abbot, 1983, p. viii.
81. Bennett, 1992, pp. 63–71, offers a useful introduction to early LSWR/ Southern publicity in North Cornwall; for a recent history of the route see David Wroe, *Pictorial History of the North Cornwall Railway*, Caernarfon, 1995.
82. Brian Stephenson, *Southern Express Locomotives*, London, 1988, p. 124.
83. H. C. B. Rogers, *Bulleid Pacifics at Work*, London, 1980, pp. 124–126.
84. D. W. Winkworth, *Southern Titled Trains*, Newton Abbot, 1988, pp. 21–22; David St John Thomas and Patrick Whitehouse, *SR 150: A Century and a Half of the Southern Railway*, Newton Abbot, 1988, p. 27.
85. T. W. E. Roche, *The Withered Arm: Reminiscences of the Southern Lines West of Exeter*, Bracknell, 1967, 2nd edn, 1977, repub. 1993, pp. 31–34.

86. Cited in Bennett, 1992, p. 68.

87. John Betjeman, *Summoned By Bells*, London, 1960, p. 33.

88. Roche, 1967 (1977, 1993), p. 48.

89. *Western Lands*, British Railways Board film, 1953; released in video form as *Yesterday's Britain No. 10: Western Lands*, London, 1991.

90. David St John Thomas and Patrick Whitehouse, *The Trains We Loved*, Newton Abbot, 1994, p. 26

91. G. Freeman Allen, *The Western Since 1948*, London, 1979, p. 11.

92. Colin J. Marsden (ed.), *The Complete BR Diesel and Locomotive Directory*, Oxford, 1991, p. 42.

93. John Vaughan, *Diesels in the Duchy*, London, 1983, p. 43.

94. John Vaughan, *An Illustrated History of West Country China Clay Trains*, Oxford, 1987, p. 15; John Vaughan, *The Newquay Branch and Its Branches*, Oxford, 1991, p. 69.

95. See Payton (ed.), 1993.

96. David Mitchell, *British Railways Past and Present No. 17: Cornwall*, Peterborough, 1993, p. 7; see also Peter W. Gray, *Steam in Cornwall*, London, 1993, p. 2, where he writes: 'Welcome to Cornwall—The Royal Duchy—characterised by the Great Western Railway as the "Cornish Riviera" '.

WHICH BASE FOR REVIVED CORNISH?

Ken George

INTRODUCTION

Cornish was spoken as a community language from about AD 600 to about 1800, and has been revived in the twentieth century (Revived Cornish). In a recent article, Charles Penglase argued that 'authenticity is the most desirable quality of a revived language'.[1] Authenticity may be a desirable goal, but absolute authenticity is quite unattainable. In the absence of native-speakers and sound-recordings of historical Cornish, any reconstruction of the grammar, syntax, phonology, lexicon, and particularly semantics, is bound to include elements of doubt. The orthography is slightly different. These aspects are discussed individually below, but firstly, the question of nomenclature must be addressed.

GETTING THE NOMENCLATURE RIGHT

The history of many European languages is divided into Old, Middle and Modern phases. The boundaries of each phase are usually not clearly definable, so different authors give different dates for them. Thus the history of English may be divided into Old English (700–1100), Middle English (1100–1500) and Modern English (1500–present). The most ancient phase of historical Cornish (600–800), which has no surviving written records, was termed Primitive Cornish by Jackson. The terms Old Cornish (800–1200) and Middle Cornish (1200–1575) are not in dispute; but there is some disagreement about the use of the term 'Modern Cornish'.

The term 'Modern Cornish' has been used to refer to:

(a) the most recent phase of historical Cornish (1575–1800), e.g. Padel.[2]
(b) the revived language of the twentieth century, e.g. Brown.[3]
(c) both (a) and (b) e.g. Saunders.[4]
(d) the form of revived Cornish advocated by Gendall (Kernuak).[5]

Because of the potential confusion, the term 'Modern Cornish' is perhaps best avoided altogether. The best name for the last phase of the historical language (1575–1800) is Late Cornish, in which the word late means both tardy (*le cornique tardif* in French) and deceased.

The revival was begun by Jenner, who based his ideas for the most part on Late Cornish.[6] Nance's reconstruction , which he called Unified Cornish, was based for the most part on the Middle Cornish phase, for reasons which are explored below.[7] Recently, the pronunciation and spelling of Nance's Cornish have been improved by the present author.[8] The principles behind the improved reconstruction, known as Kernewek Kemmyn, are discussed in the next two sections of this paper. Late Cornish has recently been re-examined by Richard Gendall, with a view to basing a revived form of Cornish entirely on that phase.[9]

Penglase seems to use the term 'Modern Cornish' not only for the last phase of historical Cornish, but also for Gendall's form of revived Cornish based upon that phase. This is merely to confuse. It is manifestly impossible for the revived language to be identical to that spoken at a given epoch before 1800, and so names which imply that it is are to be avoided. It is essential to use a nomenclature which clearly distinguishes the historical language from the revived. Although the term 'Modern Cornish' has indeed been used to describe the form of revived Cornish advocated by Gendall (Vink, Payton and Deacon, Gendall),[10] Gendall has in addition proposed the descriptions *Carnoack Tithiack* ('Traditional'–sic–Cornish), *Carnoack Nowedga, Curnoack* and *Kernuak*; this last will be used here.

A COMPARISON OF BASES FOR REVIVED CORNISH

General
Two fundamental questions may be asked, when comparing Kernewek Kemmyn and Kernuak.

Q1 Which phase is more suited for the revival of Cornish, Middle or Late?
Q2 Are the reconstructions true to the historical language (in Penglase's terms, authentic)?

Q2 is best answered by a detailed examination of the reconstructions, as compared with historical Cornish. Penglase did not
attempt this, preferring to examine the methodology. The present
author has not attempted a detailed answer, either, because the
question is somewhat sterile. There would be little point in setting up
a revived language which was known to be significantly different from
the historical (e.g. a Cornish without mutations, however desirable that
might appear to the learner!). Our knowledge of historical Cornish has
a degree of uncertainty ('experimental error') associated with it.
Provided that the revived language approximates the historical to
within the error-bounds, then it may be deemed authentic (or as
authentic as one is likely to get). If, subsequently, our knowledge of
historical Cornish improves to the point where there are demonstrable
errors in the reconstruction, then those errors should be rectified. This
is what happened to Nance's Unified Cornish, so far as the phonology
was concerned; the resulting improvement was Kernewek Kemmyn.
Authenticity is therefore relative rather than absolute. The Cornish
Language Board, which adopted Kernewek Kemmyn in 1987, is acutely
aware of the question of authenticity; for example, in its new Cornish-
English dictionary,[11] the degree of authenticity of each word is
indicated by a tripartite code, which deals with

(a) phonological and orthographic authentication;
(b) attestation;
(c) frequency of occurrence.

It is therefore Q1 which is the main subject of this article. The
doubts which Penglase expresses about a Middle Cornish base are
considered under individual headings below. When he writes 'had it
been known that Modern Cornish (i.e. Late Cornish) was in reality a
flexible, varied and distinctly Cornish vernacular', he does Nance a
great disservice. Nance was fully aware of the nature of Late Cornish,
for it was he who published most of the traditional literature from that
period, in no fewer than twenty-nine different articles, mostly in *Old
Cornwall*. The point is, that having studied the Late Cornish remains
in the minutest detail, Nance came to a rather different conclusion; viz.
that it was better to base Revived Cornish on Middle Cornish, a view
held by the great majority of Cornish speakers.

Relatively little has been published as to why this choice was made,
and this article will redress that balance. An important general point
is that Gendall's study of Late Cornish, on which his reconstruction is
based, is essentially synchronic. However, although Nance based his
grammar and syntax on Middle Cornish, his studies embraced all

phases; and he wanted to include in the revived language every scrap of Cornish that could be found, following the motto of the Old Cornwall Societies: *Cuntelleugh an brewyon us gesys na vo kellys travyth.*

Grammar

Penglase does not offer any specific criticism of the detail of Nance's grammar; he just asserts that it is in some important aspects invented. To support this sweeping statement, he quotes no primary sources, but rather the comments of Glanville Price.[12] In fact, the grammar of Middle Cornish has received considerable attention; Nance was able to refer to the work of Lhuyd, Stokes and others;[13] but in addition, he and A. S. D. Smith minutely examined, letter by letter, practically every manuscript of historical Cornish, of all phases. Their knowledge of Cornish grammar was so detailed that Smith was able to find ten pages' worth of mistakes in the second edition of Henry Lewis' *Llawlyfr Cernyweg Canol.*[14]

The only mistake which has been found in Nance's grammar in recent years is the minor one of misinterpreting the *tek a wel* construction as an exclamative.[15] This has now been corrected by Brown.[16] Another minor point has been to recommend that in Kernewek Kemmyn the singular form *ty* 'thou' be used for addressing one person, and the plural form *hwi* 'you' for addressing more than one person.[17]

A comparison of Middle and Late Cornish grammar shows that:

(a) The English plural *-s* became commoner, even for Cornish words, e.g. *poscaders* 'fishermen'.
(b) The verbal noun suffixes *-a* and *-ia* were substituted for others.
(c) Unpredictable metatheses produced words which were no longer relatable to their Breton and Welsh cognates; e.g. Late Cornish *ispak* 'bishop' (cf. Breton *eskob,* Welsh *esgob*).
(d) Mutations were indicated less frequently.
(e) Conjugated pronominal prepositions are a distinctive feature of Celtic grammar: in Cornish, they persisted into Late Cornish, but began to be replaced by more analytical forms; e.g. alongside *thym* > *them* 'to me', *(dhymm* in Kernewek Kemmyn) a form *tha vee* appeared. This may be put down to English influence during a period of terminal decline, although it should be noted that this is paralleled in Welsh by *im* ('to me') and the usual modern form *i mi* or *i fi*—not necessarily due to English influence.

Syntax

The syntax of Late Cornish appears more like English syntax than that of Middle Cornish, in that conjugated main verbal clauses were replaced by periphrastic constructions. The interrogative forms of the latter are parallelled by English:

(from *Delkiow Sevi)*	*Ra ve moas gena why?*	Shall I go with you?
(from William Rowe)	*reeg Dew lawle?*	Did God say?

Compare also

BM 979	*desempys duen alema*	At once let us go hence
CW 1331	*Gas ny tha vos a lemma*	Let us go hence

where the Late Cornish has the same form as the English.

Padel[18] pointed out numerous examples of Anglicisms in Late Cornish; e.g. in Nicholas Boson's *Dutchesse of Cornwall's progresse,* we find *iggeva setha war* 'that he is sitting upon'. In *Nebbaz Gerriau dro tho Carnoack,* there are *skoothes war* 'depended upon'; *noniel* 'neither', used as an adverb; *gwrez aman* 'made up'; *merwel akar* 'die away'; *dose tho travith* 'come to nothing'; *drez ubba* 'over here'. In addition, John Boson wrote *Termen vedn doaz* for 'time will come'. The use of the Late Cornish conjunction *tell* 'as' seems to be taken from the use of 'as' instead of 'that' in dialectal English; e.g. in William Rowe's translation from Genesis:

Preg laule theeze tell estah en noath?	Who told thee that thou wert naked?

Penglase is concerned that syntax reconstructed from Middle Cornish may not be authentic, because most of the extant Middle Cornish literature is verse rather than prose. As the author has shown elsewhere, it is still possible to recover the common word-orders from verse, without recourse to the syntax of Middle Breton. These studies also show how different word-orders could be used to emphasise a particular syntactic element. This versatility was practically lost in Late Cornish; so that the language became, not 'flexible' as stated by Penglase, but just the opposite.

Lexicon

The lexical legacy of historical Cornish is insufficient for the requirements of a modern language to be used in everyday living in the twentieth century. The gaps in the extant historical lexicon comprise:

(a) words which must have been present in historical Cornish, but do not happen to appear in the texts: these may often be deduced from Breton and Welsh cognates; e.g. the word for 'rat' was almost certainly *rath* (Breton *razh,* Welsh *rhath);*

(b) words for concepts which did not exist at the time when Cornish was traditionally spoken.

Because of the paucity of the historical lexicon, Nance did not restrict his choice of words to those found in Middle Cornish; he used in addition words from Old Cornish, Late Cornish, and those words in the Cornish dialect of English which appeared to come from Cornish (even though not recorded in traditional Cornish texts).[19] In order to fill the gaps (a) and (b), he turned to Breton and Welsh, to other dialect words, and to Middle English; he also devised new words using Cornish roots.

This policy has continued in the preparation of the dictionaries for Kernewek Kemmyn.[20] About one hundred extra words were forthcoming from Padel's study of place-names in Cornwall.[21] Otherwise, new words have been constructed according to a carefully prepared set of guidelines.[22]

A problem with Gendall's reconstruction is that Late Cornish contains only a subset of the extant historical lexicon. In his English-Cornish dictionary, he has gone backwards in time, and includes Jordan's *Creacon of the World,* dated 1611, a work which is Late Cornish in its spelling, but arguably Middle Cornish in its content; and even the Tregear Homilies, which historically belong to Middle Cornish, having been translated *circa* 1558. What is more questionable is his inclusion of many dialect words: whereas words found in the numerous texts are listed, often with variant spellings each with its own provenance, the dialect words, Cornish and non-Cornish, are all listed under the catchall label 'T' (for 'Traditional'), which includes 'material transmitted orally from 18th, 19th and 20th cent'.

Phonology

Although the testimony of Lhuyd is a help, two difficulties remain when trying to work out the phonology of Late Cornish.

(a) There is insufficient evidence to be sure about many of the phonemes.

(b) The degree of influence of English on the sounds of Late Cornish, and the source of the sounds in the dialect of West Penwith, are both controversial and indeterminate. Wakelin[22] maintained that the dialectal sounds are a reflection of seventeenth-century English, while Ó'Coileán argued that they fitted Lhuyd's description of Cornish sounds and are thus Cornish rather than English.[24]

The historical phonology of Cornish was studied in detail by the present author.[25] In his article, Penglase extensively criticises this work, but his criticisms are almost all methodological, while his questioning of the choice of computer language is merely superficial. He regards the methods as 'unconventional', but here, as in many other fields, it is the unconventional approach which leads to the successful advance of knowledge. The method used for developing Kernewek Kemmyn is summarised here for reference.

The first step was to trace the history of all the sounds of Cornish throughout its traditional phase, using a knowledge of phonetics, subject to the boundary conditions:

(a) in Primitive Cornish;[26]
(b) the evidence of Lhuyd for Late Cornish, which is sometimes contradictory;

with the aid of the following evidence, in decreasing order of reliability:

(a) the written record in texts and place-names;
(b) the development of sounds in Breton and Welsh;
(c) rhyming schemes.

Working hypotheses of the phonological history could then be tested against the evidence. This may seem like a circular argument, but in practice it worked as a spiral; successive iterations resulted in improvements to the history. With hindsight, the only change which might be made to the method would be to place more emphasis on synchronic analyses.

Orthography

The only feature of historical Cornish where one might hope to achieve authenticity is the orthography, but even here a problem arises. The following four orthographic systems may be distinguished as being used for historical Cornish:

(a) the orthography of Old Cornish,[27] which was similar to those of Old Breton and Old Welsh;
(b) the orthography of Middle Cornish;
(c) the orthography of Late Cornish;
(d) the orthography of Edward Lhuyd.

All other systems are based to some degree on one or more of these, as shown in Table 1.

With the exception of Lhuyd's phonetic system, the orthography of historical Cornish was not fixed, and was based on contemporary English orthography. Unless Lhuyd's system is used, therefore, anyone wishing to use an historical orthography as a base has to exercise an element of choice as to which spellings to use.

TABLE 1
Cornish Orthographies

Historical Orthography	*Reformist Orthographies*	
Old Cornish		Williams (1863)
Middle Cornish		Keigwin (Nance, 1926, 1927)
	→ Unified Cornish	Nance (1929)
	→ Kernewek Kemmyn	George (1986)
Late Cornish	→ Kernuak	Gendall (1992)
Lhuyd (1707)		Saunders (1979)

N.B. Jenner's orthography appears to be based on the writings of both Lhuyd and the writers of the Newlyn School (1660–1720).

It is surprising that, when choosing an orthography for Kernuak, Gendall did not use as a basis Lhuyd's system, which is far more scientific than that of the writers in the Newlyn School. He gives no reasons for this; neither does he explain the principles by which he chooses one spelling rather than another from the collection in his dictionary.[28] He has re-spelled certain words, recorded only by Lhuyd, in a fashion which is more in accordance with the style of the Newlyn School; e.g. Lhuyd's *kynyfan, kynyphan* 'nut' is re-spelled as *knuffan,* a form unattested in the historical literature.

One of the useful features of Lhuyd's orthography was the consistent distinction between /ð/ and /θ/, whereas the Newlyn School tended to use the English grapheme <th> for both phonemes. Nance followed Lhuyd, using <dh> and <th> respectively, except in final position, where /-ð/ is often realized as [θ]. Compare Breton <z> and <zh> (not always an exact correspondence); Welsh <th> and <dd>. In

TABLE 2
Words containing the reflex of Middle Cornish stressed /-i/

Kernewek Kemmyn	English Meaning	Breton Cognate	Welsh Cognate	Kernuak (Gendall, 1993)
bri	esteem	bri	bri	—
chi	house	ti	ti	choy
devri	certain	devri	difri	—
dhi	thither	di	—	—
di	thither	di	—	di
dri	to bring	—	(dyry)	—
fi	fie	—	—	—
gwri	stitch	gwri	gwni-	—
hi	she	hi	hi	hye
hwi	you (pl.)	c'hwi	ch(w)i	why
i	they	i	—	angye
ki	dog	ki	ci	kye
kri	cry	kri	cri	—
li	lunch	(lein)	—	li
ni	we	ni	ni	nye
pri	clay	pri	pridd	pry
ri	to give	reiñ	rhoi	—
ti	to roof	—	toi	—
ti	to swear	touiñ	(tyngu)	—
tri	three (m.)	tri	tri	try
yredi	surely	—	—	—

Note: There are other words in Kernewek Kemmyn which rhyme with the above, but they are not included in the figure, because they do not necessarily contain the reflex of Middle Cornish /-i/; these are *bi* 'may thou be', *gwi* 'weaves', *li* 'oath', *si* 'itch', *ti* 'house'. This makes twenty-six words in all, more than in *Kernuak*.

Kernewek Kemmyn, the distinction is made even in final position. Gendall has not availed himself of this, preferring to use English <th>: He remarks 'a working rule is difficult to form. Reference should be made to the dictionary' in order to discover which of the two phonemes is meant.

The situation is still worse when one considers the spelling of vowels. Table 2 shows words containing the reflex of Middle Cornish stressed /-i/. In Kernewek Kemmyn, all of these words rhyme; indeed they have been taken from an as yet unpublished rhyming dictionary. It is well known that the vowel sound in these words changed, in the same way and at the same time as the English Great Vowel Shift: [-i] > [-iI] > [-ΛI]; this is held to be an example of how Late Cornish was influenced by English. We would expect all of those words which survived into the Late Cornish phase to be affected in the same way, and therefore commonsense would suggest that they ought to be spelled similarly in a system based on Late Cornish. Only eleven of these words appear in Gendall's work,[29] as shown in the figure, but the vocoid therein (approximately [-I] by the year 1700) has the different spellings <oy, y, ye, i>. In his work on pronunciation, Gendall acknowledges that these four graphemes may each represent the same sound!

The orthography of Kernewek Kemmyn is an improvement on that of Nance, so as to fit the phonological base, at the same epoch. When Penglase writes of a 500-year gap between the pronunciation and the orthography, he is the victim of misinformation; the two are closely wedded, as shown in Table 3. Almost all of the graphemes used are

TABLE 3
The phonological base and its associated orthography

Phonemes	*Graphemes*
/i, I, ε, a, ɔ, o, u, œ, y/	<i, y, e, a, o, oe, ou, eu, u>
/ei, ai, ɔi/	<ey, ay, oy>
/iu, Iu, εu, au, ɔu/	<iw, yw, ew, aw, ow>
/j, w/	<y, w>
/p, t, k; pp, tt, kk/	<p, t, k; pp, tt, kk>
/b, d, g/	<b, d, g> (but <-p, -d, -k> in polysyllables)
/f, θ, x, s; ff, θθ, xx, ss/	<f, th, gh, s; ff, tth, ggh, ss>
/v, ð, h/	<v, dh, h>
/.., t.., d../	<sh, ch, j>

found in the Middle Cornish texts. The pronunciation and spelling were first explained in 1986, and have since been slightly modified.[30]

The close link between spelling and pronunciation depends upon a set of rules governing the quantity of vowels in traditional Cornish, from its beginnings *c.* 600 to about 1600. These rules were as follows:

(a) In unstressed syllables, all vowels are short.
(b) In stressed syllables, vowels are short before double consonants and groups of consonants.
(c) In stressed syllables, vowels are long in monosyllables, and half-long in polysyllables before single consonants.

The principles of the orthography of Kernewek Kemmyn are discussed further below.

The reconstruction of the verb 'to know'

Nowhere does Penglase make even one criticism of the actual details of Nance's reconstruction of Cornish, nor of the present author's improvements to it. It is these details which can and should be argued in an academic context, as has been done by Williams and George.[31] In this section, a critical comparison is offered in detail of part of the reconstruction.

Penglase asserts that: 'the Middle Cornish verb structure is complex and requires many verb parts not all of which naturally occur in the texts. Comparison with other Celtic languages was, therefore, naturally brought in to assist in the construction of these parts of the relevant verbs'.[32] The verbal structure seems complex only to English monoglots; it is no more complex than that of many major European languages, French and Spanish, for example, and has been clearly codified by Edwards.[33] Later, Penglase claims that, so far as Kernuak is concerned, 'the parts of the irregular auxiliary verbs are extant in the texts'. The validity of these statements is now tested for one of the five auxiliary verbs listed by Penglase as required to form tenses in Kernuak.

Cornish, in common with many European languages, has two verbs 'to know', semantically corresponding roughly to French *connaitre* and *savoir*. The second of these verbs has an important auxiliary function, shown by:

BM 19   *perfect ef a wore redya*   'he knows how to read perfectly'

so that the revived language needs a full paradigm for it. The paradigms presented by Brown for Kernewek Kemmyn and by Gendall for

Kernuak are shown, together with explanatory notes, in Tables 4 and 5.[34] The following observations may be made.

TABLE 4
The verb *godhvos* 'to know' in Kernewek Kemmyn

	Present	Imperfect	Preterite	Pluperfect
S 1	67 *gonn*	9 *godhyen*	0 *godhvev*	0 *godhvien*
S 2	9 *godhes*	0 *godhyes*	0 *godhves*	0 *godhvies*
S 3	82 *goer*	18 *godhya*	0 *godhva*	1 *godhvia*
P 1	8 *godhon*	0 *godhyen*	0 *godhven*	0 *godhvien*
P 2	10 *godhowgh*	0 *godhyewgh*	0 *godhvewgh*	0 *godhviewgh*
P 3	1 *godhons*	3 *godhyens*	0 *godhvons*	0 *godhviens*
I	0 *godhor*	0 *godhyes*	0 *godhves*	0 *godhvies*

	Pres. subj.	Impf. subj.	Imperative	Future
S 1	0 *godhviv*	3 *godhven*	———	1 *godhvydhav*
S 2	1 *godhvi*	4 *godhves*	3 *godhvydh*	0 *godhvydhydh*
S 3	5 *godhvo*	2 *godhve*	0 *godhvydhes*	3 *godhvydh*
P 1	0 *godhvyn*	0 *godhven*	0 *godhvydhyn*	0 *godhvydhyn*
P 2	0 *godhvowgh*	0 *godhvewgh*	7 *godhvydhewgh*	0 *godhvydhowgh*
P 3	0 *godhvons*	0 *godhvens*	0 *godhvydhens*	0 *godhvydhons*
I	1 *godher*	0 *godhves*	———	0 *godhvydher*

	Verbal noun	Past participle
	57 *godhvos*	8 *godhvedys*

Notes:

1. The verbal paradigm has been taken from Brown; all forms are given in their unmutated state.

2. The figures in front of each word indicate the number of examples of that particular tense and person being found in the Middle Cornish texts (including *Creacon of the World*); there are 302 attestations in all.

3. The data in the table are slightly different from that presented by Lewis.

4. Of the fifty-six possible forms of the verb, twenty-two are attested (39 per cent); the remainder have been reconstructed fairly easily and with little doubt in this case, because *godhvos* is a compound of *bos* 'to be', a verb which is well attested.

5. The preterite is not represented in the extant literature, presumably because its use would be confined to sudden flashes of inspiration, e.g., 'As soon as I saw her, I knew that she was the girl for me'. No such flashes are evident in historical Cornish.

6. The phonemic nature of the orthography means that the cluster /ðv/, which occurs in most of the forms, is written <dhv>. The spellings recorded in Middle Cornish reflect rather its phonetic realization in internal sandhi [θf] (>[ff]] in rapid speech).

TABLE 5
Gendall's reconstruction of the verb *gothaz/guthvaz* 'to know' for Kernuak

	Present		Imperfect	
S 1	3 *oram/orama/ora ve*		1 *oyan ve*	
S 2	1 *usta*		0 *oyas che*	
S 3m	10 *orava/ore e*		2 *oya e*	
S 3f	*ore hye*		*oya hy*	
P 1	2 *oren nye*		0 *oyan nye*	
P 2	0 *oro why*		0 *oyo why*	
P 3	0 *oranz/ore angye*		0 *oyanz/oya angye*	

	Conditional		Past subjunctive	
S 1	0 *uffeean ve*	(*uffyen*)	1 *cuffan ve*	
S 2	0 *uffeeas che*	(*uffyes*)	0 *cuffas*	
S 3m	1 *uffeea e*	(*uffya*)	0 *cuffa e*	
S 3f	0 *uffeea hye*	(*uffya*)	0 *cuffa hye*	
P 1	0 *uffean nye*	(*uffyen*)	0 *cuffan nye*	
P 2	0 *uffeo why*	(*uffyo*)	0 *cuffo why*	
P 3	0 *uffeean angye*	(*uffyenz*)	0 *cuffan'gye*	(*cuffanz*)

Notes:

1. The verbal paradigm has been taken from Gendall (1992, p. 72); where his reconstructed forms elsewhere disagree with this, the latter are indicated in brackets.
2. The paradigms for the first three of the four tenses are shown in the lenited state; the past subjunctive is shown in the provected state.
3. The figures in front of each word indicate the numer of examples of that particular tense and person which are given in Gendall (1991) (including four examples from *Creacon of the World*); there are 21 attestations in all. The figures given for the third person singular masculine form actually apply to all cases of the third person singular.
4. Gendall (1992) gives alternative forms in certain cases; these are indicated with an oblique stroke (/).
5. Of the twenty-four possible forms of the verb, eight are attested (33 per cent); the remainder have been reconstructed; as Gendall freely admits, the reconstruction of the conditional and the past subjunctive each depend on single examples in *Creacon of the World*.
6. Gendall (1991) gives the verbal noun as *gothaz/guthaz*, and the past participle as *guthvethez*. In Gendall (1992), the verbal noun is given as *gothaz/guthvaz*.
7. The present tense as given by Gendall represents a re-modelling in Late Cornish, using the third person singular as a root; the same re-modelling occurs in some Breton dialects.

(a) The full paradigm of the verb is by no means extant in the texts, and considerable reconstruction was necessary in both cases; 61 per cent for Kernewek Kemmyn and 67 per cent for Kernuak.

(b) The total number of extant examples used for Kernewek Kemmyn is approximately fourteen times that used for Kernuak, indicating that the reconstruction of the former is likely to be more reliable.

(c) No recourse to Breton or to Welsh was necessary to reconstruct the eight tenses in Kernewek Kemmyn.

(d) There are variant forms in Kernuak.

It is clear that Penglase's statements are awry so far as this verb is concerned. If, as he states, Unified Cornish and Kernewek Kemmyn are 'invented', and by implication, 'artificial', then so is Kernuak.

Richness

The sources whence Kernewek Kemmyn and Kernuak are drawn are unequal in size. Kernuak is ideologically restricted to Late Cornish as a source (though, as shown above, Gendall has borrowed extensively from dialect including the Tregear Homilies). Kernewek Kemmyn, on the other hand, although based on a date of c.1500, takes words from all phases, and re-spells them (wherever possible) to accord with the phonological base. This philosophy may appear Procrustean, but it makes the revived language immeasurably richer, and a suitable vehicle for future development, allowing the use of different registers.

This richness is also a reflection of the different status of Middle and Late Cornish. In 1500, Middle Cornish was spoken by about 33,000 people (48 per cent of the Cornish population), including an educated class which was responsible for the mystery plays, i.e. a real literature. In 1700, Late Cornish was geographically and socially restricted to about 5000 speakers (5 per cent of the population), all bilingual, 'deserted by the educated' as Gendall put it.[35] Fleuriot has asserted that when a language is spoken in a bilingual society under the influence of a dominant language, one has no longer got the true language.[36] One has only to look at Brittany today to see the truth of this statement.

Similarly, while Kernuak has no access to a historical repertoire of rich poetry and has likewise produced no contemporary literature of note, there has been an upsurge of interest in poetry in Kernewek Kemmyn.[31] A new group, Berdh Arnowydh Kernewek, has been giving public recitals of their works, in Cornish with English translation, or vice versa. Saunders and Snell are writing poetry in Cornish using specifically Celtic verse-forms. The present author has translated into Kernewek Kemmyn the whole of *Die Zauberflöte,* and made it rhyme and scan for the purposes of performance.

In short, a Late Cornish base has a reduced competence compared with a Middle Cornish base. This was effectively recognised even *c.* 1700; to obviate the problem, Keigwin went back to Middle Cornish,[38] Lhuyd drew on Welsh, while the remaining members of the Newlyn School drew on English; today Gendall turns to dialect.

Revival and planning
Since it is impossible *sensu stricto* to recover historical Cornish (of any phase), one has to question how important Penglase's goal of authenticity really is. Do we want to write Cornish in a spectral form of the original, sticking as closely as possible to the spelling of some historical epoch, or do we want Cornish to be a vibrant, living, modern, everyday language, capable of expressing ideas in more than one register?

'The real concern was language planning rather than language revival', writes Penglase. Indeed it was; and it still is. This is the nub of the argument. For the speakers of Kernewek Kemmyn, the revival phase passed long ago. To them, Cornish is a modern language in its own right, which is going its own way, keeping true to the spirit of historical Cornish, but not being straitjacketed by it.

THE ORTHOGRAPHY OF KERNEWEK KEMMYN
The principles behind the orthography of Kernewek Kemmyn were laid down by the author:

(a) It must be as phonemic as possible.
(b) It must not, however, be so phonetic as to mask the etymology of words.
(c) It should reconcile, as far as possible, the desires of different groups to pronounce Cornish in approximately Middle Cornish and Late Cornish fashions.
(d) It should not appear so different from the Unified system as to be rejected by the users of Cornish.

It is of interest to see how far these principles have succeeded.

The phonemic principle
The properties desirable in an orthography of Cornish are not the same for Middle Cornish speakers and for learners of Revived Cornish. All the players in the medieval mystery plays, one supposes, knew how to pronounce Cornish, and the writing was merely 'a visual adjunct to aural memory'.[39] Today, because most people learn Cornish from books, the orthography must be fixed, and as phonemic as possible.

The Middle Cornish orthography satisfies neither of these require-ments, and was therefore replaced by one which does. The texts are still available in their original spelling to anyone who wishes to study them, and the orthography of Kernewek Kemmyn is not so far removed from those originals. One of the valuable results to emerge from the current language debate is a wider acknowledgement that texts in historical Cornish should be published in their original spelling.

A phonemic orthography is one in which each phoneme (i.e. a minimal contrastive unit of sound in the phonological system of a language) is represented by a separate grapheme (i.e. a minimal distinctive unit of writing in a language); and each grapheme represents a separate phoneme. It is easy to learn to read languages with phonemic orthographies, such as Esperanto, because a given set of letters always stands for the same group of sounds. The orthography of Modern Welsh is often held up as a shining example of a system which is almost perfectly phonemic (for a critical examination, see Humphreys);[40] it is the result of a scientific spelling reform by Morris Jones.[41] However, it must be acknowledged that even in this 'near perfect' system there are built-in traps (as learners of Welsh soon discover) which means that sometimes only a knowledge of the etymology of a word permits one to spell it correctly.

In practice, the phonemic principle is a goal which was aspired to, but not quite reached in Kernewek Kemmyh. The principal deviations from the principle are:

(a) The occlusive consonantal phonemes /b,d,g/ are spelled <b,d,g> initially and medially, and finally in stressed monosyllables, but <p,t,k> finally in unstressed monosyllables. This takes account of the commonest realisation, and was done to reduce the changes from the Unified spelling. Thus the commonest adjectival ending appears as *-ek* rather than as *-eg* (as in Breton).

(b) The unstressed neutral vowel known as schwa has no separate distinct grapheme. This is one of the few features of the historical phonology which remains difficult; which words actually contained schwa? Lhuyd is quite helpful in indicating that the reflexive prefix contained it; this is spelled *om-* in Kernewek Kemmyn, as in Unified spelling, but elsewhere it is difficult to identify with certainty.

These deviations are minor, and any difficulties which they cause are far outweighed by the substantial benefit which a phonemic spelling brings. This benefit is that Cornish is far easier to learn. The spelling of Kernewek Kemmyn also indicates the length of vowels (which

Unified Cornish does not), by application of the quantity rules. Once beginners have mastered these rules, and the near one-to-one relationship between writing and sounds, and know how Cornish is stressed, they can read Cornish with a fairly accurate pronunciation. The result is that Kernewek Kemmyn is a great success.

Relationship to Breton and Welsh

Penglase finds it strange that Cornish orthography should be such that one can recognise the relationship of words to their Breton and Welsh cognates. As a Celtic scholar in a European context, it seems to the present author quite natural. It seems sensible to spell /i/ as <i>, the same grapheme for the same phoneme as in Breton and Welsh (see Table 2).

Reconciliation of Middle and Late Cornish pronunciations

One reasons for choosing *c.*1500 as a date for the phonological base was that it goes some way towards Late Cornish, without losing the Middle Cornish grammar. Because the orthography is based closely on the phonology (and is not, as one sometimes hears, a creation of the present author), it inherently contains the potential for some of the sound-changes which were manifest at a later date. For example, the use of <nn> for /nn/ allows those speakers who prefer the realisation [dn] readily to recognise those word which contain /nn/. Other possibilities are shown in Table 6.

TABLE 6
Realisations of selected graphemes in Kernewek Kemmyn

Phonetic environment	*Graphemes*	*Mid Cornish style*	*Late Cornish style*
after a stressed vowel	*mm, nn*	[mm, nn]	[bm, dn]
long in open monosyllables	*i, y*	[iː, Iː]	[ΔI, iː]
long in closed monosyllables	*i, y, e, a*	[iː, Iː, Eː, aː]	[iː, eː, eː, aː]
long in closed monosyllables	*oe, ou, eu, u*	[oː, uː, œː, yː]	[uː, ΔΩ, eː, iː]
unstressed	*-ek*	[-Ek]	[-ak]

Differences from the Unified system

The differences between Unified Cornish and Kernewek Kemmyn are slight. They are smaller than the differences between either and the spelling of the *Ordinalia*. Yet so sensitive are some people to the written word that they over-emphasise these differences. One change to the orthography of Cornish has probably caused more comment than any other. This is the universal use of <k> to represent the /k/ phoneme. The adoption of <k> in places where English uses <c> immediately makes Kernewek Kemmyn appear un-English, and therefore 'foreign' to those used to English orthography. Unified Cornish followed the English convention, whereby <c> is used before <a,o,u; l,r> and <k> otherwise. (In addition, the cluster /kw/ was spelled <qu>). There was a tendency to follow the same rule in Middle Cornish, but it was not absolute, however; <k> was often found before <a>, especially in *Beunans Meriasek.* The universal use of /k/ makes the mutation table easier, as shown in Table 7.

TABLE 7
Phonetic Comparisons

	Phonetics		Kernewek Kemmyn		Unified system	
radical state	[k-]	[kw-]	<k->	<kw>	<c-, k->	<qu>
lenition	[g-]	[gw-]	<g->	<gw>	<g->	<gw->
spirantization	[h-]	[hw-]	<h->	<hw->	<h->	<hw->

Although the orthography of Kernewek Kemmyn was carefully chosen so as to be as close as possible to the Unified system, while aspiring to the phonemic principle, some people have been unable to bring themselves to use it. In the main, these are people who learned Cornish many years before the reform, and had therefore been attached to the Unified spelling for a much longer period. They include some people whose written fluency is much greater than their spoken fluency.

CONCLUSIONS

Conclusions concerning the suitability of different phases of historical Cornish as a base for Revived Cornish are:

1. Because the volume of extant Middle Cornish material is greater than the volume of Late Cornish material, less reconstruction is necessary when starting from a Middle Cornish base.
2. Doubts about word-order in sentences, occasioned by the fact that most of Middle Cornish is in verse, have been resolved.

3. Middle Cornish has the potential for more than one register, offering a greater choice of styles to the author than does Late Cornish.
4. Middle Cornish is closer to Breton and to Welsh than is Late Cornish.
5. Both external and internal evidence (Table 8) indicate that Late Cornish was heavily influenced by English, which to most Cornish speakers makes it unacceptable as a base.

TABLE 8
The influences of English on Late Cornish

PHONOLOGICAL

- Changes to the vocoids [-iː], [uː], [yː], [aU] were the same in Cornish as in English
- The non-English consonant /x/ was lost or changed
- The quantity rules changed to conform with the English system

MORPHOLOGICAL

- The Cornish plural suffix *-oryon* was sometimes replaced by the English *-s*
- The pronominal prepositions were changed to an analytic form, as in English

SYNTACTIC

- Main verbal forms were replaced by periphrastic forms, as in English

Conclusions concerning the actual reconstructions are:

6. The relationship between the spelling and the recommended pronunciation is much more clear-cut (being nearly phonemic) in the case of Kernewek Kemmyn, making it easier to learn.
7. Kernewek Kemmyn is richer than Kernuak, particularly as regards the lexicon and the flexibility of word-order, so that the quality and range of literature (particularly poetry) are potentially much greater.
8. The superiority of Kernewek Kemmyn is demonstrated by the fact that it is the form of Cornish used by the majority of Cornish speakers and writers.

NOTES AND REFERENCES

1. Charles Penglase, 'Authenticity in the Revival of Cornish', *Cornish Studies: Two*, 1994.
2. Oliver Padel, *The Cornish Writings of the Boson Family*, Redruth, 1975.
3. Wella Brown, *A Grammar of Modern Cornish*, 2nd ed., Saltash, 1993.

4. Tim Saunders, 'Cornish—Symbol and Substance', in Cathal O'Luain, *For a Celtic Future*, Dublin, 1984.

5. Richard Gendall, *A Student's Dictionary of Modern Cornish*, 2nd ed., Menheniot, 1990; Richard Gendall, *A Student's Grammar of Modern Cornish*, Menheniot, 1991.

6. Henry Jenner, *Handbook of the Cornish Language*, London, 1904.

7. Robert Morton Nance, *Cornish For All*, St Ives, 1929.

8. Ken George, *The Pronunciation and Spelling of Revived Cornish*, Saltash, 1986.

9. Richard Gendall, *An Curnoack Hethow*, Menheniot, 1992.

10. Caroline Vink, 'Be Forever Cornish! Some Observations on the Ethnoregional Movement in Contemporary Cornwall', *Cornish Studies: One*, 1993; Philip Payton and Bernard Deacon, 'The Ideology of Language Revival', in Philip Payton (ed.), *Cornwall Since the War: The Contemporary History of a European Region*, Redruth, 1993; Gendall, 1990; Gendall, 1991.

11. Ken George, *Gerlyver Kernewek Kemmyn: An Gerlyver Meur*, Saltash, 1993.

12. Glanville Price, *The Languages of Britain*, London, 1984; Glanville Price, 'Cornish Language and Literature', in Glanville Price (ed.), *The Celtic Connection*, Gerrards Cross, 1992.

13. Edward Lhuyd, *Archaeologia Britannica*, 1707 (fascimile eds., Oxford, 1969; Shannon, 1971); W. Stokes, *The Life of St Meriasek, Bishop and Confessor: A Cornish Drama*, London, 1872.

14. H.Lewis, *Llawlyfr Cernyweg Canol*, 2nd ed., Cardiff, 1946.

15. Oliver Padel, 'The *mawr a beth* Construction in Cornish', *Cornish Studies* 6, 1978; Oliver Padel, 'More of the *tek a wel* Construction', *Cornish Studies* 7, 1979.

16. Brown, 1993.

17. Brown, 1993.

18. Padel, 1975.

19. Robert Morton Nance, *A New Cornish-English Dictionary*, St Ives, 1938, new ed., Redruth, 1990; Robert Morton Nance, *A Cornish-English Dictionary*, Marazion, 1955

20. George, 1993; Ken George, *Gerlyver Kernewek Kemmyn: Dyllans Servadow Sowsnek-Kernewek*, Saltash, 1995.

21. Oliver Padel, *Cornish Place-Name Elements*, Nottingham, 1985.

22. Ken George, 'The Reforms of Cornish—Revival of a Celtic Language', *Language Reform* 4, 1989.

23. M. Wakelin, *Language and History in Cornwall*, Leicester, 1975.

24. S. Ó'Coileán, 'Late Cornish: An Accurate Reconstruction of the Sound System', unpub. dissertation for BA (Hons) by independent study.

25. Ken George, 'A Phonological History of Cornish', upub. doctoral thesis, University of Western Brittany, 1984.

26. Kenneth Jackson, *Language and History in Early Britain*, Edinburgh, 1953; Kenneth Jackson, *A Historical Phonology of Breton*, Dublin, 1967.

27. See R. Williams, *Lexicon Cornu-Britannicum*, Llandovery and London, 1865.
28. Gendall, 1990.
29. Gendall, 1993.
30. George, 1986; George, 1993.
31. N. J. A. Williams, 'A Problem in Cornish Phonology', in Martin J. Ball, James Fife, Erich Poppe, and Jenny Rowlands (eds), *Celtic Linguistics: Readings in the Brythonic Languages*, Philadelphia, 1990; Ken George, 'An Delinyans Pellder-Termyn: Toul Rag Studhya an Yeth Kernewek', in G. le Menn (ed.), *Bretagne et Pays Celtiques*, 1992.
32. Penglase, 1994.
33. R. Edwards, *Verbow Kernewek*, Saltash, 1995.
34. Brown, 1993; Gendall, 1991; Gendall, 1992.
35. Gendall, 1991.
36. L. Fleuriot, pers. comm., 13 December 1986.
37. G. M. Sandercock, *Geryow*, 1995; Alan Kent and Pol Hodge, *Out of the Ordinalia*, St Austell, 1995.
38. Robert Morton Nance, 'John Keigwin's Translation of King Charles the First's letter of thanks . . . to Cornwall', *Old Cornwall*, 1:4, 1:5.
39. Tim Saunders, 'Commentary on the Two Orthographies', unpub. paper, 1979.
40. H. L.Humphreys, *La Langue Galloise—Une Presentation*, Brest, 1980.
41. J. Morris Jones, *A Welsh Grammar—Historical and Comparative*, Oxford, 1913.

VOICE FROM A WHITE SILENCE: THE MANUSCRIPTS OF JACK CLEMO

John Hurst

INTRODUCTION

An author's manuscripts are always interesting—those mute witnesses to the processes of creation. In the case of Jack Clemo they have an additional, urgent human interest. They reveal on every page the adverse conditions under which they were written. Clemo has indicated in many contexts that, even without those adversities of alternating and ultimately simultaneous blindness and deafness, his road would have been a solitary and unfashionable one. By nature he is one of those who 'hear a different drummer' (in Thoreau's phrase which lends its title to Clemo's 1986 volume of poems).[1] Those twin adversities have, however, moulded his work and its manner of creation in ways which the manuscripts reveal, and upon which it is part of the purpose of this study to cast light.

Dr Clemo deposited his manuscripts in the University of Exeter Library progressively from 1980 until his death in July 1994. Indeed, one of his final wishes was that certain manuscripts not hitherto lodged with the university should be conveyed there at an early opportunity. For the most part these were of recent work to be included in a volume in 1995 entitled *The Cured Arno*.[2] In addition, valuable earlier work was included relating primarily to a collection of poems published in 1967, *Cactus on Carmel*.[3] With the receipt of this material the processes of creation of the greater part of his published works and a considerable portion of his early unpublished fiction and verse, are available for study. The only significant omission is of some of the early tales by which he became known in Cornwall during the 1930s. Several of these were reprinted in *Bouncing Hills* in 1990.[4] The manuscripts constitute, then, a remarkable resource for students of this distinctive and unique body of work.

The manuscripts are held in the Rare Book room of the main building of the University Library where they can be studied on request and under appropriately controlled conditions. They are housed in numbered boxes in order of receipt. In consequence material is not necessarily grouped together. Work on unpublished novels may be found in the same box as manuscripts or proof copies of published poetry, or indeed of miscellanea. It has been necessary, therefore, in compiling this study to adopt the somewhat artificial method of indicating the box in which material is currently held. For example, the original handwritten manuscript of *Wilding Graft* (1948)[5] is in Box 5; the original typescript is in Box 4. There might be thought to be a *prima facie* case for consolidating related material into the same Box. The matter is not, however, so simple. Much of the work is written in exercise books (commonly red *Silvine* books). A single exercise book may well contain material in different modes. The fourth notebook for *Broad Autumn* (1975),[6] for instance, contains a valuable prose article 'Towards Christian Balance' ultimately entitled for publication in *Moorlands Message*, Summer 1974, not directly related to the poems (Box 2). Some consolidation might be possible at some time, but it is hoped that the annotated contents list which will constitute part of this study may assist in the complex task of making constructive use of the material.

THE GROWTH OF A WRITER

It is not the primary purpose of this study to provide a detailed examination of the processes involved in, for instance, Jack Clemo's development as a novelist to the point at which he turned from fiction to poetry; or to outline in detail the complex processes of rewording and recasting of all the poems. The materials available for that study will be indicated, their relationship to his situation at the time will be outlined, and the processes involved in the detailed creation of one particular poem ('The Riven Niche' in *Cactus on Carmel*)[8] examined, together with some indication of the particular problems posed by the Manuscripts.

Some outline of Jack Clemo's life is necessary as a framework if what follows is to prove fully comprehensible. Much of the story is to be found in detail in the two autobiographical volumes *Confession of a Rebel* (published in 1949) and *Marriage of a Rebel* (1980), together with the *The Invading Gospel* (1958) and the remarkable pamphlet written by his mother Eveline Clemo, *I Proved Thee at the Waters*.[9] For the immediate purpose, however, certain basic facts are relevant.

Born in 1916 into an environment rich in love and faith but materially poor (his father was killed in action in 1917), Clemo early showed unusual talent made clear in his first school years. A period of blindness when he was five was succeeded by a further attack of iritis when he was thirteen which effectively ended his schooling. Despite ability he had already discovered that his mental world lay elsewhere. 'It was obvious that I could go no further along the common scholastic road.' He read, however, voraciously, and soon turned to writing himself, publishing his first dialect story in 1931. Soon, however, his naturally solitary tendencies were to be reinforced by the onset of severe ear trouble. 'Before my nineteenth birthday I was too deaf to take part in conversation.' Nevertheless throughout the following fifteen years he worked determinedly, one might almost say doggedly, at developing his skills as a writer of fiction, the long years being at last crowned with success by the publication in 1948 of *Wilding Graft*:

> The struggle of nearly two decades, involving fifty-three rejections of my novels, including seven refusals of *Wilding Graft*, was over, and I found myself, an uneducated villager, set incongruously among the most brilliant intellectuals of the day.[10]

Already, however, the limitations of deafness for a writer of fiction were becoming clear. He speaks of how, during the Second World War 'my deafness drove me almost to despair . . . the whole district was teeming with stories I could not get at'. Unable to hear vernacular speech, he turned away from the writing of fiction just at the point at which he had found success.

But by now his creative energies had found a new and striking outlet. Clemo had written a few poems during adolescence, but had totally ceased to write in verse. 'I was therefore, astonished when, early in February 1945 I came in from a stroll . . . and immediately wrote, quite effortlessly, some lines which I knew at once were the finest poetry I had ever penned.' The poem was the celebrated and much anthologised 'Christ in the Clay-pit'. It readily found publication. One door was closing; but another had opened. He was to continue work on revising the then unpublished *The Shadowed Bed* but, failing to find a publisher, this too was laid aside, only to be rapidly revised and published in 1986.[11] Effectively he had ceased to be a writer of fiction.

He advanced, however, steadily as a poet, and his growing reputation ensured the ready publication of his first volume of autobiography *Confession of a Rebel*, and subsequently of the 'Christian manifesto' *The Invading Gospel*, and such short prose pieces as became available. Already, however, further eye trouble had developed. By the end of 1955 he was, as far as reading and writing were concerned, totally blind. The implications for his working methods were clearly far-reaching. Much of his work had been typed; but he was quite unable to touch type. Moreover he could no longer see, even in the months before total blindness developed, to write as hitherto. Faced with blindness he evolved a new style of writing.

Even the very means of communication with the world needed to be re-established as the slow and deliberate method of writing letters upon his palm was developed. Eventually he would learn to read braille, and to touch type. Formidable efforts were made to dictate *The Invading Gospel* to his mother who herself had never typed (though with great devotion she subsequently learnt to do so). The method of dictation, however, was abandoned. Clemo outlined clearly the method of working that he had developed. 'I haven't found it more difficult to write poems since I went blind. They come quickly in the atmosphere of fulfilment. I scribble them in a notebook and then type them.'[12] And, 'I think out a poem and plan it in my mind, then I type it before I have forgotten it. Yes it's a strain on the memory and I forget poems in a few months.'[13]

The Manuscripts, however, reveal a more detailed picture. The handwritten stage reveals numerous alterations, recastings and emendations. For the most part the manuscripts are carefully and systematically dated—this alone being of great assistance to their use—and it can be seen that normally a poem will be completed over a few days, even, occasionally within a single day. Less commonly, however, a longer period may be necessary. The composition of 'The Riven Niche' occupied four months and, as is not uncommon in Clemo's work, was assigned a variety of titles during this process. More recently the poem 'Schooling' in *The Cured Arno* was worked over during July 1992, again, and in a different *Silvine* exercise book, in August, and again between 12 and 21 November, before a final version was achieved. The resources of memory required are clearly considerable, not least when it is clear from the manuscripts that other poems were also claiming his attention throughout the period.

The physical appearance of the manuscripts is also significant. The early work written up to the onset of his blindness is written in an excessively crabbed and miniscule hand. Where a typed version exists it is often accompanied by interlinear handwritten alterations. Jottings for later work may well be found on the reverse. Ideas may be sketched on the back of bills or copies of letters. The drafts of the early novels are often couched in larger size exercise books or bound into folders. Pagination is by no means always consistent, and inconsistently numbered sections may be found cheek by jowl within the same binder. Paradoxically, the manuscripts written under the method developed as his blindness was encroaching are in many ways clearer. Occasionally a line will overrun the page end. Even more rarely the draft of one poem may be superimposed upon another. For the most part, however, the use of a line guide enabled him to lay his drafts out systematically upon the page. Lines are usually spaced two or three exercise book lines apart, leaving room for emendations, suggestions for development or restructuring. Handwriting is bolder than that found in the earlier work. It is printed rather than cursive, though occasionally letters may flow together. Sometimes the script may undulate around the line, but it is, for the most part, regular and well spaced. The letters are frequently not fully formed and, as might be expected, may be inconsistent in size e.g. a 'd' may be smaller than an 'a'. This can, particularly when two partially formed letters flow together, make decipherment difficult. There is, however, a systematic confidence about the presentation of this work which has struck some readers as surprising. Clemo's own comment provides all the explanation needed.

> Many people are puzzled that my poetry broadened out so much after I went blind. One would expect blindness to narrow a poet and make him pre-occupied with his own inner life. But my circumstances were exceptional. While I had good sight I was pre-occupied with my own inner life because I was lonely and had a hard financial struggle. Soon after I went blind I was in a position to marry and this changed everything for the better.[14]

MANUSCRIPTS OF FICTION

The evolution of Jack Clemo's fiction is complicated and awaits detailed study.[15] Written in conditions of isolation and spiritual introversion, the manuscripts bear witness to years of pertinacious and dedicated work, and repeated rejection by publishers. Moveover, one draft novel merges into another, whole areas of material being re-used or re-adapted while other passages are rejected. The following notes are arranged in sequence of composition and by reference to box in which currently housed.

'Travail' 1931 (Box 3); fragments of an early novel written at fifteen. Satirical comments by author written at a later date. Hand-written. Brown folder.

'March Dawn' 1931, (Box 3); reworking of 'Travail'. Read and annotated by Clemo's former schoolmaster, W. S. Pellymounter.

Satirical comments by author written at a later date. Handwritten.

'A Star Shall Lead' 1932-33 (Box 3); fifth version of above. The first format to be typed and submitted to a publisher. Manuscript version in small neat handwriting.

'The Former Rain' 1936 (Box 1); 'with personal notes, lists of early stories and poems, also some writing done by the child Barbara. The printed nature notes at the end were used as guides for the descriptive passages'. Clemo recounts his friendship with Barbara Rowse in *Confession of a Rebel*. His determined lack of interest in the natural world as a young man, also detailed in *Confession of a Rebel* rendered the Nature Notes necessary if reasonable verisimilitude was to be achieved. Pages are clearly lost from the early part of the notebook and these, presumably, contained the lists referred to which are unfortunately not present.

'Private Snow' 1936–39, revised 1945 (Box 1); early type-written portions, personal messages and drawings made by Clemo to amuse the child Barbara. This is the draft novel which Clemo submitted to Q. for his comments with the hope that he might assist its publication in some manner. Q. expressed some admiration for the quality of the novel but clearly was ill at ease with its stark portrayal of Cornish life.[16] 'Private Snow' incorporates some material from earlier work. Clemo comments revealingly on his working methods at this time; speaking of an earlier novel rejected by the publishers he says:

> it had one or two good scenes, and these were re-written and fitted into 'Private Snow', with which I was progressing slowly . . . The task was difficult, and the building up of this book alternated with an attempt to recast the one which had raised such hopes . . . The tendency to patch and re-write old incidents instead of inventing new ones was increasingly characteristic of my method, and was probably due to my deafness, the inability to get in touch with active life that would supply fresh material.[17]

Clemo subsequently worked on novels entitled 'Penance of the Seed', drafted in 1941, revised 1944–45 and finally reshaped in 1946 (Box 4), and 'Unsunned Tarn', 1937–46 (Box 3). On the title page this is described as 'incorporating "Private Snow" '. These three Manuscripts were drawn together under the title 'The Dry Kiln' in 1950–51 (Box 4). On the front cover of his typescript, he says: 'This novel is a condensed trilogy combining "Private Snow", "Unsunned Tarn" and "Pennance of the Seed", with fresh material added in 1950–51'.

While this complex process of creation was continuing, Clemo had turned, undoubtedly under the influence of the work of T. F. Powys, to the writing of a novel quite different in manner to anything he had written previously, and whose development was to be every bit as complex and protracted as that of 'The Dry Kiln'. Eventually it achieve publication in 1986 as *The Shadowed Bed*. The Manuscripts demonstrate the long process of development and during this evolution it was also variously entitled. The earliest version 1938 (Box 2) bears the title 'Lamb of the Green Bed', but attempts to reach another title are present on the title page of the typescript which indicate the words 'bed' and 'shadowed' as elements in a variety of hazarded titles. The typescript is extensively annotated between the lines and on the reverse. Page sequences in the later section are confused. At this stage the novel is not divided into Parts as it is in the 1948 and printed versions.

The 1948 version is also to be found in Box 2. It contains 386 pages of typescript with significant corrections. There is some apparently unrelated material handwritten on the reverse of pages 20–21 and pages 384-5. The novel now carries an important Preface much longer than that to be found in the printed version. It is, unfortunately, incomplete, breaking off in mid-sentence. It does not, however, carry the short poem 'in tribute to my Father' which prefixes the published novel. Prefixed quotations are from Eliot and Barth, only that from Eliot being retained for publication. The novel is at this stage divided into the three parts which were carried forward to publication. A condensed version written in 1952–53 is to be found in Box 7. The prefatory note shows affinity with the published form though has some marked differences. Tripartite structure and epigraphs are retained. The 'Poem to Father' is not yet present. The final format is to be found in Box 6—'mainly a typescript made in the early 1970s; some rewritten pages added later and final 1985 alterations stuck on'.

Wilding Graft. The development of this, the work by which Clemo established a national reputation, is less complex than that of either *The Shadowed Bed* or 'The Dry Kiln'. The original handwritten Manuscript dated 1942–46, is to be found in Box 5, and is written mainly on the reverse of sheets of earlier unpublished work. Unlike the published form it contains chapter headings and a chapter by chapter synopsis. There are extensive working corrections. The original typescript with printer's markings dated '1.9.47' is to be found in Box 4. It is clear that two leading characters were subject to a name change at a very late stage. The name of Bertha was originally Cora, and that of Martin originally Irving. On each occasion on which the original names appears a slip of paper bearing the new name in typescript has been glued on. In effect, the publication of *Wilding Graft* concluded Clemo's career as a novelist. Although *The Shadowed Bed* was not published until 1986 it was substantially complete by 1948. The short story 'The Clay Dump' published in Denys Val Baker's anthology of Cornish short stories, *One and All*,[18] in 1951 was based on a discarded chapter of a pre-war novel.

Clemo explained that 'my handicaps were beginning to hinder me as a prose writer. I had not heard a conversation since the War, and found it hard to invent spontaneous dialogue'.[19] If, however, fiction was no longer feasible, there was important work to be done in non-fictional prose.

MANUSCRIPTS OF NON-FICTIONAL PROSE

Major prose:
Confession of a Rebel 1941–45 (Box 1). A hard-back notebook contains (a) rough jottings dated 1941–45, (b) the full narrative, dated 1946–47, and (c) revisions dated 1948. Published 1949.

The Invading Gospel 1956–57. The particular conditions under which this 'Christian manifesto rather than spiritual autobiography' was written have already been referred to. The working papers are extensive consisting of (Box 5):

(a) *Max-Val* red exercise books containing 'jottings from which the book was memorised for dictation'. Some of these are dictated and are in his mother's hand, some are in his own hand.

(b) Two *Supreme* exercise books, the first containing 'jottings, synopses etc written by Jack Clemo with Bible text references written by his mother' and dated (see illustration 1). The second book contains Chapter 7 'The Rout of Tragedy' written by his mother at his dictation, and dated 1957, with a draft of the Preface at the end of the book.

(c) 'Complete Manuscripts penned by Jack Clemo's mother at his dictation' and contained in a red 'remade' exercise book, 1957. (Box 6) Manuscript for Preface of 3rd edition, 1985.

The Marriage of a Rebel (Box 1). Handwritten manuscript in nine *Silvine* exercise books; first chapter is preceded by Manuscript of essay 'Pilgrimage to Mappowder', 'the writing of which in October 1977 stimulated me to attempt another autobiography'.[20] (Box 5) contains:

(a) Typescript version of above with few alterations. 'I began writing this book at the end of 1977 scribbling small portions in notebooks and then typing them myself (I preferred typing to dictation)'. The phrase in brackets is on a slip of paper stuck over a deleted phrase. The original phrase is not fully decipherable but clearly refers to assistance from his wife Ruth.

(b) Typescript with printer's marking.

(c) Handwritten manuscript in red *Silvine* exercise book with few deletions or alterations and dated 27–28 February and 1–5 March 1988; being additional chapter 'The Palms and the Palace' for the 1988 edition.[21]

Miscellaneous prose

In addition to the article 'Pilgrimage to Mappowder' referred to above there is to be found.

(Box 2) Introduction to Newlyn Readings April 1970; located in Notebook 3 for *A Different Drummer*'; contains important note on working methods.

Article 'Towards Christian Doctrine'; dated 2–3 December 1972; published in *Moorlands Message*, Summer 1974; located in exercise book 4 for *Broad Autumn*; 'written after a meeting with Mary White-house.' Initial title (deleted), 'Those Tinkling Symbols'.

Article for Nanpean Womens' Institute; located in *Cactus on Carmel* notebook 1; dated 23 February 1949.

(Box 6) 'notes of prose Prefaces and text of Exeter University birthday celebration statement'; dated 8 March 1986; included also prose note for *A Different Drummer* and preface to *The Invading Gospel* (3rd edition).

(Box 8) Preface to Picture Book (sic) in *Cactus on Carmel* notebook 1; dated 14–17 May 1964. Text divided between back page of notebook and earlier section of book. Contains interesting argument on the aesthetic appeal of the Clay Country.[22]

MANUSCRIPTS OF POETRY

The collection is remarkably comprehensive, only a small amount of early work is missing. Moreover, because of the author's remarkably systematic manner of working subsequent to his blindness, the date of composition of the vast majority of the poems written since 1955 is identified. Earlier work is less precisely dated for the most part, but there is rarely any doubt as to the year of composition even of the earliest works. The working manuscripts are very detailed and reveal very clearly the scrupulous balancing of form and content that is so characteristic of Clemo's best work. There is much ancillary information also; various versions of titles, arrangements of the order of poems in the printed collections, drafts for annotatory notes. Taken together with the prose Manuscripts this body of material provides an almost unrivalled resource for the close study of an author.

'Twilight Where God Dwells' c 1934 (Box 5); 'These poems reflect Clemo's attachment to the girl Evelyn. He dramatized himself as an artist inspired by a girl called Brenigan'. Includes letter (dated 17 May 1934) from C.W. Daniel offering shared-cost publication but refusing to publish under full financial responsibility! Letter includes reasoned criticism. Many alterations, marginalia, doodles. Unpublished.

The Map of Clay; incorporates work published earlier in *The Clay Verge*[23] (1951), together with 'The Wintry Priesthood' (published in part in a Penguin Anthology in 1951) plus new material.

(Box 5):

(a) Manuscripts of Clemo's early poems, including draft of poems in *The Map of Clay* and unpublished portions of the original 50 poem Ms of *The Clay Verge*. Written and typed by Clemo at Goonamarris in 1955–56.

(b) 'The Wintry Priesthood'; described as 'A Poetic Sequence'. 'This Ms was placed on show in the Lion & Unicorn Pavilion, South Bank Exhibition, London, during the Festival of Britain (July 9–29 1951)'. Small unclear handwriting with many deletions and alterations; poems dated.

(Box 7): *The Map of Clay*; publisher's proof with markings; several alterations of order of printing of poems even at Galley Proof stage. Final stanzas of 'Modelled in Passion Week' supplied at proof stage. Theological proper names and pronouns consistently corrected to capitals.

Cactus on Carmel (published 1967). (Box 2): Two notebooks containing mainly material for this volume. Some material used in *The Echoing Tip* (published 1971) present. Notebook 1 contains material from 1964, 1965 and early 1966. Notebook 2 contains mainly 1966 material (see discussion of 'The Riven Niche' below). Some uncollected material. Extensive alterations and revisions. Draft order of poems for publication.

(Box 8): First handwritten draft incorporating some unpublished and uncollected poems; draft order for publication. Not in Clemo's hand. Galley proofs without publisher's markings.

The Echoing Tip 1971, (Box 2): Poems dated from May 1968–August 1971. Extensive revisions; draft order of poems. Several versions of title. Three red *Silvine* exercise books. Fragment of Alfred Wallis on brown paper mounted at front of one exercise book.

Poems for *I Proved Thee at the Waters* 1976, (Box 5): A small selection of otherwise uncollected poems appear at the end of the published book.[24] 'Some of them are new, others are slightly revised versions of poems he published in periodicals before going blind in 1955.' The drafts here are in an exercise book also containing poems for *Broad Autumn* and *A Different Drummer*.

Broad Autumn (published 1975), (Box 2): Four red exercise books glued together; handwritten with systematic revision and retitling; dated from 5 June 1972-27 March 1974. (Box 5): Several poems with poems for *A Different Drummer*. (Box 7): Proof with publisher's markings.

A Different Drummer (published 1986), (Box 2):

(a) Two *Silvine* books; poems dated from 13 March 1976–24 January 1979. The marked gap in poetic activity from 23 October 1977–19 November 1978 coincides partly with the writing of *Marriage of a Rebel*.

(b) One *A Different Drummer* poem, 'Eilidh Boadella', is to be found in another notebook also in Box 2, alongside poems to be found in *Banner Poems* and *Approach to Murano* and light verse.[25]

(c) (Box 5): Further *A Different Drummer* poems in an exercise book also containing poems for *Broad Autumn* and *I Proved Thee at the Waters* (see above).

(d) Box 6): Typescript 'rearranged by the publisher and annotated after acceptance January 1986'. This document contains interesting modifications to footnotes, usually to render them less tendentious. The original draft notes are to be found in:

(e) *Silvine* exercise book entitled 'Poems and Prose Notes 1985–1986'.

Banner Poems—A Decade of Cornish Verse (published 1989). These poems were published in the journal *Cornish Banner (An Baner Kernewek)*. The manuscripts are to be found, as indicated above, in Box 6 in two exercise books, one entitled 'Poems and Rhymes 1983–1985', the other 'Poems and Prose Notes 1985–1986'.

Approach to Murano (published 1993). Manuscripts are spread through three boxes and exercise books as follows: Box 5; 'Poems 1986–1988'; Box 6; 'Poems and Rhymes 1983–1985', also 'Poems and Prose Notes 1985–1986'. Box 8; Poems for *Banner Poems*, *Approach to Murano* and various magazines 1988-89.

The Cured Arno (published posthumously 1995). These extensive manuscripts are to be found in six exercise books in Box 8. Earlier books include poems for *Murano* and *Banner* (as above), and poems for *Cured Arno* are concentrated in the three final books bearing poems dated from 24 May 1991 to the final poem 'Quenched' on 21 May 1994.

An order of poems for publication is to be found at the end of the final exercise book. Poems show signs of intense revision in many cases and show intense poetic activity throughout the period unless interrupted by illness.

'Miscellaneous writings about but not by Jack Clemo', (Box 2): *Observer Colour Supplement* article 17 February 1980, 'A Vocation for Marriage' profile by Ena Kendall, photographs by Alain le Guernier.

(Box 5): Draft of unpublished article on Clemo by Helena Charles.

In studying the development of individual poems by Clemo it is important to be aware that most poems were originally published in a wide range of magazines, and that the magazine format may well differ in minor or significant details from the collected format. In addition to early unpublished work, a small number of later poems to be found in the manuscripts have either never been published or have not been transferred from magazine to collected format.

THE EVOLUTION OF 'THE RIVEN NICHE'

The Riven Niche
(to St Bernadette)

> A gilt-lettered phial;
> Water from the spring that flows
> Where your Lady's feet caressed the rose;
> Damp on my brow, the unfathomed sign of the Cross.
>
> Through the moist emblem
> I reach to your basilica,
> See poplars by the Gave, curved mountain shield,
> Small pounding mills
> Just clear of the forest; faggots and diadem
> On the blind earth where your heaven distils.
>
> The soft Cross of blessing
> Is a vision's gift, and the foreign features
> Melt to the inner mystery of that gaze
> Which you transmit—sometimes half-known
> In the scars of my native field.
> Barbed truth and blown veil
> Blend on the pleading stone.
>
> Before the piercing, on childhood's normal track,
> My raw life was so like yours:

Holding my pitcher to the wheezing pump
Or the valley spring-pipe, forty years back.

All waters fouled by clay sores
Around my home, except what the pump lifted
And that clear spurt in the niche
Between bridge wall and thorn-clump,
Where the poisoned brook crawled under the road.

Since then I've heard of creed-crashes,
Of broken moulds and the freedom
Of the unpierced ego to advance alone.
Does your Lady smile,
Or do the swords turn in her heart?
She rebuked the river voices,
Those glib demonic gibes of the passing current;
And now the nuclear wisdom flashes
And trimmed altars await the death-rays.

My spirit moves apart,
Dewy with the new seal, the answering
Unchanged print in the peasant mould.
Riven niche baulks river pride;
And as your baptism spreads I sense the gold
Of blooms on the feet that span the ages,
Fragrance of the wild rose guarding
Multifoliate grace, safe from the slandering tide.[26]

Jack Clemo's attention had turned towards the figure of St Bernadette of Lourdes some years before the writing of 'The Riven Niche'. He tells, in *The Marriage of a Rebel*, how at the time of the centenary of the events at Lourdes his mother had told him by writing on his palm about much of the newspaper comment on the topic, knowing his interest in visionary events.[27] At that stage he found himself comparing Bernadette's experience to that of the young American singing evangelist, Renée Martz, the exponent of what he refers to as 'God's jazz', and finding himself drawn to the vibrancy of the American girl rather than the French teenager that Bernadette had been, yet showing understanding of Bernadette's spiritual agony.

The poem 'Beyond Lourdes' in *The Map of Clay* took an uncharacteristically long period to reach its final form—four months. The same is true of 'The Riven Niche', the composition of which (from the evidence of the manuscripts) occupied from 24 May 1966 to 19

September of that year. Even the form reached at that date received further work before its publication in the *Cornish Review* in Spring 1967. The typed manuscript submitted to the journal is not present in the collection. The matter of Lourdes was clearly central to his developing vision. There is, however, clear indication that, even before the May 1966 draft, the matter had been much in his mind. During the years 1963–65 Clemo had developed a close friendship with a teacher to whom he refers as Mary. The account of this relationship, during which marriage was contemplated, is given in chapter 11 of *Marriage of a Rebel*. Though the relationship did not proceed, it was nevertheless one of great significance in his personal development and continued and deepened a process which had already started with the onset of his 'white blindness'.

Clemo describes this vital change in the Preface to the volume in which 'The Riven Niche' is printed, *Cactus on Carmel*; 'When the grey veil sealed me off I found it impossible to continue picturing the clay scenes . . . I had to broaden my range of images and subjects, using material derived from books, correspondents and family associations . . .'.[28] A major and direct result of the friendship with Mary was that it stimulated him to learn braille (and also to touch type). Together and in parallel they would read books of mutual interest—she in the conventional printed form, he in Braille. Together they read Franz Werfel's *The Song of Bernadette* in the early months of 1965. Clemo's attitude to and sympathies for Bernadette had however not been dormant in the period since the publication of 'Beyond Lourdes'. In 1961 a Roman Catholic visitor had brought him a phial of water from the Massabeille spring; 'as I sprinkled the drops on my forehead at intervals since then I had been drawn into a great mystery and benediction. Mary and I both accepted Bernadette's vision as authentic'.[29]

By the date of the first drafts of the poem in May 1966 the relationship with Mary was effectively over; but there is no indication in 'The Riven Niche' of the regret he clearly felt at the closing of a wished-for road forward. It is a poem of sensitivity and confidence.

There is a common pattern and a common difficulty to these poems of Clemo's blindness. Arising as they do from the reading of a particular book available in braille the details often relate closely to that book, though the reader is not necessarily given any clues as to the particular source being used. And so it is here. Many of the incidental details referred to in the poem relate closely to details in Franz Werfel's book, though it may well be that a close acquaintance with the more objective accounts of the Lourds appearances would provide similar information. From time to time in later volumes, especially in *A Different Drummer*, some background information helpful to the reader is supplied, but for the most part the reader has to develop an unstructured response. As part of the common pattern, Clemo will seek to relate, either in kinship or in difference, to his own experience. Both difficulty and pattern are present here. The manuscripts leave us in no doubt about the starting point of the poem—it is the phial of Lourdes water which gives the poem its initial title. First it is 'a small rubber phial'; but the second page of the first draft bears a marginal note 'gilt-lettered' and thus it remains in the subsequent versions.

A brief evocation of the Lourdes spring in similar terms to later versions leads, however, to the defining of a concern which he is later to abandon for the purposes of this poem—to establish a consistency —'no betrayal'—between his current affinity for Bernadette and his Calvinist background:

'I am not setting Lourdes against Geneva,
I only say you are elect'.

This vein continues into a second stanza which is totally absent from the final version. What is remarkable, however, is that the phrasing of this second stanza is to find its way into a much later poem—the title poem of the collection *Broad Autumn* published in 1975.

'Spirit matures without discarding
I leave no wreckage on a distant hill'

becomes in 1975:

'rue faith matures without discarding
I left no wreckage on those low rasped cones'

The draft then moves closer to later versions as it focuses on the modern religious division, modern secularism, and the ultimate expression of the evils of secularism, in Clemo's understanding of it, the nuclear threat—'the nuclear wisdom . . . the death-ray'.

Again we see Clemo reaching forward to a later poem. The subject of 'William Blake notes a Demonstration' is a CND march. Its argument is that Blake, the visionary, understands, as the marchers do not, that the nuclear threat can only be countered by spiritual renewal not secular protest. In a poem written shortly after 'The Riven Niche', 'Cactus in Clayscape', Blake and Bernadette are linked as inhabitants of 'the singing desert trodden by Blake and Bernadette'. Significantly, the sketches for that stanza are to be found at the bottom of the 19 September revision of 'The Riven Niche'.

The later stanzas of the 24 May version are close in structure and phrase to the later versions. Some refinements of phrase are still to come, along with some sharpening of perceptions, but he is still agitating the questions of his credal consistency. The parallel between his experience and Bernadette's is still to find its effective form for the purposes of *this* poem.

The version dated 6–7 June moves sharply nearer to the later form. The matter of 'credal consistency' is reduced to a single sentence:

> 'there is no betrayal
> Of my bare Bethel among Cornish kilns'

Instead there comes the vivid evocation of Bernadette's setting

> '. . . poplars by the Gave's mountain shield
> Small pounding mills
> Just clear of the forest'

And he moves towards establishing the relationship between his experience and Bernadette's as he evokes their twin responses to the Marian experience—'The soft cross of blessing'. Again the focus of the poem is moving from Clemo to Bernadette's vision. It is in this version that the opposition of natural law and miracle finds its poetic form. Referring to the incident recounted by Werfel in which Bernadette's 'lady' in the niche by her healing spring appears to still the turbulent waters of the mountain torrent (the Gave), Clemo speaks of how

> 'Riven niche baulks river pride'

The opposition of nature and grace is seen in the images of water.

Clemo has still not, however, solved to his satisfaction how to express the kinship of his experience and Bernadette's. Something is missing. Nine lines dated 3 July show him moving forward, though they are deleted in total. The link is already there. They are both of 'peasant mould'—the phrase which precedes 'riven niche baulks river pride'. The imaginative connection is established 'Lourdes hallows Goonamarris'—a new phrase that does not survive into the final form. Clemo too knew clear waters and polluted waters; the spring 'to which I held my pitcher forty years back' as he fetched water from the one local clear source in a 'raw life so like yours'. The direction is right;

the imaginative fusion established; but the passage is firmly deleted. Why?

There are, perhaps, two reasons. First as it stands it is still too abstract. He continues, in lines that did not survive:

'Local or cosmic the images abide
We are the witnesses'

He wants more image, less statement. Secondly, the 19 September stanza shows the images need a stanza to themselves. Here he is close to the final version of stanza 4 with its fully realised opposition of clear water (riven niche) and poisoned water (river pride). The correlation is established. The poem is formed. Even at this stage he is still seeking the further correlations. Two lines appended to the 19 September stanza establish yet another correlation. Again based on a phrase in Werfel he speaks of how

'I shared your gracious apathy'

but the additional correlation was seen as a diversion. The structure is now firm. The pure water-tainted water stanza becomes strongly placed as a hinge in the poem's development as stanza 4. Moreover, the title as we know it is now established. The 19 September manuscript shows three possible titles; Lourdes Water—Niche of Miracle—The Riven Niche.

Ironically, when the poem reached publication in the *Cornish Review* it had become—one feels by typographical error—The River Niche, though the phrase within the poem is printed correctly. Riven Niche it has remained; a key poem in Clemo's development. He has recognised its importance by including it in the *Selected Poems* in preference to the other Lourdes poem in *Cactus on Carmel.*

CONCLUSION

Other detailed aspects of the poem's evolution might be recounted. There is, in addition to the search for a structure appropriate to the vision, a constant refining of rhythm and of rhyme. For instance

'Men today speak of creed's ashes' (24 May)

becomes between the June draft and publication

'Since then I've heard of creed-crashes'

There is a constant balancing, refining of sound and sense. Enough has been said, however, to make clear the extraordinary power of the mental processes brought to bear, from within his world of 'white silence' upon the processes of creation. The manuscripts themselves are an extraordinary insight into these processes. Jack Clemo always resisted any concentration upon what others might regard as his handicaps. He was not, he insisted, a blind poet. He was a sighted poet who became blind. He was not a deprived poet. He was a poet, who through faith lived through deprivation to fulfilment. His final poems celebrate a still expanding world:

'I have grown and explored
In my faith's undivided world'
                              ('Broad Autumn')

ACKNOWLEDGEMENTS
The author would like to acknowledge help towards the preparation of this article to the Q. Fund which made a grant, to the staff of the University of Exeter Library (notably Mr Wyn Evans and Mrs G. Pine) for their unfailing help and courtesy, and above all to Jack Clemo himself for his continual encouragement.

NOTES AND REFERENCES
1. Jack Clemo, *A Different Drummer*, Padstow, 1986.
2. Jack Clemo, *The Cured Arno*, Newcastle-upon-Tyne, 1995.
3. Jack Clemo. *Cactus on Carmel*, London, 1967.
4. Jack Clemo, *Bouncing Hills*, Redruth, 1990.
5. Jack Clemo, *Wilding Graft*, London, 1948.
6. Jack Clemo, *Broad Autumn*, London, 1975.
7. *Moorlands Message*, Summer 1974.
8. Clemo, 1967, pp. 30–31.
9. Jack Clemo, *Confession of a Rebel*, London, 1949; *Marriage of a Rebel*, London, 1980; *The Invading Gospel*, 1958; Eveline Clemo, *I Proved Thee at the Waters*, Ilkeston, n.d.
10. Clemo, 1949, p. 240.
11. Jack Clemo, *The Shadowed Bed*, Tring, 1986.
12. Introduction to Newlyn Readings, 20 April 1978.
13. Ena Kendall, 'A Vocation for Marriage', *Observer Colour Supplement*, 17 February 1980.
14. Statement to students, 18 June 1977.

15. Throughout the discussion of the manuscripts, unattributed quotations are drawn from Jack Clemo's own entries on the manuscripts in question. Titles of works in the manuscripts are given here in inverted commas, with exception of those works subsequently published in book form which are italicised throughout.
16. Clemo, 1949, pp. 169–171.
17. Clemo, 1949, p. 135.
18. Denys Val Baker (ed.), *One and All*, London, 1951, pp. 26–69.
19. Clemo, 1980, p. 67.
20. Jack Clemo, 'Pilgrimage to Mappowder' in B. Humfrey (ed.), *Recollections of the Powys Brothers*, London, 1980.
21. Jack Clemo, *Marriage of a Rebel*, London, 1988 edition.
22. There seems to be no trace of this project or any indication that it was ever published.
23. Jack Clemo, *The Clay Verge*, London, 1951.
24. Eveline Clemo, n.d., pp. 25–38.
25. Jack Clemo, *Banner Poems*, St Austell, 1989; *Approach to Murano*, Newcastle-upon-Tyne, 1993.
26. *Cornish Review*, No. 5, Spring 1967.
27. Clemo, 1980, p. 108.
28. Clemo, 1967, p. 8.
29. Clemo, 1980, p. 122.

THE SIGNIFICANCE OF CORNISH AND SCILLONIAN NATURAL HISTORY

Stella Turk

INTRODUCTION

Many feel that Cornwall is 'a different country'. Certainly, it is almost an island with relative geographical isolation from the rest of Britain, yet with strong ancient and modern maritime links (including wildlife) with other parts of the world. Within this paradox of land isolation and sea connections, there is a key to much that characterises both Cornwall and the Isles of Scilly; indeed these factors are even more emphasised in the Scillies which warrant a separate essay. However, while the distinctiveness of Cornish history, culture and even geology is celebrated almost routinely, the individuality of Cornwall's fauna and flora is sometimes overlooked.

For its size, Cornwall has a greatly varied landscape—a veritable *multum in parvo*. North and south are different as are east and west; then there is the Lizard peninsula! Dr Paul Gainey (pers.comm.) describes this 'jewel' as being more diverse in the number of its marine and non-marine habitats and the number of species than any place of comparable size in the British Isles. It boasts 25 *Red Data Book (RDB)* species of flowering plants and 'ferns', let alone the *Red Data Book* species of mosses, liverworts and lichens. *RDB* species are those present in less that 1,610 km sqs, nationwide: one, at least, of the Lizard species is found nowhere else in the world. More can be learned of this peninsula in the publications of Bristol University Lizard Project,[1] the National Trust[2] and in Lawman.[3]

THE MARITIME CONTEXT

Looking at Cornwall in a wider setting, one can see the effects of the

Gulf Stream currents which culminate in the North Atlantic Drift. The effects of this are felt right up the west coast of Britain and Ireland, varying from the very subtle to the very obvious, but always more marked in Cornwall and the Isles of Scilly than elsewhere.

Nelson[4] shows that Cornwall has more species and specimens of Carribean drift seeds than either Ireland or Scotland which in turn have more than mainland Europe. Amongst these seeds there are great numbers produced by the Sea Pea (*Lathyrus japonica maritimus*), and Nelson[5] has shown that there are far more than could be obtained from the very few plants to be found in the South West; he concludes that they are trans-Atlantic drift seeds, a few of which find a suitable shingle beach on which to germinate. Many of the other seeds—species of *Ipomaea*, *Mucuna*, and *Entada*—have been grown from Cornish strandings as house plants after their long sea journey. For notes and illustrations of the species that have been found on Cornish shores, see Nelson.[6]

More spectacular riders of these currents are the marine turtles, of which the great Leathery Turtle can attain well over 2.5 metres in length. The smaller Loggerhead may reach our shores when quite small, and two such infants, stranded in 1984, were reared at Gweek Seal Sanctuary until they were strong enough to be flown back to the Bahamas. All turtles are now protected in our waters and there have been some brave and successful attempts to free Leathery Turtles from the crab-pot lines with which they are all too likely to become entangled, probably because they mistake the floats for the jellyfish on which they feed. Penhallurick[7] lists all the sightings and strandings for almost 250 years, and shows how the numbers of reports have increased.

The most impressive drifting incident known to the writer occurred in December 1986 when a fibre-glass speed-boat was found floating upside down off St Ives covered with West Indian marine life.[8] Seamen reckoned the boat would have been at sea for two years and that it may have been used for smuggling since it had been fitted with extra engines. Confirmation came from America that these high powered boats are used for contraband. Warm-water drift animals from the more southerly parts of their range are also carried to our shores by the dominant westerly winds which sweep up the Irish and English Channels. Some years we have numbers of *Vellella vellella*, commonly known as 'By-the-Wind Sailors', small relatives of the Portuguese Man o' War; species of *Janthina*, the Violet Sea-snails; and *Lepas fascicularis*, the Buoy Barnacle, so-called because it secretes its own float. The Channel is a great seasonal migration route for many marine mammals, birds and fishes. Dolphins and Basking Sharks are amongst the many animals that move up the Channel and Irish Sea from the more southern parts of their range in the spring.

Eckman,[9] writing of the Mediterranean-Atlantic fauna states that there 'is one coastal region which represents the northern limit of a larger number of species than any other coast; that is the western limit to the English Channel'. He gives decapod crustaceans (crabs, shrimps and prawns) as examples, with 9 per cent stopping in the area of northern Spain and 28 per cent at the entrance to the Channel. The entrance and adjacent area is also the southern limit for many northern species. This mix of warm and cold water species on Scillonian and Cornish coasts results in a rich biodiversity of marine life. During a recent analysis of marine mollusc species of the Scillies it was found that over three quarters (333 out of 416) of the species include the Mediterranean in their range, and over a quarter (109) reach their northern limits in the British Isles.[10]

It is important to remember that the British Isles as a whole have a wealth of marine life, with hundreds of species reaching their northern limits in our seas. Many of the marine species extend up the west coast to find their northern limit on the west coast of Scotland or the Scottish islands, but these same species are generally commoner in the far South West. Here, it is the scale that makes the phenomenon!

HABITATS

The following combination of attributes have dictated the sorts of wildlife that exist in Cornwall:

* Geographical position as the most south-westerly part of UK.
* Wetness, with sea mists as well as rain. Indeed, the humidity in Cornish homes means a higher proportion than elsewhere in Britain of such fellow travellers as silverfish, house spiders, moths, fleas, mites and so on, not to mention the proclivity of bathrooms to become blackened with moulds.
* Warmth, with winters that have been described as languid springs. Certainly Cornwall's oceanic climate yields very equable temperatures which accommodate plants and animals from every continent.
* A winding coastline which is longer (some 250 miles of open coast) and narrower than any English county, nowhere being more than 15 or so miles from the sea.
* Cross-country drainage, so streams are short and fast-flowing and the rivers small. Typically, the dominant fauna clings to stones, examples being river limpets and flat-bodied stonefly nymphs.
* Weather which is said to be 'exciting' in its unpredictability. There

are few days without some wind, and it is often very wild. The Cornish know how to take their bearings from the wind-pruned trees, which stream towards the north-east.

* Complex and varied geological formations, especially in the Lizard peninsula. Geology dictates the nature of coastline, shores and soils, and there are more types of soil (some due to the excavating efforts of Cornish miners!) than in any other part of the UK.

All the above features combine to make a unique Cornish mix, within which exists a great number of habitats—many of them unusual, whether natural or man-made.

WETLANDS

Loe Pool is our largest lake, formed by a great shingle beach bar. There is a very interesting flora in the lake itself as well as on the shingle—and a unique subspecies of moth.[11] The trout in Loe Pool were said to be a distinct variety, but any genetic difference will have been diluted by the introduction of trout from elsewhere. Dr P. E. O'Sullivan and his colleagues have written a number of papers on the palaeolimnology of Loe Pool.[12] Swanpool is also a bar lake formed at the last retreat of ice about 10,000 years ago and now brackish: Barnes, Dorey and Little[13] in one of a series of papers on Swanpool, wrote 'It is impossible to over-emphasize the uniqueness of Swanpool. Dilute brackish environments are rare, and often temporary places.'[13] It is now the only British site for the small rare colonial animal *Victorella pavida*, described as new to science in 1870 from specimens found in Victoria Docks, but now extinct there.

Dozmary Pool, on Bodmin Moor, is a mile across and can claim to be Cornwall's largest natural lake, in distinction to bodies of water formed by bars. It is famous for its legends and its wildlife. It even has two small rare crustaceans, one a water flea (*Drepanothrix dentata*) and another, a copepod (*Diaptomus wierzejskii*).[14] New and enlarged reservoirs have added further diversity to Cornish wildlife habitats, but it is not always realised that the legacy of pools from alluvial mining has resulted in a quantity and quality of aquatic life that would not otherwise have been achieved. Such pools abound on Red Moor in the east and Porkellis in the west. There is marked variability of vegetation and invertebrate life between the diferent pools, dictated by aspect, depth and perhaps the particular cocktail of minerals present. The deep pools resulting from china clay mining which dominates the St Austell area likewise have a wealth of aquatic life, and many have been stocked with fish that are not native to Cornwall.

Large reed beds—those over two hectares in area—are rare enough to be of UK national importance; Marazion Marsh at 16.4 hectares is the largest in Cornwall and is now managed as a Royal Society for the Protection of Birds (RSPB) Reserve.[15] Par Marsh is also dominated by reeds, and like Marazion it is a wildlife haven especially for birds. The marsh at Loggans Moor, a Cornwall Wildlife Trust Reserve, is a fen: the calacareous sand blown in from the dunes has created a very different flora and fauna from the typically acid Cornish marsh. The very acid bogs of Goss and Bodmin Moors, holding in their depths the pollen of ancient landsacpes, add yet another ingredient to the complex jigsaw of Cornish natural history.

MINERALISED LAND

Many plants and animals have become specially adapted to thrive on the mineralisd land on which they live and its importance is summarised by Johnson and Holliday who state:

> Mining and biological conservation would seem, at first sight, to be mutually exclusive and there is little doubt that man's former mining activities have contributed significantly to the large acreage of derelict land of the present day. Paradoxically, however, the various extractive industries have also created landscape features of considerable ecological significance and conservation value . . . they have developed by natural colonisation over many years, and they have a 'wilderness' quality which contributes significantly to their biological conservation value.[16]

Spalding and Haes[17] stress the importance to many invertebrates of the open nature of the land scarred by mining. They point out that bare ground is a rare commodity and that Cornwall, with more derelict land (4888 hectares) than any English county, should value this wildlife asset. Tin-streaming in Cornwall is a 4,000-year-old industry, and Penhallurick[18] discusses it in a world-wide context; the illustration that he includes of Red Moor 'sometime between 1900 and 1914', and now a valuable Cornwall Wildlife Trust Nature Reserve, causes one to marvel at the adaptibility of plants and animals. The potentiality of the Red River Valley as a Nature Reserve was seen as long ago as the early 1970s.[19]

WOODLANDS

The paucity of trees is partly due to felling in historic times for mining activities, namely the production of charcoal for tin-smelting. By the mid-16th century, the tinners had to obtain their wood and charcoal from Devon and even the Isle of Wight according to Thurstan[20] who also cites the destruction of trees in parks during the Civil War in the reign of Charles I, as well as the disparking of land for cultivation; he quotes E. A. Rees as saying that apple trees were preferred by the smelters at Chyandour, Penzance 'because they were said to prevent the molten metal from spitting'. Perhaps apple was widely used; that it used to be common is attested in the many place names in which 'avalon' appears. Trees were also barked for tanning purposes, although they were usually from managed coppiced wood, so the woodlands were not destroyed. Much of even the very exposed north coast may have looked like Dizzard Wood in North Cornwall where stunted oaks spill over the cliffs. In bays, coves and valleys there are remains of ancient submerged forests that resulted from a combination of rising sea levels and sinking land, associated with the last retreat of ice. Ancient woods in valleys once filled the basins of the Fal—the third largest natural harbour in the world—and the Helford. The Helford Woods are discussed in detail by Rackham.[21]

RIAS, ESTUARIES, BAYS AND OPEN COASTS

All these major habitats have their own special communities according to the substrate. The type of rock and the way it has weathered, perhaps with rock pools, boulders, shingle, gravel, or soft sediments, will effect the type of plants and animals to be found. Gradation from eel-grass beds to mud flats and then salt marsh unfolds a succession of wildlife. Not suprisingly the most varied marine life is to be found in the drowned valleys (rias) which combine full salinity with shelter. Where else might one find dolphins swimming near oak trees, as in the Helford 'River'[22] and the Fal? Information on the Fal can be found in Burrows[23] and in Deeble and Stone,[24] whilst S. M. Turk[25] writes generally about the significance of Cornish and Scillonian marine life. There are many marine reports and unpublished surveys held in the Cornish Biological Records Unit at the Institute of Cornish Studies, including those commissioned by statutory bodies.

TOWANS (SAND DUNES)

Cornish dunes (*towans,* from the Cornish language) are amongst the highest in Britain and being rich in lime from blown shell sand they are correspondingly rich in lime-loving plants and animals which would otherwise not be found in Cornwall. Indeed, half the British species of flowering plants and ferns can be found on dunes. By their very nature, dunes are unstable and, even in the eighteenth century, marram-grass was being planted to prevent their destruction.[26] Their climax vegetation is relatively short term as they have their periods of development and stability followed by further sand accumulation. Profiles show humus layers where former plant cover was present, and this is where buried shells and archaeological remains may tell us something of past times. As Caseldine states, 'Workers face a record that is fragmented and often difficult to interpret . . . but with the mass of archaeological remains and the likely presence of fossil landscapes rather than isolated archaeological sites, Cornwall may yet prove an important focus for future palaeoenvironmental studies'.[27] Dunes are prime areas for golf-courses, camping/caravanning and sand extraction for a countryside which is otherwise starved of lime. Such activities can lead to conflicts for conservation.

HEATHLANDS

In contrast to vegetation typical of limy soils, the heathlands support various species of heather, with gorse and other acid-loving plants. Eleven per cent of all UK lowland heath (i.e. under 250 feet) is in Cornwall. The importance of the upland heaths of the Lizard Peninsula,[28] Bodmin Moor[29] and Goss Moor is recognised and all now have some protection, although all are reduced in area. The plant communities depend on the pH of the soil as well as the topography and degree of exposure to wind and salt-spray. Coombe and Frost[30] recognise four main heathland associations in the Lizard, namely Rock Heath, Mixed Heath, Tall Heath and Short Heath. Chadwick[31] gives information on heathland in general and the threats it is now under.

CLIFFS

Cliffscapes are amongst the glories of Cornwall. The 430 foot Pliocene Platform is a reminder that the land that now towers above the sea was formerly submerged. The plant cover of the great cliffs varies from maritime heath to maritime grassland with brilliant colours in due season. Woodland plants like bluebells and primroses grow where soil accumulation allows bracken to flourish, acting like a woodland canopy. Lack of grazing on cliff areas has resulted in a great increase in bracken, the poisonous properties of which are inimical to most wildlife.

CULM GRASSLANDS

Apart from extensive areas in Devon, these are found only in North East Cornwall. They are characteristic of soils derived from carboniferous sandstone and shales which produce wet acidic clay land noted for its 'distinctive intricate mix of fen meadow, rush pasture and wet heath',[32] rich in insect and bird life.

MEADOWS

Herb-rich meadows have largely disappeared since silage offered such advantages to farmers. However, some 'old-fashioned' farming practices still obtain in the far south-west, and both the Cornwall Wildlife Trust and the National Trust have been promoting such farming. Allaby [33] describes the spread of life over space and through time to be found in an 'ordinary' field.

CORNISH HEDGES

Meneer[34] quotes Johnson and Rose[35] who recognise twenty-one types of Cornish hedge whilst he (Meneer), for simplicity, uses three: 1) the typical Cornish hedge, as broad as it is high, and tapering, is built of two outer near-vertical layers of stone with a subsoil core; 2) the turf hedge, sometimes known in East Cornwall as a 'Devon bank', and consisting of an earth core within two near-vertical skins built up in layers of turf, varying in height from one to two metres, topped with planted trees; 3) the stone hedge, usually built with loose stone core tightly packed between two outer near-vertical layers of coursed stone, including slate and hard shales. The first and third types are virtually unique to Cornwall, although a few extend into North Devon and some occur in Brittany. Their importance as shelters and food reservoirs for wildlife cannot be over-stressed. They vary in appearance and in the plants and animals they support according to the type of stone, structure, site, height, aspect, age and proximity to the sea. Their study involves geology, geography and history as well as natural history and they were described by Donald H. Gray, an American Professor of Civil Engineering, as 'a unique man-made ecosystem and a quintessential biotechnical structure'. The importance of Cornish hedges is stressed by Meneer, who describes how to increase their wildlife by management.

GARDENS

The great legacy of landscape gardens, developed in Cornwall from the mid-eighteenth century onwards, adds another dimension to Cornish wildlife. Indeed, Tim Smit, 'finder' of the lost garden of Heligan, has recently described Cornwall as 'the gardening capital of the world'. The foreign trees and shrubs that can be grown in Cornish gardens, a large number of them frost-tender, are listed in Thurstan with a short inventory of Cornish gardens. Hunt and Pett[36] give more detailed information on 224 Cornish gardens, many of which are being reclaimed by private or public efforts, and their first introductory lines state 'Cornwall, not being in the mainstream of English fashion, has its own distinctive garden history.' Cornwall Gardens Trust is always concerned that surveys should also be made of the native plants and animals that often flourish in the shelter and warmth of old walled gardens, surrounded by trees. Little gardens too, whether in town or country, are important for many species and the smallest of ponds can support populations of newts and frogs.

FARMLAND

It is impossible to consider this as an entity since it can be so varied, often incorporating several of the above habitats, quite apart from the various types of arable land. The Cornish Branch of the Farming and Wildlife Advisory Group (FWAG) encourages farmers to maintain diversity and protect any scarce or rare plants or animals on their land. FWAG also advises on Set Aside projects.

Many of the above habitats are widely scattered in Cornwall but even the small fragments create those in-between areas (ecotones)— margins of woods, margins of wetlands, margins of the sea—which are especially rich in wild life—some of it unexplored.

FLORA AND FAUNA

There is an abundance of UK nationally rare plants and animals in Cornwall, but some Cornish rarities are common elsewhere in Britain. Moreover, there is a tendency for species to be found in habitats that are different from those in which they normally occur elsewhere in Britain, whilst some of the insects have different food plants. This may be partly due to isolation bringing about genetic changes in the population, and partly to enforced adaptations due to changes that humans have wrought e.g. deforestation and mining. Every group has specialties! There are rare moths, beetles (of which there are more than sixty *Red Data Book* species in Cornwall) crabs and even aphids. A Cornish *Red Data Book* is in preparation.[37]

Accidental and deliberate introductions have added to the vast inventory of fauna and flora, of which 22,000 species and close on a million records have so far been recorded in the databank of the Cornish Biological Records Unit. A list of all naturalised flowering plants and fern groups is now available,[38] and other check lists will follow. Not all introductions have continued to be welcome even when brought in, like Japanese Polygonum (*Fallopia cupidatum*, known in Cornwall as Donkey Rhubarb), as a highly desirable addition to the Victorian garden. Approximately a third of the 1,600 species of wild flowers to be found in Cornwall have been introduced in the past few centuries: this figure includes those which have spread from other parts of the UK. Many are completely naturalised, such as Sycamore, Turkey Oak, Ivy-leaved Toadflax and Slender Speedwell (*Veronica filiformis*). This last was introduced from the Caucasus as a garden plant at the end of the nineteenth century, and has become one of the most persistent and dominant of all lawn weeds. The first Cornish record was as late as 1945 and it is now abundant.[39] Flowering plants from every continent have found the Cornish climate and soils congenial. Many of these look very exotic and often flourish at the expense of our native flora; such are the succulent Hottentot Figs (*Carpobrotus* species) from South Africa.

In evaluating our flora, it is accepted that an ancient lineage is very important in considering worthiness of a species for protection and conservation. If rarity and beauty are added, its claim is even higher. Such a one is Cornish Heath (*Erica vagans*) which covers acres of land on the Lizard peninsula, yet is a rare *Red Data Book* species, known nowhere else in Britain apart from two other small sites in Cornwall. There is also a small site in Ireland but its native status is doubtful. In mainland Europe it is restricted to France and Spain. A hybrid, unique to the Lizard, is formed by Cornish Heath x Cross-leaved Heath. By contrast, Pygmy Rush (*Juncus pygmaeus*) is a diminutive and inconspicuous Cornish rarity otherwise found only in the Hebrides, a variety of Fringed Rupturewort (*Hernaria ciliota*) is only known from the Lizard and the Channel Isles whilst Western Ramping Fumitory (*Fumaria occidentalis*) occurs only in the Isles of Scilly and Cornwall. The Cornish Early Gentian (*Gentianella anglica*) has produced a subspecies (*Cornubiensis*) unique to Cornwall where it lives on the north coast sand dunes. The Dwarf Pansy (*Viola kitaibeliana*) is so adapted to living on the boulder beaches of Tean in the Scillies (its only location north of the Channel Isles) that it can actually benefit from a storm that destroys much else.[40]

Cornwall's clean moist climate is particularly favourable to the growth of ferns, lichens, mosses and liverworts. The diversity of the lichens is renowned, and there are many rare species. Boconnoc in East Cornwall is said to have more species than any site of comparable size in Europe.

The fauna, too, has a mix of native and introduced species. Subspeciation usually indicates a population that has been long-isolated from other populations of the same species. The Isles of Scilly, cut off from mainland Cornwall and mainland Europe for thousands of years, have a unique mammal, the Scillonian Shrew (*Crocidura suaveolens* subspecies *cassiteridum*) with a counterpart in the Channel Isles and Southern Europe. The islands also boast a subspecies of the Meadow Brown Butterfly (*Maniola jurtina* subspecies *cassiteridum*). Isolation is also believed to account for a subspecies of moth (the Sandhill Rustic *Luperina nickerlii leechi*) found only on Loe Bar in Cornwall. Parasites may also provide evidence, not only of their host species but the comparative length of time they have been separated as subspecies. The strange mite *Myobia blairi* occurs, uniquely, on the Scillonian Shrew but the feather mites of birds and the gall mites of plants have yet to be studied in detail.

Some of the introduced plants have brought with them their own fauna: a very rare pine aphid (*Cinara schimitscheki*) has been found living on just one example its host plant, Austrian pine;[41] a Japanese aphid (*Takecallis arundicolens*) lives on the common—and often naturalised—Japanese bamboo, *Pseudosasa japonica*; the North American Lupin aphid (*Macrosiphon abifrons*) wrought widescale damage on the tree lupin that is used to vegetate the St Austell clay tips.[42]

Curiously, the New Zealand land-hopper (*Arcitalitrus dorrieni*) was discovered new to science, not in New Zealand, but on Tresco; it has since spread throughout Cornwall, and has been recorded as far north as Argyll.[43] Also from New Zealand are the stick insects of which four species are now naturalised. Less desirable is the flatworm, *Geoplana sanguinea*, native of both New Zealand and Australia, which feeds on earthworms. It is not as destructive as its larger New Zealand relative *Artioposthia triangulata* which is likely to reach Cornwall eventually.[44] These flatworms, like so much of our fauna—including rats, silverfish and the many species of moths and beetles that feed on dried store products— have been introduced accidentally by humans, and continue to live in close proximity to us. Many of these synanthropic species are listed by Turk and Turk.[45] The most recent arrival is a Mediterranean species of mollusc (the Girdled Snail, *Hygromia cinctella*) which has been naturalised in Devon since 1950:

in 1993 it was first found in Cornwall and has now appeared in three different localities.[46]

The Cornish fauna is also replenished seasonally by the migrant birds and insects which regularly reach Cornwall as well as those casuals that may be blown off course. It is obvious that the colonisation of Cornwall, as of all areas, is a dynamic process. New species still arrive. Well-known examples which have arrived by their own volition are the Fulmar and the Collared Dove, and in the last few years the Long-winged Cone-head (*Conocephalus discolor*—a type of bush-cricket) has extended its range to include Cornwall and the Isles of Scilly. Some species are brought in by humans, accidently or deliberately. Others become extinct. The mix is never quite the same from one period to the next. This process has been happening since the last retreat of the ice some 10,000 years ago. In the early days of re-colonisation (assuming that the perma-frost was too intense for life to have existed in Cornwall with its present coastline) those species which would have been pushed southwards by the advancing cold would have moved northwards from the refuges provided by the greater expanse of land exposed by low sea levels.

Many Cornish habitats are small and demand conservation measures exercised by the Cornwall Wildlife Trust which now has 4000 members. We cannot know too much of what we have, and the inventory of the flora and fauna of Cornwall in the Cornish Biological Records Unit at the Institute of Cornish Studies continues to grow. The broad monitoring implicit in computerising records of all these species allows us, for instance, to compare the numbers of dolphin strandings year by year.

CONCLUSION

Obviously, there are elements of continuity throughout the whole of the South West Peninsula. But that 'difference' west of the Tamar noted by historians and other scholars, where Cornwall is so often to be considered an entity in its own right, is also borne out scientifically by the many extremes ('most' as well as 'least') that are expressed in Cornish wildlife. As this article has argued, there is in Cornwall a quality and quantity of features, habitats and species that adds up to a remarkable inventory. It is this inventory which makes Cornwall a unique place, a Mecca for naturalists of all kinds as still more of its treasures are revealed.

ACKNOWLEDGMENTS

The author is indebted to Mr R.D.Penhallurick for reading the script and making many helpful suggestions which have been incorporated.

NOTES AND REFERENCES

1. Bristol University Lizard Project (1981–90). During these years, under the leadership of Dr Lewis Frost, twenty-three Reports were compiled—mainly on the flora but also one on the birds of the Peninsula.
2. National Trust. The Cornish properties of the Trust's Biological Survey Team were the first in the country to be surveyed in 1979; further surveys on the Lizard were carried out in 1989.
3. J. Lawman, *A Natural History of the Lizard Peninsula*, Redruth, 1994.
4. E. C. Nelson, *Catalogue of European Drift Seeds*, Computerised list, 1986.
5. E. C.Nelson, 'Sea peas among tropical drift seeds', *BSBI News*, No. 44, 1986b.
6. E. C. Nelson, 'Exotic Drift Fruits and Seeds from the Coasts of Britain and Adjacent Islands, *Journal of the Royal Institution of Cornwall* (New Series), 10, 1988.
7. R. D. Penhallurick, *Turtles off Cornwall, the Isles of Scilly and Devonshire*, Truro, 1990; 'Turtle Occurrences off Cornwall and Scilly in 1990', *Zoological Cornwall and the Isles of Scilly* , No. 1, 1991; 'Turtle Ocurrences off Cornwall and Scilly in 1991 and1992', *Zoological Cornwall and the Isles of Scilly*, No. 2, 1993.
8. S. M. Turk, 'Christopher Columbus and *Pteria colymbus*', *The Conchologists' Newsletter*, No. 105, 1988.
9. S. Eckman, *Zoogeography of the Sea*, London, 1967.
10. S. M. Turk and D. R. Seaward, *Marine Mollusca of the Isles of Scilly*, in preparation.
11. A. Spalding, 'Notes on the Population of *Luperine nickerlii leechi* Goater (Lepidoptera: Notuidae) at its Site in Cornwall, 1987-89', *British Journal of Entomology and Natural History*, 44, 1991..
12. P. E. O'Sullivan, M. A. Coard, S. M. Cousen and D. A. Pickering, 1984. 'Studies of the formation and deposition of annually-laminated sediments in Loe Pool, Cornwall, U.K.', *Verh. Internat.Verein. Limnol.*, 23, 1984; H. Simola, M. A. Coard, and P. E. O'Sullivan, 'Annual Laminations on the Sediments of Loe Pool, Cornwall', *Nature* 290, 1981. In preparation are items of the pool's history, sediment stratigraphy, chronology, varve formation andeutrophication.
13. R. S. K. Barnes, A. E. Dorey and C. Little, 'An Ecological Study of a Pool Subject to Varying Salinity (Swanpool, Falmouth)', *Journal of Animal Ecology*, 40, 1973.
14. A. L. Galliford, 'Notes on the Fauna of Dozmary Pool', *Microscopy* 30, 1967.
15. D. J. Flumm, 'Marazion Marsh: a RSPB Reserve for Cornwall', *Zoological Cornwall and the Isles of Scilly*, No. 1, 26, 1991.

16. M. S. Johnson and R. J. Holliday, *Ecological and Conservation Value Assessments and their Integration with Proposed Alluvial Tin-Mining–Porkellis Moor, nr Helston, Cornwall*, Liverpool, Environmental Rehabilitation Unit, 1978.
17. A. Spalding and E. C. M. Haes, 'Insect Species as Habitat Indicators on Contaminated Land', *Land Contamination and Reclamation* 3, 1995.
18. R. D. Penhallurick, *Tin in Antiquity* London, 1986.
19. F. A. Turk, 'Tin Streaming Valley into Wildlife Reserve' in E. Dennis (ed.), *Everyman's Nature Reserve: Ideas for Action*, Newton Abbot, 1972.
20. E. Thurstan, *British and Foreign Trees and Shrubs in Cornwall*, Cambridge, 1930.
21. O. Rackham, *The Helford River Woods: Their History, Ecology and Conservation—A Report for Kerrier District Council*, 1987.
22. See the several publications of the Helford Voluntary Marine Conservation Area.
23. R. Burrows, *Wildlife of the Fal Estuary*, Local Wildlife Series No. 3, Dartmouth, 1984.
24. M. Deeble and V. Stone, *Exploring Underwater in a Cornish Estuary*, St Agnes, 1985.
25. S. M. Turk, *An Introduction to the Sea-shore Life of Cornwall and the Isles of Scilly*, Truro, 1971.
26. W. Borlase, *The Natural History of Cornwall*, Oxford, 1758.
27. C. J. Caseldine, 'Environmental Change in Cornwall During the Past 13,000 years', *Cornish Archaeology*, No. 19, 1980.
28. Bristol University Lizard Project, *Reports*, 1–23, 1981–90;. National Trust, *Reports on The Lizard*, 1979 and 1989.
29. C. Brewster, *Bodmin Moor: A Synoptic Study and Report on a Moorland Area*, Redruth, 1975; Cornwall Wildlife Trust, *The Bodmin Moor Natural Area*, Truro, 1994.
30. D. E. Coombe and L. C. Frost, 'The Heaths of the Cornish Serpentine', *Journal of Ecology*, 44, 1956.
31. L.Chadwick, *In Search of Heathland*, Durham, 1982.
32. G. Wren and D. West, 'Caring for the Culm', *Enact*, 2, 1994.
33. M. Allaby, *A Year in the Life of a Field*, Newton Abbot, 1981.
34. R. Meneer, *Wildlife Revival in Cornish Hedges*, Redruth, 1994.
35. N. Johnson and P. Rose, *Bodmin Moor: An Archaeological Survey—1: The Human Landscape*, London, 1993.
36. D. Hunt and D. E. Pett, *Historic Gardens in Cornwall*, 1991.
37. A. Spalding, (ed.), *Red Data Book for Cornwall*, in preparation.
38. C. N. French, (ed.), *Check List of Flowering Plants and Ferns of Cornwall and the Isles of Scilly*, 1994.
39. J. A. Paton, *Wild Flowers in Cornwall and the Isles of Scilly* Truro, 1968; L. J. Margetts and R.W.David, *Review of the Cornish Flora, 1980*, Redruth, 1981.
40. P. Sargeant, 'The Great Scillonian Storm Versus the Dwarf Pansy,' in A. Spalding and C. French, (eds), *Crises and Biological Records:*

Proceedings of the National Federation for Biological Recording Conference, 29–31 July 1993, Redruth, 1995.

41. C. I. Carter, 'A Rare Pine Aphid Established in Cornwall', *Zoological Cornwall and the Isles of Scilly*, No. 2, 4, 1993.

42. C. I. Carter, D. F. Fourt and P. W..Bartlett, 'The Lupin Aphid's Arrival and Its Consequences', *Antenna*, 8, 1993.

43. R. J. Lincoln, *British Marine Amphipoda: Gammaridea*, London, 1979.

44. S M. Turk, 'The Turn of the Worm', *Wild Cornwall*, No. 65, 1994.

45. F. A. Turk and S. M. Turk, 'The Occurrence in Cornwall of Animals Alien to the British Fauna', *Cornish Biological Records*, No. 3, Redruth, 1980.

46. S. M. Turk and H. Meredith, 'A New Snail for Cornwall', *BRICS Journal*, No. 1, 1995.

SELECT BIBLIOGRAPHY

There are thousands of items written on Cornish natural history. The publication of the *Victoria County History of Cornwall* (Vol. 1) in 1906 was a landmark, with its compilation of known records for marine and non-marine species. Also in 1906, Norman and Scott published *The Crustacea of Devon and Cornwall* and over the next few years papers by James Clark on Cornish fish and Crustacea appeared in the *Zoologist*. In 1948, B. H. Ryves' *Bird Life in Cornwall* was published. Flowering plants and fern groups were covered in F. H. Davey's *Flora of Cornwall* of 1909. Since the appearance of these pioneering works many more books, papers and articles have appeared. The following are a few of the larger items which have appeared since 1960, and which cover the whole of Cornwall and/or the Isles of Scilly.

D. Barker, 'A Potted History, 1931–1980', *Jubilee Issue of the Cornwall Bird Watching and Preservation Society*, 1981.

R. M. Barton, *An Introduction to the Geology of Cornwall*, Truro, 1964.

R. Bere, *Wildlife in Cornwall*, Truro, 1970.

R. Bere, (ed.), *The Nature of Cornwall*, Buckingham, 1982.

R. L. Bowley, *The Fortunate Isles: The Story of the Isles of Scilly*, Isles of Scilly, 1990.

R. Burrows, *The Naturalist in Devon and Cornwall*, Newton Abbot, 1971.

E. A. Edmonds, M.C.McKeown and M. Williams, *British Regional Geology: South West England*, 4th edn, London, 1975.

P. G. Embrey and R.F.Symes, *Minerals of Cornwall and Devon*, London, 1987.

C. N. French, 'The Sub-fossil Flora of Cornwall and the Isles of Scilly', *Cornish Biological Records*, No.8, 1985.

M. Groves, *Exploring Underwater: The Isles of Scilly*, St Agnes, 1988.

E. C. M. Haes, 'Grasshoppers and Related Insects in Cornwall', *Cornish Biological Records*, No.12, 1990.

E. C. M. Haes, 'Grasshoppers and Their Allies', *Zoological Cornwall and the Isles of Scilly*, No. 1, 1991.

E. C. M. Haes, 'Grasshoppers and Their Allies 1991 & 1992', *Zoological Cornwall and the Isles of Scilly*, No. 2, 1993.

M. R. House and E. B. Selwood, 'Palaeozoic Palaeontology in Devon and Cornwall', in K. F. G. Hosking and G. J. Shrimpton (eds), *Present Views of Some Aspects of the Geology of Cornwall and Devon*, Penzance, 1964.

D. Hunt and D. E. Pett, *Historic Gardens in Cornwall*, 1991.

J. E. Lousley, *Flora of the Isles of Scilly*, Newton Abbot, 1971.

L. J. Margetts and R. W. David, *Review of the Cornish Flora, 1980*, Redruth, 1981.

L. J. Margetts and K. L. Spurgin, *The Cornish Flora Supplement 1981–1990*, Zennor, 1991.

R. Meneer, *Wildlife Revival in Cornish Hedges*, Redruth, 1994.

M. Nicholson, 'Reptiles and Amphibians in Cornwall: An Interim Report', *Zoological Cornwall and the Isles of Scilly*, No. 2, 1993.

J. A. Paton, *Wild Flowers in Cornwall and the Isles of Scilly*, Truro, 1968.

J. A. Paton, 'A Bryophyte Flora of Cornwall', *Transactions of the British Bryological Society*, 5, 1968.

R. D. Penhallurick, *Birds of the Cornish Coast*, Truro, 1969.

R. D. Penhallurick, *The Birds of Cornwall and the Isles of Scilly*, Penzance, 1978.

R. D. Penhallurick, 'Ornithology in Cornwall, BC to 1931', *Jubilee Issue of Cornwall Bird Watching and Preservation Society*, 1981.

R. D. Penhallurick, *Turtles off Cornwall, the Isles of Scilly and Devonshire*, Truro, 1990.

A. D. Smith, *Bats in Cornwall: A Summary of Their Status, 1960–1985*, Truro, 1985.

J. E. Smith, (ed.), *Torrey Canyon Pollution and Marine Life*, Plymouth, 1968.

K. G. V.Smith and V. Smith, *A Bibliography of the Entomology of the Smaller British Offshore Islands*, 1989, (references to the Scillies are on pages 12-16).

A. Spalding, *Cornwall's Butterfly Heritage*, Truro, 1993.

A. Spalding, *Atlas of the Butterflies*, Redruth, 1993.

F. A. Turk, 'Distribution Patterns of the Mammalian Fauna of Cornwall', *Cornish Studies*, No. 1, 1973.

F. A. Turk, 'The Sub-fossil Fauna of Cornwall and the Isles of Scilly', *Cornish Biological Records*, No. 7, 1984.

S. M. Turk, *An Introduction to Sea-shore Life in Cornwall and the Isles of Scilly*, Truro, 1971.

S. M. Turk, 'Cornish Marine Conchology', *Journal of Conchology*, 31, 1983.

S. M. Turk, 'Non-marine Conchology of Cornwall and the Isles of Scilly', *Journal of Conchology*, 31, 1984.

S. M. Turk, 'Cornish and Scillonian Marine Studies, Past and Present', in S. Fisher (ed.), *Man and the Maritime Environment: Exeter Maritime Studies No. 9*, Exeter, 1994.

In addition to the many UK societies and journals with records and papers on Cornish natural history, there is a number of Cornish (and Devon) societies with publications that contain details of Cornish and Scillonian wildlife. Notable examples are: *Camborne-Redruth Natural History Society, Caradon Field and Natural History Club, Cornwall Badger Group, Cornwall Bat Group, Cornwall Birdwatching and Preservation Society, Cornwall Branch of the National Cactus and Succulent Society, Butterfly Conservation (Cornwall), Cornwall Dolphin Watch Group, Cornwall Garden Society, Cornwall Garden Trust, Cornwall Otter Group, Cornwall Reptile and Amphibian Group, Cornwall Wildlife Trust, Helford Voluntary Marine Conservation Area Group, Kernow Microscopical Society, North Cornwall Natural History Club, Royal Society for the Protection of Birds: Cornish Branch.*

THE IMPORTANCE OF METALIFEROUS MINING SITES IN CORNWALL FOR WILDLIFE (WITH SPECIAL REFERENCE TO INSECTS)

Adrian Spalding

INTRODUCTION

Cornwall has more 'derelict land' (4888 hectares) than any county in England.[1] The bulk of this lies in Kerrier and Carrick, but with sizeable areas in the other districts (the figure excludes large areas of land in the china clay district of St Austell). Derelict land is defined for this purpose as 'land so damaged by industrial or other development that it is incapable of beneficial use without treatment'.[2] Metalliferous mining sites form by far the largest proportion of dereliction justifying reclamation, according to the Department of the Environment.[3] With such a large area of derelict land in Cornwall (0.01 per cent of the total area of Cornwall), it is not surprising that there is a considerable amount of interest and controversy generated by the subject. Two conferences have been called recently within Cornwall to discuss the problem (one on contaminated land by the Camborne School of Mines in 1993 and one on derelict land by the Institute of Cornish Studies in 1994[4]) and several local pressure groups have been established (notably the Red River Valley Protection Group).

RECLAMATION

The term 'derelict' is a loaded word, implying something bad. Barr wrote an angry book about derelict land, partly in response to the Aberfan disaster of October 1966, and his emphasis was on doing things: 'The holes should have been filled, the heaps dismantled, the scars healed'.[5] Even now, the emphasis of papers in journals such as *Land Contamination and Reclamation*[6] is on positive action, doing something with derelict land. Once the decision has been made to reclaim these areas, choices have to be made between conflicting interests. For example, the objectives set by Cornwall County Council to be considered when tackling derelict land include dealing with hazardous sites, enhancing the economic potential of Cornwall, improving the environment, creating recreational and leisure facilities and preserving Cornwall's industrial heritage.[7] Since 1989, when the goverment published new guidelines, there has been more consideration to 'soft' end-use, partly as a cheaper option than 'hard' end-use.[8] Caradon District Council[9] has recognised the importance of nature conservation and suggests that isolated rural areas may best be reclaimed in a way which suits an amenity or wildlife use; but there still apppears to be a presumption for positive action, not leaving things as they are. Out of 835 sites restored to 'soft' after-use between 1978 and 1984, for only four was priority given to nature conservation.[10] Priorities have to be set for each site to be reclaimed. For example, the debate between the archaeology and ecology of derelict land is set out in an interesting account by Clark.[11]

ECOLOGY OF DERELICT LAND
Particularly since the classic book by Bradshaw and Chadwick,[12] there has been greater consideration of the ecology of these areas. Bradshaw and Chadwick advocated the conservation of wild species on some of these sites and the proper ecological integration of the reclaimed area into the surrounding landscape. Although a major step forward, the overall theme was still one of treatment. Box went further, pointing out the importance of naturally revegetated derelict land sites as a part of the ecological framework of the British landscape.[13] The Department of the Environment now recognises that the extraction of minerals can create new types of wildlife habitat in areas where they were formerly absent.[14] Unusual biological communities linked to industrial sites can be unique and non-recreatable.[15] Patience is often necessary when awaiting natural recolonisation (often very slow) of recent industrial sites.[16] Work on revegetating china clay sites has shown the importance of colonisation by semi-natural wildlife communities and the need to replicate habitat loss.[17] In fact, the offical definition of derelict land does not recognise the inherent value of many of these sites for wildlife.[18] It does not recognise the complexities of wildlife communities on these sites, or their importance for education, research and

amenity, or their value as reservoirs of wildlife in the midst of industrial or agricultural landscapes.

CORNWALL'S WILDLIFE

Before elaboration on these points, it is necessary to establish briefly the place of plants and animals in the context of Cornwall as a mosaic of plants and animal communities in a fragmented landscape. The key wildlife areas are generally considered to be those (often isolated) reserves of high nature conservation interest, such as managed by organisations like the Cornwall Wildlife Trust and English Nature. This tends to be an elitist view of nature conservation, which can exclude the local community; it is wildlife for the specialist and expert, rather than the general public. In some cases, the rarer the species, the more likely it is that only an expert can look at it. This view also ignores the fact that many important species occur outside nature reserves. For example, all the most important sites of the nationally-scarce blue-tailed damselfly are on the old tin mining areas of West Cornwall outside protected areas.[19] Concentration on the protection of key nature reserves has meant that nine sites for this species have been lost in West Cornwall since 1980. In many ways, Cornwall is different from the rest of Britain, and what is common here might be rare elsewhere and vice-versa e.g. the buzzard, the scarlet tiger moth and Cornish heath. Some of the most extensive habitats in Cornwall (such as willow carr and acid grassland) are important in UK national terms because they reach their fruition in this region for reasons of geology, climate and history. Despite this, we tend to take them for granted because they are so familiar to us.

We need to consider landscape as a whole, to take a three-dimensional view which integrates high nature conservation areas with the totality of Cornwall, both to protect wildlife areas as isolation increases their vulnerability, but also to place a higher value on those areas in between which are an essential part of the nature conservation fabric. In many cases these areas can be upgraded for wildlife more easily than Sites of Special Scientific Interest and nature reserves. We especially need to consider the history of the area as this gives us our 'sense of place', a sense of continuity with those who have gone before. This is recognised by the Trevithick Trust, which in a publicity leaflet emphasises that the landscape associated with Cornish mining and engineering is an essential part of our heritage.[20] In a non-elitist approach, bringing a sense of continuity to nature conservation can bring together not just naturalists but all those who are concerned for the history and identity of their area. This is conservation for the community. Awareness of the development of the wildlife of a place as it has changed over centuries and been modified by man's activity constructs our 'moral geography' of the countryside and emphasises our part within it— drawing the boundaries of our world and where we fit into it. Too often, we see wildlife, particularly animals, as there despite us, when in most cases it is there because of us, the numbers and distribution of species directly influenced by our activities, past and present. One well-known example is the rabbit, which was deliberately introduced into Britain probably in the twelfth century (there were rabbits in the Isles of Scilly in 1176) and then subjected to a deliberate attempt at extermination by the introduction of myxomatosis in 1953.[21]

The wildlife forms part of the history of a site. The presence or absence of a species gives us clues as to how the habitat has developed and changed over the years, what was there before and what is there now, even what the surrounding area was like. The presence of these historical indicator species in the wildlife sites of Cornwall gives them an importance over and above the mere presence of UK nationally rare species, for here in Cornwall (one of the birthplaces of the industrial revolution) everywhere has history, from the effect of the Ice Ages and recolonisation from continental Europe, to the Neolithic clearances of Bodmin Moor, to the medieval tin-streaming sites, to the beginning of the china clay extraction over 200 years ago and the great boom years of deep mining in the nineteenth century. The history of the Cornish industrial landscape can be seen as the triumph of nature over man's endeavours, nature getting its own back. Many of the key sites for nature conservation in Cornwall are old industrial sites e.g. Goss Moor, Luxulyan Valley, Croft Pascoe, Ventongimps Pond.

WILDLIFE AND MINING SITES

Nature adapts to the diversity created on these industrial sites, and wildlife communites develop according to the influence of soil structure, nutrient levels and availability, alkalinity/acidity, toxicity, pre-industrial wildlife and industrial history and the sequence of colonisation.[22] In fact, the vegetation present on a site can provide a useful indication of the metals present and any remedial treatment required. Even woodlice can serve as bio-indicators of metal pollution, although they need to be crushed and the metal content examined.[23]

Derelict mining sites are a coherent part of the landscape easily identified by the local community; they stand out in a largely treeless countryside (such trees as there were, were cut down for use in the mines). Here gorse scrub takes the place of woodland. Typically, these sites have been colonised by gorse, willow, grasses and heathland, all typical of Cornwall; but as we have seen, what is common in Cornwall can be rare and important in a UK national context. Gorse and willow scrub are unlikely to be important wildlife habitats in themselves, although they do provide shelter for birds and small animals, and act as wildlife refuges particularly important in urban areas. The presence of these habitats makes a site more interesting and varied; they combine with the derelict buildings and complex surface levels often characteristic of these sites to provide secret, sheltered areas and sudden changes of view.

PLANTS

Metalliferous mining has generally been inimical to plant establishment and growth, especially where heavily compacted and toxic nutrient-poor soils have been produced. Several factors inhibit plant growth on metalliferous mines, including compacted and unstable soils, toxic elements, steep slopes, extremes of temperature, wind and water erosion, the absence of soil and associated micro-organisms, and low nutrient status.[24] These factors have led to the formation of an interesting mix of habitats and commmunities reflecting these unusual environmental conditions. The presence of the metals copper, zinc, lead and arsenic has particularly led to the evolution of plants (pseudo-metallophytes) that are genetically different to the ones growing on normal soils—an example of evolution in action, sometimes involving rapid genetic variance[25]—and especially to the genetically metal tolerant populations of common grasses e.g. Common Bent (*Agrostis capillaris*). Many plant species evolve tolerance only to one metal not others, so that the presence of Yorkshire Fog (*Holcus lanatus*) for example indicates that copper is absent, as in Devon at least this grass has not developed tolerance to copper.[26] We also find unusual associations of such metallophyte plants e.g. thrift forming large swards as an early coloniser alongside Ling. Thrift is a local metallophyte (i.e. occurring locally on metalliferous soils but more generally in non-metalliferous habitats) associated particularly with copper mine wastes[27] and occurs at many copper mining sites in Cornwall, e.g. in the Poldice Valley.[28] Specialist metallophyte vascular plants, lichens and bryophytes can be used in the assessment of the conservation status of these sites on a national basis.[29]

These sites are also important for the number of species in Cornwall which they provide habitat for. Tables 1 and 2 show the numbers of flowering and lower plants in Cornwall associated with derelict land sites.[30]

TABLE 1
Flowering plants on derelict land in Cornwall

	No. of Species	No. Of Rdb* Species
Mines	40	2
Quarries	59	4
China Clay	13	0
Old Railways	86	3

Extracted from data in L. J. Margetts and R.W. David, *A Review of the Cornish Flora, 1980*, Redruth, 1981, and L. J. Margetts and K. L. Spurgin, *The Cornish Flora Supplement 1981–1990*, Zennor, 1991.
**Red Data Book.*

TABLE 2
Bryophytes on derelict land in Cornwall

	No. of Liverworts	No. of Mosses
Mines	30	64
Quarries	40	131
China Clay	27	43
Gravel Pits	4	4

Extracted from data in J. A. Paton, 'A Bryophyte Flora of Cornwall', *Transactions of the British Bryological Society* 5:669–756, 1969.

Using our knowledge of what grows on these metalliferous mine sites, the Cornish Biological Records Unit at the Institute of Cornish Studies has established a list of plants suitable for planting on derelict land sites in west Cornwall (Table 3). Cornwall is particularly rich in bryophytes and lichens, mainly because of its position, geology, climate and industrial history.[31] Derelict land in Cornwall offers bare, contaminated soil surfaces suitable for colonisation by bryophytes but which exclude those higher plants that might out-compete the lower plants. There are about 420 moss species in Cornwall, representing about 60 per cent of the total for the British Isles.[32] Over 230 of these can be found on mine and quarry sites (Table 2). Of especial interest is Cornish Path-moss (*Ditrichum cornubicum*) which is only known from one site in the world (Phoenix Mine, near Liskeard), although it used also to be found near Lanner.

TABLE 3
List of plants suitable for planting on derelict land
sites in west Cornwall

Flowering Plants	Grasses	Trees and Shrubs
Bell Heather	Cock's-foot	Alder
Bird's-foot Trefoil	Common bent	Ash
Broom	Creeping bent	Blackthorn
Buck's-horn Plantain	Yorkshire Fog	Downy Birch
Common Centaury		Dwarf Cherry
Devil's-bit Scabious		Grey Willow
European Gorse		Hawthorn
Ling		Sycamore
Lousewort		
Oxeye Daisy		
Sea Plantain		
Sheep's-bit		
Thrift		
Yellow rattle		

ANIMALS

In their pioneering paper on wildlife conservation on metalliferous mine sites in Wales, Johnson et al. mention that the ruderal habitats created by mine workings are exploited by a wide range of birds, mammals and invertebrates, in addition to the better studied plants.[33] The heterogeneity of these habitats provides a broad spectrum of environmental conditions in which these animals can survive. In Cornwall, such sites may be important for bats (especially underground, as at Tresavean[34]), nesting birds (particularly the peregrine, which is reported as nesting on several derelict land sites in Cornwall) and reptiles such as the common lizard and slow worm. Little is known about the invertebrates of these sites; the only insect mentioned in a recent government report is the Herald Moth, recorded in casual records as hibernating underground.[35]

INSECTS AND HEATHLAND

Insects are too often a forgotten part of the ecosystem of derelict land sites, despite occupying an important place in wildlife habitats both as pollinators and a large part of the food chain. In their book of the restoration of land, Bradshaw and Chadwick have one sentence on insects (and then in the context that they give rise to concern over the spread of disease).[36]

Perhaps the most valuable habitats on metalliferous mining sites are the heathland and bare ground areas. Heathland on these sites is generally dominated by Ling (*Calluna vulgaris*), in a climax self-regulating community where toxic, compacted ground inhibits other plant growth. The tolerance of heavy metal contamination by Ling may be due to the presence of mycorrhizae fungi associated with it.[37] Many invertebrates use heather as an architectural feature.[38] Ling is also an important nectar source for insects in the autumn. The author and E. C. M. Haes observed twenty-six insect species nectaring on Ling during recent survey of twelve metalliferous mining sites in Cornwall. Heathland is typically poor in nectar in spring and early summer, when ruderal plant species such as ragwort growing by old buildings are especially im- portant.[39]

Initial surveys of sites in Cornwall have revealed several insects which are key heathland indicator species. Examples are the Heath Assassin Bug and Heath Damsel Bug, which have both been recorded at Binner Downs, a site especially rich in heathland species. For some heathland species, metalliferous mining sites form a major resource in Cornwall (based on records in the ERICA database at the Cornish Biological Records Unit). For example, mining sites form a large pecentage of the total recorded sites in Cornwall for the following species:

Heath Damsel Bug	20%
Beautiful Yellow Underwing	25%
Heath Assassin Bug	50%
Methoca ichneumonides	50%

Methoca ichneumonides is especially interesting as the female (which is parthenogeneticic) is flightless and therefore slow to colonise new sites.[40] The male is very rare. The larvae parasitise tiger beetle larvae, in Cornwall the Green Tiger Beetle which is associated with warm areas of bare ground. There are only two post-1960 recorded sites in Cornwall for *Methoca ichneumonides*, one of which is at Wheal Busy.

BARE GROUND

The importance of bare ground as a habitat in its own right is all to often unrecognised.[41] For many invertebrates it is essential, of vital importance for burrowing, basking and hunting.[42] Many metalliferous sites have large expanses of bare ground, where the soil is toxic to plants and so heavily compacted that little or nothing can grow in it. Such denuded lands as these recolonise very slowly if at all and any vegetation surviving is prone to being removed by sheet and gully erosion.[43] Many of these soils are stained dark with metals and are quick to absorb solar radiation, heating up quickly in the sun. In Cornwall, there are several insects associated with these areas which require warm open areas to survive. Even on north-facing sites, bare ground on metalliferous mining sites can be warm enough for insects such as the Grayling. This butterfly requires areas with high cumulative temperatures (because of its relatively slow larval development) and also bare, dry, warm soil conditions for rapid pupal development. It is likely that open ground is also favoured because it houses fewer arthropod predators.[44] A typical site is at Watchcroft in West Penwith, where Grayling have colonised open mine spoil.[45]

Other bare ground specialist insects include the Mottled Grasshopper, which requires hot, open spaces with short turf and little shade.[46] Hard-packed ground is particularly important for many solitary bees and wasps for construction of tunnels, e.g. mining bees such as *Colletes succinctus* and *Andrena fuscipes*.[47] The richest sites for these species were Tolskithy and Binner Downs. These metalliferous mining sites are generally more important for bare ground specialists than for heathland species. It should be remembered that these results are based on a survey of just twelve mining sites; it is likely that the results of further survey work (on additional sites and at different times of year) will further emphasise the importance of these sites for nature conservation.

For some bare ground insects, metalliferous mining sites as a whole form a major resource in Cornwall (based on records in the ERICA database). For example, mining sites form a large pecentage of the total recorded sites in Cornwall for the following species:

Andrena fuscipes (mining bee)	50%
Colletes succinctus (mining bee)	40%
Mottled Grasshopper	20%
Grayling butterflyover	10%

Futher survey work will add to the importance of these sites in the context of the Cornwall distribution of these species.

HISTORICAL INDICATORS

Many of these insect species are historical indicators and give clues to the history of the site and the surrounding areas. The presence of Mottled Grasshopper at Wheal Jonny (Kehelland) is a good example. Although winged, the Mottled Grasshopper is generally slow to colonise new habitats and its presence on this isolated site indicates that:

(a) there has been a small area of heathland here since the mining activity ceased
(b) high quality heathland was present at the site before (and during) mining operations
(c) much of the surrounding countryside was heathland when mining started here

The presence of other key species can also indicate long-term continuity. Both *Andrena fuscipes* and *Colletes succinctus* are excellent indicators of continuity of (heathland) habitat.[48] The presence of the sand wasp *Ammophila sabulosa* indicates continuity of warm, open habitat at the sites where it has been recorded (e.g. Tolskithy).

BINNER DOWNS

Binner Downs is a good example of a disused metalliferous mine that is now rich in wildlife. Copper mining began here over 250 years ago and continued until 1838.[49] Tin was at first discarded on dumps and then reworked on the surface sometime after 1838. It is likely that much of the original vegetation would have been destroyed during the mining process. Despite this, the site is now important for several species, including Grayling, Heath Assassin Bug, Heath Damsel Bug, Lesser Cockroach and Beautiful Yellow Underwing Moth. The site is surrounded by heathland, from which species would have been quick to recolonise once heathland and associated habitats returned to the site. This emphasises the importance of having reservoir colonies from which species can move onto new areas. Recolonisation becomes more difficult in a fragmented landscape.

RECLAMATION, RESTORATION OR LEAVING ALONE?

The key question is whether we want land 'restored' or whether we want to enhance what is there now? Natural recolonisation and regeneration, although slow, has the advantage of being cheap. They are low input, low output options, involving natural processes such as weathering and habitat succession; they fit nicely with sustainable development policies. In contrast, large-scale schemes require management, monitoring, correction, replanting schemes and 'gardening'. The pressure for planting trees on these sites does not meet the need to retain habitat and species diversity on these site (and ignores the need to retain any geological features).[50] Start-up grants for large-scale schemes are relatively easy to obtain, but follow-up grants are much scarcer. A good example for future action is the work on the Prince of Wales Quarry near Tintagel, funded by Derelict Land Grant. Here the mix of industrial and wildlife heritage was met largely by allowing the natural colonisation of the site by vegetation.[51] The great copper mines at United Downs (last mined in the 1860s, although with dumps re-worked later) have become well vegetated in unmanaged areas, where in places a rich ground flora has developed.[52] Tree planting here has been largely unsuccessful, and in any case it is the author's opinion that trees are out-of-place in such a highly exposed industrial site. If planting is required at a particular site, then the practice of the Cornish Biological Records Unit is to ask landowners and managers to use species that are already found in Cornwall (see Table 3 for recommendations as to which species to plant).

PROTECTION

In assessing the nature conservation objectives for Cornwall, it should be a high priority to establish a register of derelict land sites showing their nature conservation interest, followed up by the detailed survey and protection of the mining sites. Protection should include adequate representation of the best sites, perhaps as Local Nature Reserves or as reserves owned by Cornwall Wildlife Trust or local bodies such as the Dandelion Trust. One deep-mining site should be protected as a Site of Special Scientific Interest as an example of a particular habitat type. English Nature has adopted certain criteria to use in the assessment of sites for the selection of SSSIs.[53] The primary criteria are: size, fragility, diversity, naturalness, rarity, and typicalness. These sites are difficult to assess using these methods and we need to look again at the criteria used. We need to highlight the importance of recorded history for the site, which gives us a greater understanding of the site and its wildlife value. The presence of species indicating long-term historical continuity can give added value to the recorded history. It should also be recognised that a site can be important even if it is surrounded by agricultural land (such as Wheal Jonny). Furthermore, a site can be important despite (or because of) being small, especially if it has a long history. The author suggests the following critera for site evaluation and selection for conservation of metalliferous mine sites in Cornwall: size, habitat types, number of rare plants, number of rare animals, recorded history, elapsed time since mine last worked, surrounding area type, access, ecological assessment.

THE FUTURE

We are so impatient nowadays. There is great public pressure to restore and 'green' derelict sites as quickly as possible.[54] Nowadays, we would not wait for Goss Moor or Breney Common to clothe themselves with a natural succession of vegetation from open water to reed-bed, swamp and mire, heathland and willow scrub. The living landscape that we see now has taken time to develop, and cannot be re-created as it is without the essential ingredient of passing time. The importance of these sites for wildlife lies as much in their history as what is there now. Future action requires a greater sympathy towards these sites, to allow natural processes to produce a wildlife habitat that fits the area. This 'soft end-use' is cheap, leads to more natural results and is community-based. Not all sites can be protected and treated in this way, not all are suitable or of high enough quality—and we cannot turn the whole of Cornwall into one large museum. Nevertheless, these sites are important as they are for amenity, education/research and recreation; we need to preserve the best examples as they are as living memorials to the industrial and wildlife heritage of Cornwall.

ACKNOWLEDGEMENTS

The author would like to acknowledge the important work of E.C.M. Haes during the invertebrate survey, as well as advice on the ecology of particular insects. The Hymenoptera were identified by Mike Edwards. Thanks also go to Helen Pryor for extracting vascular plant and bryophyte data used in Tables 1 and 2, and to David Holyoak for information on mosses in Cornwall.

REFERENCES

1. D.o.E., *Survey of Derelict Land*, London, 1988.
2. D.o.E., *Derelict Land Grant Advice: Derelict Land Grant Policy (DLGA 1)*, London, 1991.
3. D.o.E., 1988.
4. See A. Spalding (ed.), *Derelict Land: A Challenge for Conservation and Community—Synopses of the Conference Proceedings*, Redruth, 1994.
5. J. Barr, *Derelict Britain*, Harmondsworth, 1969, p. 13.
6. *Land Contamination and Reclamation*, Richmond. But see in this Journal

A. Spalding and E. C. M. Haes, 'Contaminated Land—A Resource for Wildlife: a Review and Survey of insects on Metalliferous Mine Sites in Cornwall', 3:25–29, which summarised part of the preparatory work for the Derelict Land Conference in October 1994 and marked a new direction for this Journal.

7. Cornwall County Council, *Derelict Land Strategy, 1993–1996, incorporating a rolling programme submision to the Department of the Environment for 1993/4–1995/6,* Truro, 1974.

8. See, for example, Land Capability Consultants, *Cost Effective Management of Reclaimed Derelict Sites,* London, 1989.

9. Caradon District Council, *Derelict Land Policy and Strategy Statement, Consultation Draft,* Liskeard, 1994.

10. Land Capability Consultants, 1989, p. 3.

11. C. Clark, 'The Brown Debate: Archaeology, Ecology, and Derelict Land', in L. Macinnes and C. R. Wickham-Jones, *All Natural Things: Archaeology and the Green Debate,* Oxford, 1992.

12. A. D. Bradshaw and M. J. Chadwick, *The Restoration of Land: The Ecology and Reclamation of Derelict and Degraded Land,* Oxford, 1980.

13. J. Box, 'Conservation or Greening? The Challenges of Post-industrial Landscapes', *British Wildlife* 4, 1992.

14. D.o.E., *Planning Policy Guidance: Nature Conservation (PPG9),* London, 1994, p. 9, section 42.

15. J.Box, *Conservation or Greening? The Challenge of Post-Industrial and Derelict Sites,* Regro Conference, June 1994.

16. Box, 1994.

17. Wardell Armstrong/D.o.E., 1993. *Landscaping and Revegetation of China Clay Wastes: Summary Report,* London, 1993, pp. 4–5.

18. D.o.E., 1991.

19. Steven Jones, pers. comm.

20. *Trevithick Trust* membership leaflet (nd): 'The objective of the Trust is to identify, preserve, protect, manage and interpret for the benefit of the people in Cornwall and of the public at large throughout the world whatever of the historical, architectural and engineeering heritage may existin the form of buildings, artefacts, documents, records and land associated with Cornish mining and enginering'.

21. C. Lever, *The Naturalized Animals of the British Isles,* London, 1977.

22. Bradshaw and Chadwick, 1980.

23. Hopkin and Hames, 1994; Zinc, among a 'cocktail' of metal pollutants, is responsible for the absence of the terrestrialisopod *Porcellio scaber* from the vicinity of a primary smelting works, see *Ecotoxicology* 2.

24. G. T. Goodman and S. A. Bray, *Ecological Aspects of the Reclamation of Derelict and Disturbed Land,* NERC, 1975.

25. M. Macnair, 'Heavy Metal Tolerance in Plants: A Model Evolutionary System', *Tree* 2, 1987.

26. For an interesting account of plant metal tolerance in Devon, especially

on the Gawton Mine see M. Macnair, 'Metal Tolerance on Mines in Devon: A Natural Evolutionary Experiment', *Naturein Devon*, n.d.

27. A. J. M. Baker and J. Proctor, 'The Influence of Cadmium, Copper, Lead and Zinc on the Distribution and Evolution of Metallophytes in the British Isles', *Plant Systematics and Evolution* 173, 1990.

28. D.o.E. (Minerals Division), *The Reclamation and Management of Metalliferous Mining Sites*, London, 1994, pp. 97–98.

29. B. Sellars and A. J. M. Baker, *Review of the Metallophyte Vegetation and its Conservation*, Peterborough, 1987.

30. The information for Table 1 has been extracted from data in L. J. Margetts and R. W. David, *A Review of the Cornish Flora*, Redruth, 1981 *and* L. J. Margetts and K. L. Spurgin, *The Cornish Flora Supplement 1981–1990*, Zennor, 1991. The information for Table 2 has been extracted from data in J. A. Paton, 'A Bryophyte Flora of Cornwall', *Transactions of the British Bryological Society* 5, 1969.

31. N. Hodgetts, 'Low Life: Lower Plabts on Derelict Land in Cornwall', in A. Spalding, (ed.), *Derelict Land: A Challenge for Conservation and Community. Synopses of the Conference Proceedings*, Redruth, 1994.

32. David Holyoak, pers. comm.

33. M. S. Johnson, P. D. Putwain, and R. J. Holliday, 'Wildlife Conservation Value of Derelict Metalliferous Mine Workings in Wales', *Biological Conservation* 14, 1978.

34. See D.o.E. (Minerals Division), 1994, p. 99.

35. D.o.E. (Minerals Division), 1994, p. 29

36. Bradshaw and Chadwick, 1980.

37. R. Bradley, A. J. Burt, A. J. and D. J. Read, 'The Biology of Myrcorrhiza in the Ericaceae. VIII. The Role of Mycorrhizae Infection in Heavy Metal Resistance', *New Phytologist* 91, 1982.

38. P. Kirby, *Habitat Management for Invertebrates: A Practical Handbook*, Sandy, 1992.

39. Kirby, 1992.

40. M. Chinery, *Collins Guide to the Insects of Britain and Western Europe*, London, 1986.

41. Kirby, 1992, p. 5.

42. R. Fry and D. Lonsdale, *Habitat Conservation for Insects—A Neglected Green Issue*, Middlesex, 1991, p. 135–36.

43. Goodman and Bray, 1975.

44. R. L. H. Dennis, 'Islands, Regions, Ranges and Gradiants', in R. L. H. Dennis, (ed.), *The Ecology of Butterflies in Britain*, Oxford, 1992, pp. 15–16.

45. T. Edwards, S. Hocking, E. C. M. Haes, A.Spalding, *A Biological Survey of Watchcroft: A Report to the National Trust*, Redruth, 1994.

46. J. A. Marshall and E. C. M. Haes, 1988. *Grasshoppers and Allied Insects of Great Britain and Ireland*, Colchester, 1988.

47. Kirby, 1992.

48. E. C. M. Haes, pers. comm.

49. K. Brown, 'The Mines', in A. T. Jenkin (ed.), *Leedstown In Our Lifetime,* Leedstown, 1994, p. 31.
50. Box, 1994.
51. See the leaflet produced in conjunction with Cornwall Archaeological Unit by the North Cornwall Heritage Coast Service in 1990 on the Prince of Wales Quarry and Engine House.
52. D.o.E. (Minerals Division), 1994, pp. 94–96.
53. Nature Conservancy Council, *Guidelines for Selection of Biological SSSIs: Rationale and Operational Approach and Criteria*, Peterborough, 1989.
54. Box, 1994.

MOVERS AND STAYERS: A COMPARISON OF MIGRATORY AND NON-MIGRATORY GROUPS IN CORNWALL, 1981–91

Malcolm Williams and Eric Harrison

INTRODUCTION

This article presents some recent work conducted at the University of Plymouth on population change in Cornwall. The research uses longitudinally linked Census data to examine some of the socio-economic characteristics of migrating and non-migrating groups between 1981 and 1991.

The most profound of the social changes that followed the collapse of mining in Cornwall was the slow leaching of population, which continued well into this century. Rossler notes that between 1860 and 1900 the gross emigration rates from Cornwall (after allowing for return migrants) were about twenty per cent for men and ten per cent for women.[1] By 1939 the population was 309,000, 60,000 less than in 1861.[2] Though wartime evacuees gave rise to a brief increase it was not until the 1960s that there was any kind of large scale, or sustained population growth. From the late 1960s onwards, however, things were very different. Between 1961 and 1991 Cornwall's population grew from 343.3 thousand to 470.2 thousand.

The years of population decline were mainly those of economic stagnation, yet the 'turnaround' in population levels was not matched by any kind of large scale economic recovery. Whilst Cornwall did enjoy brief periods of relative prosperity between the mid-1960s and mid-1970s[3] this was mainly due to relatively short-lived economic initiatives such as the decentralisation of enterprises, mainly from the South East and the Midlands, and for much of the decades 1971–91

Cornwall has remained one of the poorer parts of Britain.[4] Indeed, the population increase has actually masked a level of out-migration possibly as great as that of the late nineteenth century. At the end of each of the periods 1971–81 and 1981–91, 11 per cent of the Cornish population were enumerated outside of Cornwall in England and Wales. To this figure we would have to add all of those who left for destinations other than England and Wales.

Cornwall appears to be unusual not so much in respect of its repopulation, which is shared by many other rural areas, but in the high levels of population 'turnover'. Economically linked out-migration from a 'deprived' area such as Cornwall is not that unusual, but what takes some explaining is why more people come to Cornwall than leave it, given its economic characteristics? This question has been addressed by others, notably Perry et al.[5] in the mid-1980s, where it was argued that migration to Cornwall was associated more with 'lifestyle' factors, such as the enjoyment of previous holidays or preferred environment, rather than economic ones.

This article describes and contrasts the socio-economic characteristics of those who leave Cornwall, those who move to Cornwall, and the long term population. It is popularly held in Cornwall that in-migrants enjoy considerably greater economic advantage than the Cornish, but at the same time have failed to regenerate the economy. Whilst it is undoubtedly true that many in-migrants have prospered we will offer evidence to suggest that the economic situation of in-migrants is in fact complex. The evidence we present is that the economic fortunes of out-migrants not only improve in comparison to those who remain in Cornwall, but also that they do 'better' than those who move to Cornwall. Secondly, whilst in-migrants are likely to enjoy economic advantage upon moving to Cornwall many of them begin to resemble the long term population after they have been in Cornwall for ten years.

We will conclude, therefore, that in-migrants to Cornwall are not an homogeneous group and that their subsequent economic fate may rest upon reasons for moving to Cornwall and the conditions under which they make the move.

METHODOLOGICAL ISSUES

One of the problems associated with studying the characteristics of migrants is that one is usually restricted to describing 'one off' samples of particular populations. Certainly, it is possible to talk about the overall characteristics of an area such as Cornwall and infer these from nett migration trends. However, when there are likely to be important differences between in and out-migrating groups and these in their turn represent a large portion of the aggregate population, suitable comparative data are hard to find. The OPCS Longitudinal Study (LS) is one of the few data sets allowing comparative analyses, over time, between migrating and non-migrating groups. However, the LS is possibly the only data set to offer large enough numbers for analysis in an area as small as Cornwall. In this paper four different populations are compared:

> *the 'long term' population of Cornwall (i.e. enumerated in Cornwall in 1981 and 1991).*

> *those who moved into Cornwall (i.e. enumerated outside of Cornwall in 1981 and enumerated in Cornwall in 1991).*

> *those who moved out of Cornwall (i.e. enumerated in Cornwall in 1981, and outside of Cornwall in 1991).*

> *the population of England and Wales (i.e. enumerated outside of Cornwall in 1981 and 1991).*

The LS is a set of records of various events held by the Office of Population, Census and Survey (OPCS) relating to just over one per cent (about 500,000 people) of the population of England and Wales (and Cornwall). These can be linked in a variety of ways for analysis. Initially, all people born on each of four dates each year were selected from information given in the 1971 Census. From 1971, as new births occur on these four dates each year and as immigrants with these birth dates register with the NHS, these people join the LS. Another sample of all those giving the selected birth dates was taken from the 1981 Census and their Census records were incorporated into the LS. This procedure was again repeated after the 1991 Census. Thus the LS represents a continuous sample of the population rather than a sample taken at any one time point only. Census information is also included for all people living in the same household as the LS member.

The LS permits the linking of records of individuals over three time points, but the analyses reported here, with one exception, link the records of individuals between 1981 and 1991. The reasons for this are threefold. Firstly, if the LS sample was to include all of those enumerated in 1971, 1981 and 1991 a rather narrow age distribution would result. Only those alive in 1971 and who were still alive in 1991 could be included. Secondly, a characteristic of analyses of the kind reported here is that cross-sectional comparison between longitudinally defined groups is equally as interesting as comparisons within the groups. Thirdly, with few exceptions, the comparative positions of each of the migrant and non-migrant groups remained very similar, though of course each group experienced historic change between 1971 and 1991.

Because of the nature of the sample, LS data are unclustered and excellent coverage is available at county levels—indeed comparisons with county level data, for Cornwall, show a very high level of agreement. In Cornwall the total LS sample enumerated in 1991 was 3,981 which is 0.84 per cent of the Census population. This sample is slightly under the one per cent because in order to select a longitudinal sample it must include only those alive at both dates.

WHENCE THEY COME, WHITHER THEY GO?
One of the ironies of migration to and from Cornwall is that the principal destination region of out-migrants is the same as the principal

TABLE 1
Origins and destinations of migrants into and out of Cornwall
1981–91 (%)

Region 1991	Origin of in-migrants 1981	Distination of out-migrants 1991
South East	43.5	35.2
North West	6.1	3.3
Yorks/Humber	4.2	3.7
North	1.8	2.0
West Midlands	8.6	6.3
South West	25.2	37.8*
East Anglia	2.0	3.9
East Midlands	4.8	4.3
Wales	2.9	3.7
Other	0.9	—
n=	1044	493

*Many migrants to other parts of South West Britain are short distance migrants to neighbouring Plymouth.

region of origin of in-migrants. Table 1[6] shows that excluding short
distance migration to and from the South West of England, the principal
destination of out migrants and principal region of origin of in-migrants
is the South East. Moves to the South East might be explained by the
desire to move from an area of high unemployment and low wages to
an 'escalator region'. In this respect out-migration from Cornwall would
be little different to that from other economically-depressed regions.
However, the question of why people are moving from a region of
economic prosperity to a relatively 'poor' area requires a different kind
of explanation.

There would appear to be two possibilities: a) that the migrants
to Cornwall, though originating from an economically dynamic region,
are themselves less 'prosperous' b) economic or cultural perceptions
of Cornwall act as important pull factors. The current research indicates
that in-migrants are more likely to be from non-manual classes and
more likely to be economically active than the long-term population,
or out-migrants prior to leaving Cornwall.

Nevertheless, the picture may not be that clear. Whilst the
proportion of in-migrants from other regions are individually very
much smaller than those from the South East, together they comprise
over 31 per cent of total in-migrants. Many of these would have
originated in localities with similar economic profiles to Cornwall and
may represent, in many cases, a type of economic migrant particular
to the 1980s—those who wish to begin a new life with redundancy
money! We shall return to this idea in our conclusion. Conversely, it
is possible that migrants from the South East may be over-represented
in the service class of Cornwall—itself dominated by in-migrants.

AGE AND HOUSEHOLD STRUCTURE
Whilst retired people are over-represented amongst Cornwall's long-
term population, migrants to and from Cornwall are much more likely
to be of working age. Table 2 contrasts the age of heads of households
of migrant and non-migrant households.

The age profile of both migrant groups is rather lower than long
term residents and comparable with England and Wales generally,
but with a particular over-representation of very young heads of
household in 1991 amongst the leavers. Analyses of age of LS member
(not shown here)[7] indicates this is a result of a very high proportion
of leavers under twenty-nine years old in 1981. Many of these would
have been students after leaving Cornwall and went on to form new
households by 1991.

Those who move into Cornwall are very much more likely to have

TABLE 2
Age of heads of household by migration 1981–91 (%)

	In Cnwll 1981/91		Out of Cnwll 1981/In Cnwll 1991		In Cnwll 1981/ Out of Cnwll 1991		England and Wales	
	1981	1991	1981	1991	1981	1991	1981	1991
15–29	9.0	6.9	16.6	11.5	17.3	23.7	13.0	10.2
30–44	38.6	26.7	39.9	37.1	35.8	36.7	39.6	32.0
45–59	31.0	32.2	29.3	25.3	28.7	16.9	30.0	29.6
60–69	12.8	17.1	10.3	16.3	11.8	8.9	11.4	14.6
70+	8.5	16.9	3.9	9.8	6.4	14.0	5.6	13.7
n=	2910	2870	1016	1010	471	473	394559	392154

a head of household under forty-five than the long term population. This is true both before moving to Cornwall and ten years on. That the proportion of heads of household under twenty-nine in 1981 is significantly higher than that of England and Wales and moreover that the proportion in the 45–59 age group is likewise not greatly different suggests that there is no great preponderance of late career migration associated with promotional moves within the service classes. Moreover, despite the 'ageing effect' built into a cohort sample such as this the very elderly were under-represented in this group in 1991. There is then no evidence of any large-scale migration of retirement, or near retirement, age people to Cornwall. That the long term population is more likely to be headed by an older person is explained by the correspondingly high levels of out-migration amongst those of working age.

Given the foregoing, it is not altogether surprising, then, that those who move to Cornwall are more likely to live in 'traditional' nuclear families than any other arrangement (Table 3). Moreover, after being in Cornwall for ten years, members of this group were more likely to be living in such households than any other group. Conversely, in both 1981 and 1991 there were fewer 'elderly' households amongst in-migrants than those enumerated in Cornwall at both censuses.

There were other important differences amongst the groups. Most

TABLE 3
Household structure by migration 1981 and 1991 (%)

	In Cornwall 1981/91		Out of Cnwll 1981/In Cnwll 1991		In Cnwll 1981/Out of Cnwll 1991		England and Wales	
	1981	1991	1981	1991	1981	1991	1981	1991
Single person 65 or over	3.0	6.9	1.3	3.4	2.1	4.7	2.4	6.3
Elderly Couple	6.8	12.4	3.8	11.3	6.8	10.6	4.6	9.2
Single person 65 or under	2.7	5.0	2.5	5.5	3.0	7.4	3.2	5.5
2 or more adults no elderly	2.6	6.0	5.3	6.6	3.8	15.4	4.1	7.5
Couple no dependent children	12.6	13.3	15.2	17.9	11.9	15.0	11.6	13.1
Couple with dep. children	38.6	19.9	38.6	27.5	38.4	25.8	38.3	22.8
Cple. dep. children + adult	12.5	9.4	11.8	7.4	16.1	4.2	9.5	8.9
Cple. + adult, no dep. children	8.8	11.6	9.9	5.2	5.3	4.4	9.5	12.2
One parent families	5.3	5.9	5.9	6.8	6.5	7.4	6.0	6.6
Complex households	7.0	9.7	5.8	8.3	5.9	5.1	6.4	7.7
n=	2910	2870	1016	1010	471	473	394607	392144

notable was the tendency of the 'stayers' to be over-represented in complex households with more than two generations present, or where another adult who was not a member of the same family was present. There is a growing body of evidence to indicate that this characteristic is associated with 'hidden homelessness', whereby housing need is absorbed into existing households.[8] Nevertheless, given the relatively small size of this household category, there has been a sizeable increase of those living in complex households amongst incomers, suggesting that housing need may increase in this group after residence in Cornwall for ten years. Indeed, the only group in which this household category has declined has been out-migrants.

Migration to and from Cornwall appears to be associated with relatively younger people of working age. Those who leave are more likely to be under thirty and single, whereas in-migrants are concentrated in the twenty-five to thirty-nine age group and are more likely to live with other family members. Twenty two per cent of all out-migrants were between fifteen and twenty-four and thus many are likely to be leaving Cornwall to enter higher education.

RE-MIGRATION

Relatively few of those who leave Cornwall return during their working lives. Table 4 shows migration flows over the twenty years between 1971 and 1991.

TABLE 4
Migration flow in and out of Cornwall 1971–91 (%)

| In 71 | In 71 | In 71 | In 71 | Out 71 | Out 71 | Out 71 |
| In 81 | In 81 | Out 81 | Out 81 | In 81 | Out 81 | In 81 |
In 91	Out 91	Out 91	In 91	In 91	In 91	Out 91
48.7	4.6	7.9	1.3	11.9	20.1	5.4

n = 3826

Some care is needed in reading this table in that it represents a cohort of all those enumerated at the 1971, 1981 and 1991 censuses. Those under twenty in 1991 are therefore excluded as are many elderly (those who died during the period). This means that return migration amongst those who are retired is underestimated. Nevertheless, of this cohort only 1.3 per cent who were out-migrants in 1981 were enumerated back in Cornwall in 1991. What is perhaps more surprising is that 5.4 of the cohort were people who were outside of Cornwall in 1971, enumerated in Cornwall in 1981 and outside of Cornwall in 1991. In other words, these were the in-migrants who left! Again, this figure probably underestimates levels of in-migrants who subsequently out-migrated, not only because of the age distribution in the sample, but because the LS is still a series of snapshots. An unknown number of people will have migrated into and then out of Cornwall between censuses.

SOCIAL CLASS

Whilst class is a less reliable predictor of life chances than it used to be, it remains the case that there are important differences between

Cornish Studies: Three

non-migrants and each of the migratory groups. Table 5 compares the social classes of the heads of households of migrants and non-migrants.

TABLE 5
Heads of household social class 1981–91 (%)
(*Excludes retired persons and those without attributed social class*)

	In Cnwll 1981/91		Out of Cnwll 1981/In Cnwll 1991		In Cnwll 1981/ Out of Cnwll 1991		England and Wales	
	1981	1991	1981	1991	1981	1991	1981	1991
I	3.0	3.7	7.3	5.8	8.2	13.7	5.9	6.1
II	27.0	29.4	35.1	39.7	35.0	38.5	24.7	30.1
IIN	11.3	9.7	14.7	15.9	14.3	17.2	12.1	13.1
IIIM	36.6	33.8	27.1	24.0	24.5	16.3	35.7	30.3
IV	16.3	16.6	12.6	11.4	13.7	12.0	16.4	15.4
V	5.7	6.7	3.1	3.2	4.4	2.3	5.3	5.0
n =	2246	1946	848	691	343	343	325706	283226

Though the gradient of change was in the same direction for all groups, one of the most striking features is the scale of the shift from manual to non-manual classes, particularly to Class I, by the out-migrants. Though this is partly explained by the transition of many in this group from higher education (the likely reason for leaving Cornwall) to service class jobs, a logistic regression analysis of factors associated with out-migration indicated that people who were unemployed were over seven times more likely to leave Cornwall than those in a job. Though cross tabulations of social class change and age are not available it would seem that there is an age dichotomy, whereby younger out-migrants leave mainly for education and training, whilst those who are older are leaving to seek work.

The class changes associated with in-migration are a little more ambiguous. In comparison to the long-term population there was a greater shift to non-manual classes, but this was rather less than for the population of England and Wales. Indeed, there was a reduction in the proportion in Class I for this group between 1981 and 1991. This may be further evidence to suggest that those who make 'career' moves to Cornwall are earlier in their career and 'lower' in the class hierarchy.

In class terms those who leave Cornwall do 'best', indeed better than England and Wales generally, whereas the long-term population of Cornwall does 'worst' of the three groups. Nevertheless, those who move to Cornwall appear to do worse than those who remain in England and Wales.

EMPLOYMENT AND EARNERS

The Census does not measure prosperity particularly well. Two of the better 'proxies' available are those of numbers seeking work in the family and number of earners in the family. Whilst each of the groups had fewer persons seeking work in the family in 1991 than 1981, once again those who left Cornwall fared very much better than both England and Wales generally and those who were in Cornwall in 1991 (Table 6). What is perhaps more surprising is the fate of the in-migrants. Whilst in 1981, prior to moving to Cornwall, they had fewer seekers of work in the family, by 1991 their position was rather similar to the long-term population. Indeed, they were the only group to experience an increase of two or more persons seeking work in the family.

TABLE 6
Those seeking work in the family by migration 1981–91 (%)

	In Cnwll 1981/91		Out of Cnwll 1981/In Cnwll 1991		In Cnwll 1981/Out of Cnwll 1991		England and Wales	
	1981	1991	1981	1991	1981	1991	1981	1991
None	68.0	77.2	70.3	77.7	59.7	81.7	68.9	77.3
One	25.9	17.6	25.8	17.6	28.9	16.6	25.1	17.7
Two or more	6.1	5.2	3.9	4.7	11.4	1.7	6.0	5.0
n =	2606	2426	912	870	412	367	352941	328729

The relative positions of the groups remains much the same when we consider numbers of earners in the family (Table 7). All groups experienced an increase in the 'no earners' category between 1981 and 1991 but this is largely attributable to the 'ageing effect' in the cohort. What is important, however, are the comparative positions between the groups. In-migrants experienced a dramatic increase in the number of 'no earner' families in comparison to the other groups—despite the fact that this group has a younger age profile than the long-term population. Perhaps even more surprisingly, long-term residents were very much more likely to have three or more earners in 1991 than were in-migrants.

Once again the position of in- migrants deteriorated between the censuses. Prior to moving to Cornwall, they were very much less likely to have no earners in the family than those enumerated in Cornwall in 1981, or England and Wales generally.

TABLE 7
Earners in the family by migration 1981–91 (%)

	In Cnwll 1981/91		Out of Cnwll 1981/In Cnwll 1991		In Cnwll 1981/Out of Cnwll 1991		England and Wales	
	1981	1991	1981	1991	1981	1991	1981	1991
None	20.5	27.7	11.8	31.1	21.1	24.8	15.4	24.6
One	43.9	29.0	42.4	27.9	43.0	23.4	37.9	26.0
Two	26.4	32.6	34.3	35.9	29.4	46.6	33.5	37.1
Three or more	9.2	10.6	11.4	5.0	6.6	5.1	13.2	12.3
n =	2606	2426	912	870	412	367	352941	328729

These data have to be considered in relation to changes in part-time working in the decade. Whilst there was an increase in part time working across all groups in the decade 1981–91, in 1991 of those in employment 21.6 per cent of the long-term population were in part-time jobs as were 20.7 per cent of in-migrants (Table 8). Whilst slightly more of the latter group were thus in full-time work, the percentage of this group in either full or part-time work fell very much more dramatically than that of the long term population.

TABLE 8
Full time and part time employment 1981–91
(*as % of those in employment*)

	In Cnwll 1981/91		Out of Cnwll 1981/In Cnwll 1991		In Cnwll 1981/Out of Cnwll 1991		England and Wales	
	1981	1991	1981	1991	1981	1991	1981	1991
Full time	82.2	78.4	85.8	79.3	87.7	86.9	82.7	80.6
Part time	17.8	21.6	14.2	20.7	12.3	13.1	17.3	19.4
n =	1212	1296	542	473	171	268	189187	198693

The expansion of part-time working, whilst increasing the numbers of earners in households, does not necessarily increase household income. Whilst Cornwall was undoubtedly in the latter phases of industrial decline in 1981, increased part-time working since has almost certainly been a symptom of the decrease in jobs in the extractive/ manufacturing sectors, the corresponding increase in jobs in the service sector, and the erosion of job security in the workforce at large brought on by the 'marketisation' of the public sector. Multi-earner households may be 'work rich'[9] but this does not make them 'income rich'. Thus the increase in three-earner households amongst the long-term population may be more as a result of changes in the labour market than any real growth in prosperity. Furthermore, the slight increase (against the UK national trend) of heads of household in social classes IV and V may also be attributable to particular economic changes in Cornwall.

From the data available we must conclude that both the long term population of Cornwall and in-migrants did 'worse' than the population of England and Wales between 1981 and 1991. However, the most dynamic group by far were those who left Cornwall during the decade. Whilst it is also apparent that incomers to Cornwall were 'doing better' in 1981 than those enumerated in Cornwall in that year, the position is less clear cut ten years on. From the economic characteristics described here there is little to indicate in-migrants are 'doing better' than locals and, indeed, in some respects might be said to be 'doing worse'! Nevertheless, the picture painted here compares each group as a whole with the other. To claim that as a group in-migrants come to economically resemble the local population does not preclude a 'wealth gap' whereby the very wealthiest members of Cornish society are themselves incomers.

MOTIVES FOR MIGRATION

Despite its central role as a redistributor of populations and therefore public resources, we still know far too little about the reasons for people's migratory motivations. The LS data, of course, cannot help us here. But although a neglected topic for a long time, geographical mobility has recently been linked with the career strategies of the middle classes. Savage et al.[10] note the existence of three such strategies for social mobility, based on the deployment of three types of assets which they term property assets, organisation assets and cultural assets. In brief, these refer to firstly those who accumulate capital through either business and/or housing moves and use this as a basis for self-employment; secondly those who are required to move geographically within an organisation or group of organisations (the so-called internal labour market); thirdly, those with professional and thus transferable qualifications who move for accelerated career advancement. There is a some evidence (Table 5) to support the existence of all three strategies. Internal labour market transfers could be said to operate within the military services, strongly represented in various locations in Cornwall and nearby Plymouth. Finally, many professionals running Cornwall's public services are in-migrants, as are large numbers of professionals in education, the law and the health service.

A second possibility is that some in-migrants make Cornwall their 'home' but continue to work elsewhere, commuting long distances to other parts of Britain and even Europe. Our data say little about this, though what we know from the 1991 census and anecdotally suggests quite small numbers in this category. Such is Cornwall's distance from London and other European capitals that this is simply not a realistic option. As another study of North Devon remarked, in-migrants had come 'to escape commuting, not to participate in it'.[11]

What this suggests is that 'people are giving more attention to "quality of life" considerations at the expense of economic, or indeed strictly employment, factors'.[12] What we have termed 'lifestyle migration' would appear to be one explanation for the influx of people into an economically disadvantaged area. However, while the middle classes are in a good position to benefit from quality of life gains such as lower house prices, pollution and crime, there is always an element of risk for those without a firm footing in the labour market. In common with Bolton and Chalkley's study of South Molton, our data suggests that counter-urbanization 'is a phenomenon of the masses'; however, it also suggests a high failure rate among those whose migrations are what we might call 'speculative'.

Various studies in the 1970s and 1980s[13] explored reasons for moving to Cornwall. The Perry et al. study in 1983, and the Cornwall County Council study in 1975, indicated that economic considerations were not foremost in decisions to move to Cornwall.[14] Reasons commonly cited as pull factors were preferred environment, to re-join friends/ relatives and in the Perry et al. study, the enjoyment of previous holidays, whilst 'push' factors included 'to escape the rat race'. In other words lifestyle considerations played a key role in decisions to move to Cornwall. These findings, as Mitchell noted,[15] contrast with those from the County Council's New Households Survey conducted in 1986. In this study 'job related' reasons were cited as the most important factor in moving. Mitchell suggests that the contrasting evidence may be explained either by the way in which each of the surveys was constructed,[16] or because the latter survey was conducted only in private housing estates. He also speculates on whether the occupants of the private housing estates surveyed (who were shown by analysis of other questions in the survey to be relatively affluent) were also more materialistic in terms of the factors which influenced them.

If the incomers had been in Cornwall for some time, then their prosperity was not typical of the in-migrant group as a whole. It is thus possible that the respondents in the County Council survey were mainly of the first (or even second) type of migrant described above. Their move to Cornwall was the result of material motivations and this in turn may explain why they chose to live in relatively new estates rather than traditional housing. Nevertheless, 22 per cent of the estate dwellers, in the County Council survey, did indicate that the environment of Cornwall was a motivating factor, whilst a further 5 per cent cited 'escape from the city' as a key reason for moving. It might then be hypothesised that whilst migrants of the first (and possibly second) type favour newer housing, not all of those in newer housing are economic migrants.

Sadly LS data on dwelling type is rather inconclusive on the question, though not surprisingly it does show that in-migrants are over-represented in detached housing and under-represented in terraced housing. Nevertheless, all of the in-migrants interviewed in a 1993 ethnographic study comparing the housing circumstances of Cornish families with in-migrants, reported in Buck et al.,[17] had moved into older housing stock which they had carried out at least some renovation work. Moreover, all of the households were 'speculative' movers without jobs to move to in Cornwall and all were motivated to move as a result of lifestyle rather than economic factors. Economic activity since moving to Cornwall was mainly self-employment or casual work. This study, though statistically unrepresentative, provided rich biographical household data which points firmly toward the existence of lifestyle migration.

What this demonstrates is the increasingly complex nature of long-distance migration in recessionary Britain. In economic terms a move from Cornwall would appear to make better sense than a move to Cornwall. However, this varies considerably with the labour market situation of an individual and their household. Just as we have to recognise Cornwall's specificity within South West Britain, it is also necessary to acknowledge the heterogeneity of the Cornish labour market. While some migrants bring their jobs with them and set up small businesses, many move into existing jobs (e.g. in the public sector) or become unemployed. The most attractive locations (to in-migrants) seem to have the greatest concentration of problems. In the late 1970s, for example, two-thirds of Newquay's jobless were recent (largely seasonal) in-migrants and these were concentrated in the 20–30 age group. Even so, a more extensive Department of the Environment survey undertaken in 1978 found evidence to suggest that in-migrants were 'job consumers' rather than 'job creators'[18]. It would be unsurprising if speculative migrants experienced greater difficulties than locals in obtaining jobs. Whilst there is evidence to suggest that the indigenous Cornish suffer discrimination[19] and that this may extend to the workplace, they are more likely to be part of existing local and cultural networks which, as Gallie and Vogler have noted, are so important to identifying and securing employment opportunities.[20]

CONCLUSION

Migration from Cornwall has traditionally been associated with economic factors and, whilst LS data cannot establish reasons for migration (from or to Cornwall), it does seem likely that contemporary out-migration is mainly motivated by material considerations. Whilst out-migration continues to be high there is clear evidence that out-migrants do better economically than those who remain in Cornwall.

The situation of in-migrants is altogether more complex. As a group they appear to fare better before coming to Cornwall than ten years on when their economic fortunes appear to have become little different to the long term population. From this, however, we should be wary of concluding that those who move to Cornwall end up being somehow 'poorer' than the Cornish. A more realistic scenario is that migration to Cornwall is far from uniform, and that whilst most who move to Cornwall are comparatively 'better off' before moving, economic fortunes may depend upon whether migration is economically motivated, or the result of lifestyle decisions. Even so, these categories should be seen as 'ideal types' and economic and lifestyle reasons for migration may be combined.

Whilst internal labour market moves to Cornwall are possibly little different to elsewhere, doubtless the attractions of Cornwall, such as environment and ease of local commuting, play a part in encouraging job applications from professionals. Thus whilst the latter are primarily concerned with career advancement and depend upon the 'cultural assets', described by Savage et al., secondary lifestyle considerations may determine a choice between Cornwall or Coventry!

Each of the strategies of Savage et al. described originate in material considerations, yet to make sense of much of the migration to Cornwall we would suggest it is necessary to cite non-material factors as primary motivations for a large group of people. For many, economic strategies adopted after moving to Cornwall are secondary, and in some cases the results of the unintended consequences of the original non material reasons for moving. The findings of the study by Buck et al., referred to above, was that whilst property assets realised upon moving to Cornwall were an important economic factor *after* the move, they were not the main motivation *to* move. Moreover, the accumulation of capital as a result of realising housing assets may be insufficient to provide the basis for secure long-term self-employment. This is particularly so given the vicissitudes of tourist and related business, the favoured options of many in-migrant entrepreneurs.

Furthermore, though this latter group might be said to be realising their 'property' assets there are other in-migrants, though not falling into the previous two categories described by Savage et al., who have few or no assets to realise. Only those who move from areas where property prices are higher will accrue economic advantage from moving house. For many others the principal capital asset will be redundancy money, or savings. Finally, whether or not property assets are realised not all in-migrants become entrepreneurs, preferring to take their chances in the Cornish job market.

We would suggest, then, that those in-migrants deploying 'organisation' or 'cultural' assets are those most likely to succeed economically, whereas those deploying 'property' assets mainly do so as a secondary strategy to that of 'lifestyle'. The assets of these 'lifestyle' migrants may vary considerably.

ACKNOWLEDGEMENTS

The project upon which this work is based was funded jointly by Cornwall County Council, Caradon District Council and the Department of Applied Social Science, University of Plymouth. Specific thanks go to Brian Cheal, Brian Dodgeon and Peter Mitchell.

NOTES AND REFERENCES

1. Horst Rossler, 'Constantine Stonemasons in Search of Work Abroad 1870– 1900', *Cornish Studies: Two*, 1994.
2. Peter Mitchell, 'The Demographic Revolution', in Philip Payton (ed.), *Cornwall Since the War: The Contemporary History of a European Region*, Redruth, 1993.
3. Ronald Perry, 'Economic Change and "Opposition" Economics,' in Payton (ed.), 1993.
4. Malcolm Williams, 'The Invisible People—Cornwall in Official Statistics', *Radical Statistics* 52, 1992.
5. Reported in Ronald Perry, Ken Dean and Bryan Brown, *Counterurbanisation*, Norwich, 1986.
6. The data source in each of the tables reproduced here is the LS.
7. Findings referred to but not but not reproduced in tabular form in this paper can be found in the project report, Malcolm Williams, Brian Cheal and Lyn Bryant, *Population Change in Cornwall 1971–91*, University of Plymouth, 1995 (forthcoming).
8. See, for example, Carol Williams, *Housing Need in Cornwall*, Sociology Working Paper 95/1, University of Plymouth, 1995.
9. Ray Pahl, *Divisions of Labour*, Oxford, 1984.
10. M. Savage, J. Barlow, P. Dickens, A. Fielding, *Property, Bureaucracy and Culture: Middle-Class Formation in Contemporary Britain*, London, 1992.
11. N. Bolton and B. Chalkley, 'Counter-urbanisation: Disposing of the Myths', *Town and Country Planning*, September, 1989.
12. A. Findlay and R. Rogerson, 'Migration, Places and Quality of Life: Voting with Their Feet?' in Anthony Champion (ed.), *Population Matters*, London, 1993.
13. These are described in Mitchell, 1993 p. 152.
14. Perry, Dean and Brown, 1986 p. 90.
15. Mitchell, 1993, p. 155.
16. Mitchell speculates over what difference the use of 'open ended' questions might make (as compared to a 'tick box' type): 'Do people in filling out

an open-ended questionnaire take Cornwall's environmental advantages as something understood, which do not need to be spelt out.' (1993, p.154).

17. Mary Buck, Lyn Bryant, Malcolm Williams, *Housing and Households in Cornwall—A pilot study of Cornish Families,* University of Plymouth, 1993.
18. R. McNabb, J. Barry and N. Woodward, *Unemployment in West Cornwall,* Department of Employment, 1978.
19. Surprisingly little research has been conducted in this area though a recent study by the Commission for Racial Equality did find evidence of perceived discrimination; see E. Jay, *Keep Them in Birmingham: Challenging Racism in South West England,* London, 1992.
20. Duncan Gallie and Carolyn Vogler, 'Unemployment and attitudes to work' in Duncan Gallie, Catherine Marsh, Carolyn Vogler (eds), *Social Change and the Experience of Unemployment,* London, 1993 pp. 136–7.

HOUSING IN CORNWALL: A TWO-TIER SYSTEM?

Carol Williams

INTRODUCTION

The rapid population growth that Cornwall has experienced over the last thirty years has had effects in many areas, but particularly in housing. Demand from outside of Cornwall has artificially inflated house prices in relation to the generally low wage levels in Cornwall, resulting in a 'mortgage gap' for many people trying to get access to housing from within Cornwall. Moreover, high levels of unemployment exclude many more from even entertaining the idea of a mortgage. Coupled with a decline in the quantity of both privately rented and Local Authority accommodation available, these factors have brought about what is considered by many to be a housing 'crisis' in Cornwall.[1]

Paradoxically, although the numbers reporting homeless to District Councils in Cornwall have risen in recent years, they remain at a level comparable to those in the neighbouring counties of Devon and Somerset. A study by Buck et al. in 1993 suggested that this apparent paradox may be explained by two factors; out-migration and the 'absorption' of housing need into existing household structures.[2] Williams, also in 1993, has shown that households migrating out of Cornwall are likely to display characteristics associated with housing deprivation, such as unemployment and overcrowding.[3] Indeed, a more recent study has found that those who leave Cornwall generally do so for economic reasons and are likely to improve their life chances after leaving.[4]

The second of these factors, the absorption of housing need into existing household structures, was explored by Buck et al. in a small qualitative study of Cornish households.[5] Other studies have indicated that shared households may come about as a result of housing scarcity,[6] and the evidence presented by Buck et al certainly suggests that Cornish households may be playing an important role in mitigating some of the worst effects of the housing crisis. This assistance however, is not confined to the direct provision of somewhere to live. Buck et al. suggest that the members of extended family networks may be helping to overcome housing problems in a variety of ways. This could take the form of financial assistance, the supplying of valuable information about housing opportunities, through to providing accommodation within family members' homes and shared ownership schemes.[7]

The study by Buck et al. was intended to set the parameters for a larger scale survey on Cornish housing. Indeed, the need to make more extensive comparisons between Cornish households and recent in-migrants was evident given the small number of recent in-migrants interviewed in the study. Moreover, the need for a wider overview of the housing situations of long-term residents of Cornwall and more recent in-migrants has become apparent in light of evidence which suggests that a dichotomy of housing opportunity exists in Cornwall between these two groups.[8] Long-term residents of Cornwall (specifically the indigenous Cornish) suffer housing need as they are unable to compete in the private housing market and alternatives are difficult to come by, as mentioned above. In contrast, those who can buy into the Cornish housing market from outside enjoy a great deal of housing choice.

The intention of this paper then, is to explore the extent to which this dichotomy of housing opportunity exists, using data collected in a research project which aims to uncover any differences between Cornish people and incomers in both the quality of their housing and the ways in which housing need is met.[9] Two questions are being posed; do recent in-migrants enjoy better housing chances than long-term residents, and if so, why? In attempting to answer these questions a number of issues will be explored. How do the characteristics of the recent in-migrants and long-term residents of Cornwall vary? What implications does this have for their housing chances? In addition, levels of housing need within the two groups will be explored.

THE DATA
The data were collected via a postal survey of 1500 households in Cornwall. The most comprehensive sampling frames available for Cornwall are the electoral rolls. However, conducting a random sample entirely from electoral rolls presents problems of both time and cost. Thus it was decided to use a multi-stage random sample. Fourteen electoral wards were selected from the Census county monitor on a

random basis. Within these wards, 1500 respondents were selected randomly, using the electoral rolls as the sampling frame. Each ward, therefore, had an equal chance of being selected and each person within those wards also had an equal chance of being selected.

The questionnaire elicited data on household structure, size, economic activity and housing needs. Overall, 873 questionnaires were returned completed, a response rate of 58.5 per cent. Four sub-groups were identified within the sample: recent in-migrants (up to ten years residence), in-migrants resident between eleven and twenty years, residents of twenty-one years or over, and those people who had lived in Cornwall all of their lives. The relative size of these groups was dependent upon the response rate as there was no way of identifying them beforehand to enable the sample to be stratified. Overall, 22.7 per cent of respondents had lived in Cornwall up to ten years, 17 per cent of respondents between eleven and twenty years, 21 per cent of respondents had lived in Cornwall for twenty-one years or more and 39.4 per cent had lived in Cornwall all of their lives. There is no way of knowing from the data whether or not those who have lived in Cornwall over twenty-one years but not all their life were actually born or brought up in Cornwall, have left the area and have subsequently returned, or whether they have in fact migrated into Cornwall over twenty-one years ago from elsewhere. Thus no distinction can be made between new migrants and return migrants.

CHARACTERISTICS OF THE SUB-SAMPLES

Tables 1–4 below explore similarities and differences in economic characteristics between the four sub-groups in the sample. This should highlight any variations which may have implications for housing status and access to housing opportunities. Tables 1–4 should be read from left to right, with each row adding up to 100 per cent. Thus the categories are being compared against an equal denominator.

Table 1 below shows the breakdown of the different 'length of residence' cohorts according to the age of the respondents. Some variations are inevitable. In the eighteen to twenty-four years cohort the age of the respondents will mean that the numbers in twenty-one years or over category will inevitably be very small. However, it seems that a significant proportion of the twenty-five to forty-four years age group have moved into Cornwall in the last ten years. Likewise, the forty-five to sixty-four years group are over-represented in the twenty-one years and over category, suggesting that they migrated to Cornwall as young people. The chi-square test indicates that these variations are statistically significant (chi-square statistic = 53.01321, $p < 0.00001$). This

TABLE 1
Length of residence in Cornwall by the age of the respondent (%)

	Up to 10 years in Cornwall	*Between 11 and 20 years in Cornwall*	*21 years or over in Cornwall*	*Lived in Cornwall all of life*
11–24 years	16.1	24.2	1.6	58.1
25–44 years	31.7	17.7	15.0	35.7
45–64 years	18.1	17.1	27.9	36.9
65 years +	17.6	13.8	25.7	41.9
n = 870				

would suggest that a fairly large proportion of in-migrants move to Cornwall as young people.

There is no evidence of any association between the economic activity of a respondent and their length of residence in Cornwall (chi-square = 34.81377, p = 0.1436). The only significant variations that can be found are in the 'retired' category, where in-migrants of less than twenty years residence are under-represented (this would be expected given the age structure of these groups) and those resident for twenty-one years or over are over-represented. Given that a large proportion of this group are aged forty-five to sixty-four, it is possible that these 'longer-term' migrants are more likely to retire earlier than the statutory retirement age. However, the category 'economic activity' does not differentiate between the types of occupation undertaken by those who are in some form of employment or self-employment. Thus it is important to examine differences in occupational class according to length of residence in Cornwall.

There appears to be an association between length of residence in Cornwall and occupational class which is statistically significant (chi-square statistic = 50.33919 p = ≤0.0001). It can be seen from Table 2 below that those residents who have moved into Cornwall in the last ten years are over-represented in the 'I', 'II' and 'IIIN' classification, as are those respondents who have lived in Cornwall between eleven and twenty years. Conversely, respondents who have lived in Cornwall all of their lives are under-represented in those classifications, and over-represented in 'IIIM', 'IV', and 'V'. Again those resident in

TABLE 2
Length of residence in Cornwall by occupational class (%)

	I	II	IIIN	IIIM	IV	V	Retired
Up to ten years	2.6	21.4	24.0	6.1	7.7	13.8	24.0
11–20 years	1.4	18.4	23.1	10.9	10.9	10.9	24.5
21 years +	0.5	12.0	17.5	10.4	11.5	9.8	38.2
All of life	1.2	8.6	15.7	14.5	15.4	13.0	31.7

n = 864   missing = 9

Cornwall twenty-one years or over are more likely to be retired as discussed above. Thus, those moving into Cornwall in the last twenty years are more likely to be in managerial, professional or clerical occupations, whereas people who have lived in Cornwall all their lives are more likely to be in manual occupations. This accords with the findings of other studies.[10]

This would at least suggest that those migrating into Cornwall are likely to be in a better financial position than people who have lived in Cornwall all of their lives, and thus are better able to compete in the housing market. Table 3 below shows the housing tenure of respondents according to their length of residence in Cornwall to see if this is in fact the case.

TABLE 3
Length of residence in Cornwall by household tenure (%)

	Owned outright	Buying with mortgage	Renting privately	Renting LA/HA
Up to ten years	29.0	53.9	10.4	6.7
11–20 years	30.1	55.2	8.4	6.3
21 years +	39.5	43.5	5.6	11.3
All of life	35.5	35.2	7.6	21.8

n = 843

There is evidence of an association between length of residence in Cornwall and the tenure of respondents (chi-square statistic 50.11654, p = ≥0.0001). The over-representation of in-migrants resident for less than twenty years in the 'buying with mortgage' category and the long-term residents in the 'owned outright' category may well be accounted for by age and life-cycle factors. However, those resident in Cornwall all of their lives appear to be more likely to be in Local Authority or Housing Association accommodation than any other group. When age is controlled for in-migrants of less than twenty years in the younger age groups tended to be over-represented in the 'buying with mortgage' category. In the sixty-five years and over age group, those resident in Cornwall for less than ten years were over-represented in the 'owned outright' tenure category. Respondents living in Cornwall all of their lives, however, were significantly over-represented in Local Authority/Housing Association accommodation in the sixty-five years and over age group, and slightly over-represented in all other age groups except the eighteen to twenty-four years group. Interestingly, the twenty-one years and over group were not noticeably over or under-represented in any tenure.

TABLE 4
Respondents' opinions about the condition of their accommodation by length of residence in Cornwall (%)

	Good	*Satisfactory*	*Poor*
Up to ten years	77.2	18.3	4.6
11–20 years	76.2	21.8	2.0
21 years+	77.6	20.2	2.2
All of life	73.4	24.0	2.6

n = 869

Table 4 above examines the difference between the sub-groups in terms of their opinion on the condition of their accommodation. This may give an indication of the differences in the quality of accommodation between the sub-groups. It can be seen that very small numbers of people actually described their accommodation as being in a 'poor' condition. There is no statistical evidence of any association between respondents' opinions about the condition of their accommodation and the length of residence in Cornwall (chi-square = 5.15096, p = 0.5246). However, those respondents resident in Cornwall all of their lives do seem to be slightly over-represented in the 'satisfactory' category. This may well be related to tenure. Indeed, cross-tabulation reveals an association between expressed opinion on condition of accommodation and tenure (chi-square = 67.26823, p = 0.0106). Those in owner-occupation are more likely to describe their accommodation as in good condition than those in privately rented or Local Authority/Housing Association who are more likely to describe their accommodation as satisfactory. When age was controlled for the association remained the same. There is also an association between the occupational class of the respondent (excluding the retired) and their opinion on the condition of their accommodation. Those in occupational class groups II and IIIN are more likely to describe their accommodation as 'good' than those in groups IV and V, who in turn are more likely to describe it as 'satisfactory' (chi-square statistic = 23.04464, p = 0.0106).

Examining differences in the economic characteristics between the sub-groups reveals that the main variations occur in occupational class and housing tenure. Those resident in Cornwall less than twenty years are more likely to be in a higher occupational class group and to be buying their homes than those who have been resident in Cornwall all of their lives. The latter are more likely to be in a lower occupational class group, and have a larger proportion of the group in Local Authority or Housing Association accommodation. The distribution of economic activities is comparable between the groups, with the exception of the twenty-one years or over group who are over-represented in the 'retired' category. This may be related to early retirement as mentioned above. In addition, respondents' opinions on the condition of their accommodation also vary according to occupational class and tenure. The main differences between the groups then, appear to be related to economic status. In terms of their economic situations long-term residents of Cornwall are disadvantaged which means that they are less likely to be in owner-occupation than in-migrants. This is very much as expected and accords well with the findings of other studies.[11] What needs exploring further is how the housing chances of the two groups differ once they are within Cornwall. For those buying into the housing market from outside Cornwall gaining access to accommodation is not a problem, but who is looking for accommodation from within Cornwall, and does this vary according to how long they have been resident in the county?

HOUSING NEED

Overall, 10 per cent of the sample expressed 'housing need' in some form. This was measured in two ways. The first asked the respondent if they, or anyone in their household, was actually seeking accommodation. Details of who was looking, the reason why and the type of accommodation being sought were taken. The second measure asked the respondent if they, or anyone in their household, would prefer to live in separate accommodation but were unable to do so for any reason. Details about the reason they were unable to do so were also sought. While these two measures form a very subjective account of housing need (two people in very similar situations may each have different ideas about whether or not they are in housing need), they do give an indication of 'felt need'.

Table 5 below shows who is seeking alternative accommodation. While a significant proportion of those seeking alternative accommodation were young people under the age of twenty-five (43.4 per cent), single people over the age of twenty five were also discernibly represented (21.6 per cent), as were whole households (33.3 per cent). Thus, the desire for alternative accommodation is not confined solely to young people wishing to leave the parental home. The reasons given for seeking alternative accommodation seem to substantiate this. While 31.7 per cent of those looking for alternative accommodation did cite

TABLE 5
Who is looking for alternative accommodation

	Frequency	*Per cent*
Male 25 or under	16	26.7
Female 25 or under	10	16.7
Male 26 or over	8	13.3
Female 26 or over	5	8.3
Whole household	20	33.3
Couple under 25	1	1.7
	Total = 60	Total = 100

independence as their reason for wanting to move, the range of other reasons was quite wide. Other factors cited included that current housing was in poor condition, overcrowding, family or relationship breakdown and that current housing was no longer available due to short term tenancies and homelessness.

Table 6 below shows who the people are in each household structure who are seeking alternative accommodation. In the couple with children households it can be seen that the majority are indeed young adults under twenty-five. However, there are also single people over twenty-six in this household structure and whole households who are seeking alternative accommodation. In the lone parent with children households, it is mainly the 'whole household' who is seeking alternative accommodation. This is likely to be associated with wishing to leave unsuitable accommodation (poor condition, short-term lets, and so on) due to their economically disadvantaged position. One other significant minority is the 'non-elderly couple' households who are also seeking alternative accommodation.

TABLE 6
Who is seeking alternative accommodation by the household structure currently inhabited

	One elderly person	One non-elderly person	Non-elderly couple	Couple with child/ren	Lone parent plus child/ren	Two+ non related adults	Complex households
Single person 25 or under	0	0	0	21	1	1	3
Single person 26 or over	2	1	0	6	2	2	0
Whole household	0	0	6	6	6	0	2

The two measures of housing need were collapsed into one variable, referred to here as 'housing need'. There is no evidence of an association between those expressing housing need and the length of residence of the household in Cornwall (chi-square statistic = 3.13429, p = 0.3714). However, when age is controlled for, some slight variations begin to appear. In the twenty-five to forty-four years group, those resident between eleven and twenty years seem to be slightly over-represented. In the forty-five to sixty-four years group, those resident for twenty-one years or over again seem to be slightly over-represented as those in housing need. However, these variations are not statistically significant.

The tenure of the household, however, does seem to have a bearing on housing need (chi-square statistic = 21.63584, p = ≤ 0.0001). Those households expressing housing need in some form were slightly over-represented in the privately rented sector, and under-represented in the owned outright group.

We know that there is an association between the tenure of the respondent and their length of residence in Cornwall, so it is important to assess the effect of 'length of residence' on this association between housing need and tenure. When 'length of residence' is controlled for, the association disappears in all of the sub-groups except the eleven to twenty years group. Thus it appears that some of those in housing need are likely to have lived in Cornwall between eleven and twenty years and live in privately rented accommodation. A note of caution is necessary here, the three-way cross-tabulation breaks down the 'housing need' variable into very small numbers from which it may be difficult to generalise.

Housing need, then, is found in in-migrant households as well as long term residents of Cornwall. Young adult off-spring from all of the four sub-groups expressed a desire for alternative accommodation. These adult off-spring seem to be mainly still living in their parents homes who in turn are predominantly buying their homes with a mortgage. However, a proportion of the housing need is located in the privately rented sector, and this does appear to be affected by length of residence in Cornwall. Indeed, those respondents expressing housing need in the privately rented sector are over-represented in the eleven to twenty years of residence sub-group.

Given that it has already been shown that those who have lived in Cornwall all of their lives are generally in an economically disadvantaged position compared with more recent in-migrants, this would lead one to expect them to be over-represented in housing need. Why then, there is an over-representation of housing need in the privately rented sector of people who have been resident for eleven to twenty years clearly needs explaining. It is possible to argue that these are simply the exceptions to the rule—the economically disadvantaged in-migrants. This could be younger people who have migrated into Cornwall from neighbouring counties in the South West in search of seasonal employment. While in-migrants may be over-represented in the higher occupational class groups, this does not mean that they are all in higher occupational class groups or even in employment.

Alternatively they could be people who migrated into Cornwall with their parents and have subsequently left the parental home, or whose parents have only stayed a short while in Cornwall. It has already been demonstrated that the adult off-spring of in-migrants are in the same situation as 'locals' in terms of housing need.

However, if this can be explained economically, then why are not all the sub-groups equally represented in housing need in the privately rented sector? The answer to this may well be cultural. It was noted earlier in the paper that a study by Buck et al and interviews at the start of this research showed Cornish families to be playing an important role in overcoming and meeting housing need for family members. Thus, the presence of family and kinship networks within the community acting as mechanisms for resolving housing problems may mean that the long-term residents of Cornwall are less likely to express housing need. Given that those in privately rented accommodation are likely to be in vulnerable housing situations due to short-term and winter lets, it is not altogether surprising that this group is generally over-represented in housing need. However, it may be that long term residents of Cornwall are less dependent on this sector because of the role played by kinship networks than more recent in-migrants who are forced to seek accommodation through the housing market.

Furthermore, given that the measure of housing need in the survey was a subjectively expressed one, it is possible that acceptance of the situation, a degree of fatalism, results in long-term residents being less likely to express housing need. This will certainly require further investigation.

CONCLUSION

This article set out to examine the extent to which a dichotomy of housing opportunity exists within Cornwall between long-term residents and more recent in-migrants. Access to housing is generally dependent upon economic factors, this is particularly so in Cornwall as alternatives to owner-occupation are severely limited. An examination of the data collected then, certainly reveals that recent in-migrants are generally in a better economic position, and are therefore better able to compete in the housing market. Indeed, they are more likely to be in owner occupation than long-term residents, even when life cycle factors are controlled for. However, it seems that this relative advantage in the housing market is limited to those in-migrants who sold properties outside of the region and subsequently purchased within Cornwall. The adult off-spring of in-migrants experience the same difficulties in gaining access to independent accommodation as young people who have lived in Cornwall all of their lives. Moreover, they may actually find themselves further disadvantaged as they lack the benefit of a wider kinship group attempting to meet and overcome some of the housing problems experienced by family members. This latter point requires further investigation. As this article comes from research in progress, it is hoped that further ethnographic investigation into the ways in which both recent in-migrants and long term residents of Cornwall attempt to overcome their housing need will reveal if this is actually the case.

NOTES AND REFERENCES

1. See Andrew George, *Homes for Locals in Cornwall*, Truro, 1990; Bernard Deacon, Andrew George, Ronald Perry, *Cornwall at the Crossroads?*, Redruth 1988; Joy Lennon, *The Homeless in Cornwall*, Truro 1991; Malcolm Williams, 'Housing the Cornish' in Philip Payton (ed.), *Cornwall Since the War: The Contemporary History of a European Region*, Redruth, 1993.
2. Mary Buck, Lyn Bryant and Malcolm Williams, *Housing and Households in Cornwall: A Pilot Study of Cornish Families*, Plymouth, 1993.
3. Williams, 1993.
4. Malcolm Williams, Brian Cheal and Lyn Bryant, *Population Turnaround in Cornwall 1971–1991*, Plymouth, 1995 (forthcoming).
5. Buck et al., 1993.
6. See Janet Fitchen, 'On the Edge of Homelessness: Rural Poverty and Housing Insecurity', *Rural Sociology* 57 (2); Irene Rauta, *Who Would Prefer Separate Accommodation?*, London, 1986; Christine Lambert, Syd Jeffers, Paul Burton and Glen Bramley, *Homelessness in Rural Areas*, Salisbury, 1992.
7. For further details, see Mary Buck, Lyn Bryant and Malcolm Williams, 'Housing the Cornish: Containing the Crisis', *Cornish Studies: One*, 1993.
8. Williams, 1993.
9. The data were collected in the early stages of research for a PhD. which is funded primarily by a University of Plymouth Research Studentship (HEFCE). Additional funding was made available by the Department of Applied Social Science at the University of Plymouth to enable a postal survey to be undertaken.
10. See Perry et al., 1986; Williams et al., 1995.
11. Perry et al., 1986; Williams et al., 1995.

BOOK REVIEWS

Mark Stoyle, *Loyalty and Locality: Popular Allegiance in Devon During the English Civil War*, University of Exeter Press, 1994, xvi.pp + 330.pp, ISBN 0 85989 428 2, £25.00.

One of the most significant (and fascinating) areas of historical debate since 1945 has been that surrounding the Civil War(s) in these islands in the mid-seventeenth century. A succession of interpretations has produced a range of emphases and perspectives, not to say conflict, for—as Christopher Hill has written—'History is not a narrative of events. The historian's difficult task is to explain what happened. The years between 1603 and 1714 were perhaps the most decisive in English (sic) history.' Hill himself, some fifty or more years ago, replaced Clarendon's notion of 'rebellion' with the more historiographically modern concept of 'revolution', arguing that the events of the Civil War were in fact '*England*'s Revolution', a precursor of those of France and America. But, as more recent writers such as Taylor Downing and Maggie Millman have noted, the powerful paradigm of the 'Puritan revolution' was itself replaced (or at least complemented) in the 1960s and 1970s by a more diffuse model which pointed to a complex inter-play of historical processes, a blend of 'predisposing' and 'pre-cipitating' factors.

In turn, the late 1970s and 1980s produced a revisionist focus on the detailed events of the mid-1600s, with scholars arguing that the War was not the inevitable outcome of the interaction of historical forces but represented the failings of otherwise responsible men (the 'rational actors' of modern international relations parlance) to produce a peaceful settlement. More recently, others have sought to set the Civil War in the wider context of relationships within the British Isles, not least with regard to events in Ireland and Scotland, and against the background of a 'centre-periphery' analysis which indicates a territorial dichotomy between the generally 'Parliamentarian' Midlands and

Southern England on the one hand and 'Royalist' Wales, Cornwall and the North on the other. The importance of purely local issues in determining allegiance has been emphasised, while there has also been a return to religious conviction as an explanation for political action. But while the focus on locality has encouraged some historians to return to a more conservative perspective, emphasising the (alleged) role of the gentry as the principal determinant of attitudes and behaviour in the early modern period, it has also led to a new concern to explore in detail the nature and impact of popular belief and action in the Civil War. This has been reflected in the often controversial work of David Underdown, but an important new contribution is that made by Mark Stoyle.

Mark Stoyle's concern is popular allegiance in Devon during the Civil War but his book is also a significant contribution to Cornish Studies. In addition to the inherent comparative value for us of considering events in neighbouring Devon, Stoyle goes out of his way to present his material in the wider context of loyalty and locality (there is discussion of Wales, Lancashire, and other areas) and draws explicit contrasts between the experiences of Cornwall on the one hand and Devon on the other, highlighting the significance of ethnic identity in Cornwall in this early modern period. As such, Stoyle's work reinforces the recent academic focus on Cornish 'difference' and is in that respect a major contribution to the new Cornish historiography.

Although a cursory reading of Devon's Civil War history might lead broadly to the conclusion that the county was in the main 'Puritan' in sympathies and 'Parliamentarian' in politics, Stoyle's more detailed and penetrating analysis shows that seventeenth-century Devon was diverse in culture and loyalties. While South, South-East and even remote North Devon were generally supportive of Parliament, mid-Devon was noticeably more Royalist. As Stoyle notes, Royalist sympathy was especially characteristic of the Dartmoor tinners, who in this and other respects (as in the rebellion of 1549) shared more in common with the Cornish than with their Devon compatriots—perhaps not surprisingly so, given their status as Stannary men and subjects of the Duchy of Cornwall. And as this indicates, in Devon as elsewhere long-standing and deep-rooted traditions of cultural and religious behaviour were the principal determinants of popular allegiance in the Civil War.

It is in this context that Stoyle's observations on Cornwall have an especially powerful resonance. He considers that:

To begin a discussion of Civil War allegiance in Devon by examining local ethnology may well seem perverse, for the county possessed few large minority groups during the seventeenth century. Nevertheless it is too often forgotten that Devon was a marcher (or border) county, the River Tamar forming a racial frontier between Anglo-Saxon England and Celtic Cornwall. (p. 149)

The most fascinating part of this frontier is, for Stoyle, the far North East of Cornwall around Stratton. Remote from the rest of Cornwall and characterised by English rather than Celtic place-names, Stratton Hundred was—as Clarendon wrote—'the only part of Cornwall eminently disaffected to the King'. In 1645 the parishes of Stratton, Whitstone, Bridgerule, Marhamchurch, Launcells and Poundstock rose against the Royalists, and in 1646 there was a further rising in Morwenstow and Kilkhampton. Stoyle's explanation is that the Stratton district was in effect an 'English enclave in north-east Cornwall', a 'little England in Cornwall' where sympathies were Parliamentarian rather than Royalist and where the inhabitants 'preferred to co-operate with the people of north-west Devon rather than with their fellow Cornishmen'. An intriguing aside here is that Stratton Hundred was the home of Sir Bevill Grenville, beloved leader of the Cornish Royalists, an indication that—as Stoyle argues—in Cornwall and elsewhere popular allegiance was a function of culture and religion rather than deference to the preferences of local gentry.

Moving to the rest of Cornwall, Stoyle complains that ever since Mary Coate's great study of 1933, Cornish Royalism has tended to be played down. He insists instead that 'The vast majority of the common people supported the King, a fact that was demonstrated again and again as the war progressed', with Parliamentary sympathy generally restricted to some of the gentry and clergy. Stoyle concedes that West Cornwall was more solidly for the King than the East but he notes that Bodmin, Liskeard and the countryside around Saltash were clearly Royalist areas. And just as Stratton remained unmoved by Grenville's Royalism, so the tenants of Lord Robartes of Lanhydrock in South East Cornwall were not persuaded to embrace his Parliamentary enthusiasms. Again the deference model is discredited, and Stoyle argues that explanations for Cornwall's support for the King must be sought in the institution of the Duchy of Cornwall and in religion and culture.

In particular, the Stannaries (an integral part of the Duchy structure) played a vital role in securing Cornwall for the King and the Cornish tinners were the backbone of the small Cornish army which time and again defeated superior Roundhead forces. To this institutional link with the Crown was added the religious conservatism of the

Cornish (Roundhead pamphleteers described Cornwall as 'a corner of ignorants . . . a place full of superstitious and popishly affected persons . . . a pagan principality'). And, as Stoyle notes, in the far west of Cornwall in 1642 there was still a substantial monoglot Cornish-speaking population, linguistically and culturally resistant to English influences—not only to Puritan religious teachings but to the stream of scurrilous ballads and newsheets which did much to tarnish the monarchy elsewhere in the years before the outbreak of war.

In setting the experience of the Civil War in Devon in its wider comparative context, Stoyle makes much of the similarities between Wales and Cornwall in this period. Not only were both areas hotbeds of popular Royalist allegiance but both were singled out for particular contempt by English Roundhead pamphleteers. One accused the Welsh and Cornish of 'paganisme' and went on to predict that 'when posterity shall see the Gospell shine cleere there, they will know what Turks their ancestors were, and what advantage this rebellion against the Parliament had from thence by their forefathers' ignorance'. Far more than in Cornwall, the existence of a widespread population that knew no English was a major barrier to the spread of advanced Protestant views in Wales, although it is significant that the one part of Wales to demonstrate unreserved support for Parliament was Pembrokeshire—the heavily anglicised 'Little England beyond Wales'. That these subtleties of local allegiance were not lost to contemporary observers was evident in the commentary of Sir John Birkenhead, the perceptive editor of the Royalist *Mercurius Aulicus* who wrote that:

> Pembroke is the only remnant of Wales (if it be true Welch) which rebels against his Majestie, for as Pembroke (still called little England beyond Wales) forsook their allegiance when all other Welch counties stood loyal to his Majestie; so Cornwall (which is little Wales beyond England) proved themselves true Brittaines, when no English county stood intirely for his Majestie. (p. 241)

Stoyle goes further to argue that in Wales and Cornwall, as in Ireland and Scotland, ethnic and religious factors fused to produce a Royalism that was an integral part of national identity. Here Stoyle has successfully combined his micro-study of one specific locality with macro-generalisations that offer broader explanations (a technique that often eludes local historians), an approach that allows him to refute those historians of the 1970s who discarded the traditional map of Civil War territorial allegiances in favour of more diffuse models. Stoyle concludes that, after all, the traditional view of a Royalist North and West pitted against a Parliamentarian South and East is not far from the truth, at least as far as popular allegiance is concerned, and he declares that 'It is time to start looking at the old map again . . . to return to the old canvas, to revise it, to correct it and to bring it up to date'.

For Cornwall, this message is indeed a timely one, as we move towards a greater understanding of the perpetuation of 'difference', and it is to be hoped that the energy and refreshing originality of Mark Stoyle's analysis will be applied in even greater measure in the future to early modern Cornwall—surely a 'suitable case for treatment' if ever there was one?

Philip Payton,
Institute of Cornish Studies.

P. A. S. Pool, *The Second Death of Cornish*, Dyllansow Truran, Redruth, 1995, iv.pp + 12p, ISBN 185022 079 4, £1.00.

This slim volume pulls no punches. Written very much as a polemical pamphlet in response to the Cornish Language Board's decision to embrace Ken George's phonemic revision ('Kemmyn'), this book will be welcomed by defenders of Unified Cornish and the Nancean inheritance. But it will also be seen by a wider audience as an important contribution to the on-going 'language debate', furnishing as it does a fascinating insight into both the ideological position of Unified supporters and the depth of feeling that has been generated by the current split in the language movement.

Peter Pool needs little introduction to those familiar with the world of Cornish Studies. A former Honorary Research Fellow of the University of Exeter, he was also, as his book reminds us, the first General Secretary of the Cornish Langauge Board and later its Treasurer. He is also a Bard of the Cornish Gorsedd.

Pool begins with a brief review of the Cornish language revival, noting that after the death of Robert Morton Nance in 1959 there was in the then tiny band of Cornish speakers a determination to perpetuate his work, 'and nobody doubted that this should be through the medium of Unified Cornish, which had served its purpose so well'. This led, amongst other things, to the foundation of the Cornish Language Board in 1968. The two decades or so after 1968, argues Pool, were a time of expansion and optimism. But 'In the last six years, all has been lost;

clarity has been replaced by confusion, and unity by discord. What', asks Pool rhetorically, 'went wrong?'.

Pool's answer is that the emergence of two new, competing forms of Cornish, at variance with each other as well as with Unified, led inevitably to a split in the language movement which produced three rival groups, each with its own societies, publications, funds and supporters. As he explains,

> One group, led by Kenneth George, favours a system known as Common Cornish (or *Kemyn*—sic), which like Unified is based on medieval Cornish, but with entirely different spelling. The other group, led by Richard Gendall, favours a system known as *Kernuak*, which is based (like Jenner's original system) on the Late Cornish of the decline. (p. 5)

Although Pool is critical of Gendall's intervention, considering it part of the process of fragmentation, he has some supportive words for the Kernuak (Modern) camp:

> It can be said for Kernuak that it does resemble Cornish as at one time used by Cornish people; it has a natural and genuine ring, and is really a unified form of Late Cornish, evolved in much the same manner as Nance evolved his Unified from Middle Cornish. Had the revivalists of the 1920s decided to continue with Jenner's spelling, we should probably by now had been using something very like Kernuak. (p. 6)

In contrast, Pool's harshest words are reserved for George's phonemic revision, for:

> Kemyn is something quite different, an artificial creation which does not resemble Cornish as used by Cornish people at any time in history. To those accustomed to Unified, as indeed to those who prefer Kernuak, Kemyn has an alien and somewhat sinister ring, as if the language had somehow been taken over by robots and reduced to the status of a code. Every principle of sound and spelling, claim the supporters of Kemyn, must be followed to its logical end and strictly observed, however weird the outcome. (p. 6)

At the practical and organisational level, Pool's principal regret is that, in his opinion, the Cornish Language Board is no longer an umbrella body for the revival as a whole but has become a pressure group dedicated to the promotion of one particular faction. Although believing that for any language revival to be successful it should have unanimity on issues such as spelling and pronunciation, Pool recognises that consensus will now be difficult to achieve and 'that the best outcome we can hope for is to ensure that Cornish never again dies out'. For Pool this involves pointing to the 'folly and ingratitude' of the Language Board as well as continuing to insist upon the qualities of Unified: 'Unified bears a strong and deliberate resemblence to Cornish at its prime, when it was the first language of most Cornish people and the vehicle of major works of literature'.

Pool concludes by recalling the advice of John of Chyannor in the well-known Cornish folk-tale of that name: *Na-wreugh why gasa an forth coth rag an forth noweth*—'Never leave the old road for the new road'. While many have indeed left the old road for the new, whether it be Kemmyn or Kernuak, there is still—as evidenced by the latest (1995) reprint of Pool's *Cornish for Beginners* and the continuing demand for Nance's dictionary (reprinted in 1990 and again in 1994)—a strong body of opinion in favour of Unified Cornish.

A few years ago it was fashionable to insist that the language debate in Cornwall was all but over. However, it may be (as the appearance of Pool's book suggests) that after an initial period of dislocation it is only now that extended debate is being joined. If that is the case, then Pool has made a passionate defence of Unified that will delight its supporters as well as catching the attention of others interested in the wider issues of culture and identity in modern Cornwall.

Philip Payton,
Institute of Cornish Studies

David Gordon and Ray Forrest, *People and Places: Social and Economic Distinctions in England*, SAUS Publications, Bristol, 1995, viii.pp + 135.pp, ISBN 1 873575 66 1, £19.95.

People and Places 2, produced by the School for Advanced Urban Studies at the University of Bristol, provides a fascinating analysis both in tabular and atlas form of social and economic distinctions in the 366 English and Cornish Districts. The atlas uses data from the 1991 Census, largely derived from the 10 per cent sample. Thirty-six variables are examined, ranging from social class to aspects of poverty.

They are ranked and then mapped according to which quartile they have been allocated.

The data as it is presented in the publication certainly assists in addressing the problem of 'statistical invisibility' which besets Cornwall. 'Statistical invisibility' is the process by which data is presented in such a way that Cornwall is submerged within data for a Devon and Cornwall or South West region, a problem outlined recently in a report produced by the Institute of Cornish Studies and funded by the Rural Development Commission. The atlas format of *People and Places 2* should lead readers to a ready recognition of Cornwall's socio-economic distinctiveness. It is also evident that Cornwall is not part of a prosperous South West and that although there are similarities with Devon, there are also critical differences.

The use of maps as a means of identifying areas with similar characteristics has both advantages and disadvantages. An initial appraisal indicates those areas of the country which have a similar status. However, converting data into map form has its limitations. In particular, by its very nature it results in a simplification of the information. Therefore, closer analysis is often necessary, looking beyond the maps to scrutinise raw data in detail. In the context of comparing Cornwall and Devon, there are some cases where the atlas suggests a close affinity between the two areas but closer anaylsis reveals important differences. For the student of contemporary Cornwall, then, *People and Places 2* provides an at-a-glance indication of Cornish socio-economic conditions but requires closer and careful perusal if 'statistical invisibility' is to be avoided entirely and the full extent of Cornwall's problems appreciated.

What is immediately obvious from many of the maps is that the Cornish Districts together stand out as a distinct territory, and that the greatest contrast between Cornwall and Devon is to be found in the data relating to those groups which have been defined as the *emarginati*—those on the margins of society. Several variables are an indication of the status of these groups, namely—'men on the scrap heap', the level of youth unemployment, percentage of youth on government training schemes and poor children.

The phrase 'men on the scrap heap' refers to the proportion of men aged between fifty-five and pensionable age who are neither retired or in work. It is an indication of the severity of unemployment in an area. All six Cornish districts are in the upper quartiles, compared to four of the ten Devon districts. The average for the Cornish districts is 15.7 per cent compared to 11.1 per cent for the Devon districts. Kerrier and Penwith emerge as the worst areas in Devon and Cornwall, with 19.2 per cent and 18.5 per cent of men in this category. Comparable areas include inner London, and old industrial centres in Lancashire, Yorkshire, Merseyside and Birmingham as well as rural Lincolnshire. The details for the sixteen districts are shown in Table 1.

TABLE 1
'Men on the scrap heap'

	%	*Ranking*
Kerrier	19.2	49
Penwith	18.5	53
Plymouth	17.4	63
Restormel	16.4	76
Torbay	14.6	99
Carrick	14.0	110
Caradon	13.8	115
North Cornwall	12.4	146
Teignbridge	11.2	183
Torridge	11.2	183
North Devon	10.5	202
South Hams	9.8	226
West Devon	9.6	234
East Devon	9.2	248
Exeter	8.7	270
Mid Devon	7.9	298

Unemployment, particularly amongst sixteen to seventeen year-olds, is a good indicator of the level of disadvantage in a community. This is expressed as a percentage of those who are unemployed in this age group as a percentage of those in work. With the exception of Carrick, all the Cornish districts are in the top two quartiles, compared to only three of the Devon districts. The mean for the Cornish districts is 27.4 per cent, for the Devon districts 20 per cent. Again, Cornwall has a close affinity with inner London, Manchester and Tyneside.

As is to be expected, there is a link between unemployment data and the percentage of sixteen to seventeen year olds on Government training schemes. Again, Cornwall is included amongst those areas with a high percentage of young people in this category. All six districts are in the upper quartile and, with the exception of Carrick, in the top fifty ranking. The contrast with Devon is quite clear, the mean for the Cornish districts is 48.6 per cent, for Devon 32.2 per cent.

Data on poverty amongst children is expressed as the number of children in non-earner families as a percentage of all children in households. Five of the Cornish districts are in the two upper quartiles (13 per cent or more), while in comparison only four of the Devon districts are in the same position. The incidence of poverty declines as one moves from west to east in Cornwall; Penwith and Kerrier emerge as the worst off, while Caradon has the lowest level.

The Department of the Environment's index of local conditions is in essence an indicator of deprivation and is used as a means of allocating resources to local authority districts. With the exception of Caradon, the Cornish districts are in the second tier of deprived areas. In Devon, Plymouth is in the first tier, with three districts in the second. One difficulty here is that the criteria used in the index is open to criticism. Of the thirteen variables, three, namely—households lacking a car, level of educational participation and low educational achievement levels, penalise Cornwall. For example, car ownership in rural areas is invariably higher than in urban areas and is not a reliable indicator of income or wealth (more pertinent factors here might be lack of public transport provision, and the relative age of cars). Similarly, high participation in education may reflect, paradoxically, the lack of employment opportunities in Cornwall.

The 1991 census asked about the number of households containing one or more members with a long-term limiting illness. The report links this data with the number of health care professionals available and tabulates this as a ratio. Again the Cornish districts are amongst the worse off, with the exception of Carrick (probably due to Treliske Hospital) all are included in the upper quartiles. The mean for the Cornish districts is seventy-three per health care worker. This compares to the overall district mean of sixty-two; while that for the Devon Districts is forty-eight. Within Cornwall, the spatial variation is quite wide, ranging from 146 in North Cornwall to thirty-three in Carrick.

A high proportion of young families is usually associated with the older industrial urban centres, and here again Cornwall is seen to have more in common with the industrial North than with Devon. Each of the Cornish districts has an above average level of households in this category. Four—Kerrier, Restormel, Caradon and North Cornwall— are in the first quartile. In Devon, the only district found here is Torridge. An appraisal of economic factors also shows some important differences. *People and Places 2* maps out the importance of the informational economy in each district. As expected, the London and Home Counties area emerges as the core area for this activity. Both the Cornwall and Devon regions are deficient in this activity, but whereas four of the Devon districts are listed in the second quartile, only one district in Cornwall—Carrick—is in the same position. Its neighbour Restormel has the dubious distinction of coming bottom of the table in Cornwall.

As noted above, there are some areas where the atlas presentation of data suggests Devon and Cornwall share certain characteristics, but where further analysis indicates a degree of difference. For example, the atlas shows that Cornwall and Devon have a high percentage of workers in the construction industry (expressed as a percentage of the resident working population) and both areas are included in the upper quartiles. But looking at the data itself reveals that, in general, the Cornish districts have a higher percentage of construction workers than the Devon districts. With the exception of Penwith, Cornish districts are in the top fifty ranked districts. By comparison, only three of the Devon districts are included there. Another important variable is the free or hidden economy, essentially those who carry out unpaid work or look after the home. Here Cornwall, Devon, Somerset and Dorset are all in the upper quartile. However, closer examination reveals that Cornwall's position is far worse than an initial perusal would indicate. All six districts are ranked in the top eighteen. The figures reveal that 35.5 per cent in Penwith and 33.3 per cent in Restormel work in the free economy.

As expected, when the data for income is examined, the Cornish Districts are in the lower quartiles; indeed Penwith and Kerrier are in the bottom fifty districts. Devon districts generally have a higher level of income. *People and Places 2* also indicates the degree of inequality within each district, an important source of information to social scientists. What emerges here is the high level of inequality in most Cornish districts. Kerrier ranks thirty-three out of all Districts, Penwith thirty-five, Carrick sixty-three, Restormel eight-one, Caradon 110 and North Cornwall 214. Not only are people in Cornwall poorer than on average but the gap between rich and poor is higher than in most areas. In general, incomes in Devon are higher, and the distribution is more equitable.

To summarise, *People and Places 2* serves to illustrate the high levels of socio-economic deprivation experienced in Cornwall compared to other regions. It also indicates that in many areas there are clear differences between Cornwall and Devon, a factor that becomes even more apparent if the reader is prepared to look beyond the maps themselves to consider the raw data. Although situated in the 'South' of Britain, Cornwall has in fact more in common with the decaying industrial areas of the 'North', a fact often obscured by its inclusion for statistical and planning purposes in a wider South West or Devon-and-Cornwall region. The planners of Cornwall County Council have come to recognise that in socio-economic as in other areas Cornwall remains *A Land Apart* (the title of a recent Structure Plan document), while Cornish Studies as an academic discipline is increasingly addressing itself to the problems of modern Cornwall. *People and Places 2* can only serve to assist in this process.

Peter Wills,
Institute of Cornish Studies